How to Make a Million Dollars an Hour

How to Make a Million Dollars an Hour

Why Hedge Funds Get Away with Siphoning Off America's Wealth

Les Leopold

John Wiley & Sons, Inc.

Jacket Design: Wendy Mount
Jacket Photograph: © John Kuczala/Getty Images

Published by John Wiley & Sons, Inc., Hoboken, New Jersey
Published simultaneously in Canada

For general information about our other products and services, please contact our Customer Care Department within the United States at (800) 762-2974, outside the United States at (317) 572-3993 or fax (317) 572-4002.

Wiley also publishes its books in a variety of electronic formats. Some content that appears in print may not be available in electronic books. For more information about Wiley products, visit our web site at www.wiley.com.

Library of Congress Cataloging-in-Publication Data

Leopold, Les.
    How to make a million dollars an hour : why hedge funds get away with siphoning off America's wealth / Les Leopold.
      p. cm.
    Includes bibliographical references and index.
    ISBN 978-1-118-23924-7 (cloth); ISBN 978-1-118-43814-5 (ebk);
    ISBN 978-1-118-43811-4 (ebk); ISBN 978-1-118-43812-1 (ebk)
      1. Hedge funds.   2. Investment advisors.   3. Wealth.   4. Income distribution.
      I. Title.
  HG4530.L423 2013
  332.64'524—dc23

                                              2012025744

Printed in the United States of America
10 9 8 7 6 5 4 3 2 1

With love to Frank,
Alvina, and Darlene Szymanski

CONTENTS

Introduction   1

Step 1   Reach for the Stars—and Beyond   5

Step 2   Take, Don't Make   25

Step 3   Rip Off Entire Countries Because
         That's Where the Money Is   48

Step 4   Use Other People's Money   62

Step 5   Create Something You Can Pretend
         Is Low Risk and High Return   78

Step 6   Rig Your Bets   97

Step 7   Don't Say Anything Remotely Truthful   113

Step 8   Have the Right People Whispering in Your Ear   136

Step 9   Bet on the Race *after* You Know Who Wins   159

Step 10 Milk Millions in Special Tax Breaks   183

Step 11 Claim That Limits on Speculation Will Kill Jobs   204

Step 12 Distract the Dissenters   221

Conclusion   237

Acknowledgments   241

References   243

Index   251

Introduction

So, you want to make a million dollars an hour? Who wouldn't? Just think of what you could do. Work ten minutes and buy yourself a Ferrari. Work another half hour and retire. Or tough it out for just one day and make as much as the average family makes in 179 years!

You're about to learn the secrets that enabled America's top hedge-fund managers to pull down astounding sums in the space of minutes.

Maybe you're a little hesitant, though. You have a few questions you need answered first. Like, what would you have to do, exactly? What *is* a hedge fund, anyway? How does it make so much money? And do you have to be Einstein to get that rich?

If you're a do-gooder, you might also want to know whether running a hedge fund does any harm. Does it suck blood from the poor around the world? Does it rob widows and orphans? Does it profit from arms smuggling or global warming?

If you're really righteous, you won't worry just about the damage done. You will also ask whether hedge funds do any good for anyone other than those hauling in a million an hour. You might even worry about whether, as a newly minted hedge-fund billionaire, you might be undermining democracy itself. That's a heavy load—so heavy, in fact, that it might keep you from concentrating fully on making a million an hour. We understand. No one wants to be accused of wrecking society.

Well, don't fret. We've got you covered on all fronts. As you'll soon see, I'm obsessed with these questions. I'm especially worried about whether the million-an-hour crowd produces anything positive at all for our society and economy.

It's a perverse question, I know. Most people (and economists) assume that if hedge funds make piles of money, they *must* be creating value. The more they make, the more value they produce by definition. Who cares what value hedge funds actually produce or whether the activity is socially useful. Those guys are rich, and we wanna be, too!

A lot of people, including most people who write books about hedge funds, just can't stop gushing about these financial elites. They're the best of the best of the best, and they deserve every billion they get. So what if a couple of the big guys get busted (think Bernie Madoff, Raj Rajaratnam, and Allen Stanford)? So what if a couple of the big hedge funds were primary instigators of the greatest financial crash since the Great Depression.

If you want to know what hedge funds really do, however, you'll soon discover that a straight answer is hard to come by. Mostly, these guys (and yes, they are nearly all guys) keep their efforts well hidden from view. Trade secrets and mystical lore shroud their every move. Neither regulators nor the public have any idea how so much money is minted.

So, who is our ideal target audience for this book? You. I'm thinking about average workers who haven't seen a real raise for years, who don't know whether their jobs will be there next week, who watch health-care deductibles rise higher and higher while coverage shrinks, and who see their retirement funds going nowhere. I'm also thinking of teachers, firemen, police officers, and other public servants who serve as piñatas for self-promoting politicians and pundits, only because they still have decent jobs with reasonable benefits. Meanwhile, because of the Wall Street crash, those jobs and benefits are being cut, cut, cut. And, of course, I'm thinking about their kids, who are struggling to pay for college, who get saddled with enormous debts, and who then search for jobs that don't exist.

What about professionals? Don't worry, I'm thinking about you as well. When the top money managers make twenty thousand times more per year than the average pediatrician, you've got to wonder what's up. You work hundred-hour weeks tending to sick children, while some snot-nosed kid in a hedge fund makes more in *one hour* than you'll earn in *ten years*.

So, all you production workers, nurses, school teachers, cops, students, and professionals, welcome aboard. You must be damn curious about how these hedge-fund honchos are making so much, doing God knows what. You may even wonder if you can get there, too. After all, this is America! At the very least, I'm sure you want to know whether their hedge-fund wealth comes from picking your pockets.

We can find the answers, but it requires that you join us in a walk on the wild side of fantasy finance. Please follow our twelve-step guide to accumulating vast riches. This book is all you'll ever need to peer into the million-an-hour club and maybe, just maybe, become a member, or, at the very least, a fierce opponent.

STEP 1

Reach for the Stars—and Beyond

If you live in America, chances are, you want to be rich. Winning big is our national religion, and the competition to the top sure is tough these days. A recent study of the twelve richest countries shows that nine of them have more upward mobility than we do ("A Family Affair," 2010). So, it isn't going to be easy to break through.

I'm going to assume you're middle class, so let's anchor ourselves in what it means to be middle class in the United States today. The median American family—at the halfway point in income distribution—earned $45,800 in 2010. Sadly, that's 7.7 percent below what it was in 2007. We'll refer to this median household as "the average family" (Bricker 2012, 1–5).

The good news for the rich, though, is that they're getting richer. We now have the most skewed income distribution since records started in 1928. One clear indicator is the gap between CEO pay and worker pay. In 1970, for every one dollar earned by a nonsupervisory production worker (nearly 80 percent of the workforce), the top hundred CEOs averaged $45. By 2006, the top hundred CEOs earned a whopping $1,723 for every dollar earned by the average worker—quite a jump.

Or look at the share of income that goes to the richest 1 percent of Americans. In 1970, these very fortunate individuals possessed 8 percent of our national income. Today they're taking in nearly 24 percent.

So, who occupies the very top rungs of the income ladder? And just where will you fit in as a top hedge-fund honcho?

CELEBRITIES

The surest way to get to the top of the celebrity income pyramid is to host a show about yourself. No one does it better than Oprah, and Oprah is certainly a money machine. In fact, she brings up the average for celebrities in a big way. Thanks to her, the top ten celebrities had an average yearly income of $119.8 million in 2010, or $57,596 per *hour*. Not bad, but a far cry from our million dollar an hour target.

By the way, the hourly rate assumes 2,080 working hours in a year—your average 40-hour workweek. This assumes that the celebrities don't get any vacation time, which is unrealistic, but it also assumes they work only 40 hours a week. Simon Cowell (number six on the list) may work more than that, but, as far as I can tell, Elton John isn't putting in those kinds of hours anymore.

It would take the average American family a lot longer than a year to earn as much as these folks received in only one hour.

Top Ten Highest-Paid Celebrities, 2010

Celebrity	Yearly Income (millions)	Hourly Income
Oprah Winfrey	$290.0	$139,423
U2	$195.0	$93,750
Bon Jovi	$125.0	$60,096
Elton John	$100.0	$48,077
Lady Gaga	$90.0	$43,269

Simon Cowell	$90.0	$43,269
Dr. Phil McGraw	$80.0	$38,462
Leonardo DiCaprio	$77.0	$37,019
Howard Stern	$76.0	$36,538
Tiger Woods	$75.0	$36,058
Average	$119.8	**$57,596**

It would take the average family **1 year and 94 days** to make what the average top celebrity makes in **one hour**!

Source: "The World's Most Powerful Celebrities 2011." *Forbes*. http://www.forbes.com/lists/2012/celebrities/celebrity-100_2011.html.

Are you surprised by who didn't make the cut? I was. Rush Limbaugh ($64 million) and Paul McCartney ($64 million) just missed breaking into the top ten. Ellen DeGeneres ($45 million) and David Letterman (also $45 million) didn't make it, either. Yet they did beat out Glenn Beck ($40 million). It was also news to me that within the entertainment industry, producer/directors are the highest-paid stars. So I decided to look into that. Here are the top five:

Top Five Highest-Paid Directors/Producers, 2010

Director/Producer	Yearly Income (millions)	Hourly Income
James Cameron	$210.0	$100,962
Tyler Perry/Michael Bay	$125.0	$60,096
Jerry Bruckheimer	$100.0	$48,077
Steven Spielberg	$100.0	$48,077
George Lucas	$95.0	$45,673
Average	$126.0	**$60,577**

It would take the average family **1 year and 118 days** to make what the average top director/producer makes in **one hour**!

Source: "The World's Most Powerful Celebrities 2011." *Forbes*. http://www.forbes.com/celebrities/#p_1_s_a0_Directors/Producers.

Honestly, I thought that movie stars would come next. Nope, it's pop musicians.

Top Ten Highest-Paid Musicians/Groups, 2010

Musician/Group	Yearly Income (millions)	Hourly Income
U2	$195.0	$93,750
Bon Jovi	$125.0	$60,096
Elton John	$100.0	$48,077
Lady Gaga	$90.0	$43,269
Michael Bublé	$70.0	$33,654
Paul McCartney	$67.0	$32,212
Black Eyed Peas	$61.0	$29,327
The Eagles	$60.0	$28,846
Justin Bieber	$53.0	$25,481
Dave Matthews Band	$51.0	$24,519
Average	$87.2	**$41,923**

It would take the average family
334 days to make what the average top
musician makes in **one hour**!

Source: "The World's Most Powerful Celebrities 2011." *Forbes*. http://www.forbes.com/celebrities/#p_1_s_a0_Musicians.

Although top athletes and movie stars are by no means suffering, their incomes in 2010 were only about half those of pop musicians. The top authors are also doing quite well.

Top Ten Highest-Paid Athletes, 2010

Athlete	Yearly Income (millions)	Hourly Income
Tiger Woods, golf	$75.0	$36,058
Kobe Bryant, basketball	$53.0	$25,481
Lebron James, basketball	$48.0	$23,077

Roger Federer, tennis	$47.0	$22,596
Phil Mickelson, golf	$46.5	$22,356
David Beckham, soccer	$40.0	$19,231
Cristiano Ronaldo, soccer	$38.0	$18,269
Alex Rodriguez, baseball	$35.0	$16,827
Lionel Messi, soccer	$32.3	$15,529
Rafael Nadal, tennis	$31.5	$15,144
Average	$44.6	**$21,442**

It would take the average family
171 days to make what the average top
athlete makes in **one hour**!

Source: "The World's Most Powerful Celebrities 2011." *Forbes*. http://www.forbes.com/celebrities/#p_1_s_a0_Athletes.

Top Ten Highest-Paid Movie Stars, 2010

Movie Star	Yearly Income (millions)	Hourly Income
Leonardo DiCaprio	$77.0	$37,019
Jerry Seinfeld	$70.0	$33,654
Johnny Depp	$50.0	$24,038
Charlie Sheen	$40.0	$19,231
Adam Sandler	$40.0	$19,231
Will Smith	$36.0	$17,308
Tom Hanks	$35.0	$16,827
Ben Stiller	$34.0	$16,346
Robert Downey Jr.	$31.0	$14,904
Angelina Jolie	$30.0	$14,423
Average	$44.3	**$21,298**

It would take the average family
170 days to make what the average
top movie star makes in **one hour**!

Source: "The World's Most Powerful Celebrities 2011." *Forbes*. http://www.ranker.com/list/forbes_s-most-powerful-celebrities-2011/worlds-richest-people-lists?page=1.

(Wow, where are the women? Angelina is on her own at the bottom of the list. Still, it's hard to complain about $14,423 an hour.)

Top Ten Highest-Paid Authors, 2010

Author	Yearly Income (millions)	Hourly Income
James Patterson	$70.0	$33,654
Stephenie Meyer	$40.0	$19,231
Stephen King	$34.0	$16,346
Danielle Steel	$32.0	$15,385
Ken Follett	$20.0	$9,615
Dean Koontz	$18.0	$8,654
Janet Evanovich	$16.0	$7,692
John Grisham	$15.0	$7,212
Nicholas Sparks	$14.0	$6,731
J. K. Rowling	$10.0	$4,808
Average	$26.9	**$12,933**

It would take the average family **103 days** to make what the average top author makes in **one hour**!

Source: "The World's Most Powerful Celebrities 2011." *Forbes*. http://www.forbes.com/celebrities/#p_1_s_a0_Authors.

CEOs

Let's assume, though, that if you could hit a hundred-mile-an-hour fastball, write songs as well as the Beatles, or create one of the best-selling young adult books of all time, you'd be doing that right now. So, if you're just a paunchy, middle-aged white guy in a suit, does that mean being a gazillionaire is out of reach? Not in America, my friend!

Those who run our largest, most prosperous nonfinancial corporations also have no trouble making ends meet. They might be pleased to know (if they don't know already) that they did a bit better than the top movie stars and sports heroes. Five of the top ten CEOs, however, are also in the entertainment business, proving once again that America's dream factories are doing much better than its industrial ones.

Top Ten Highest-Paid Corporate CEOs, 2010

Corporate CEO	Yearly Income (millions)	Hourly Income
Philippe Dauman, Viacom	$84.5	$40,625
Ray Irani, Occidental	$76.1	$36,587
Lawrence Ellison, Oracle	$70.1	$33,702
Leslie Moonves, CBS	$56.9	$27,356
Richard Adkerson, Freeport-McMoRan Copper/Gold	$35.3	$16,971
Michael White, DIRECTV	$32.9	$15,817
John Lundgren, Stanley, Black and Decker	$32.6	$15,673
Brian Roberts, Comcast	$28.2	$13,558
Robert Iger, Walt Disney	$28.0	$13,462
Alan Mulally, Ford Motor	$26.5	$12,740
Average	$47.1	**$22,644**

It would take the average family **180 days** to make what the average top CEO makes in **one hour**!

Source: Equilar. "2010 Executive Compensation." http://www.equilar.com/ceo-compensation/2011/index.php.

But where are the Wall Street bankers? Aren't they raking it in again? Of course, they are, but I suspect they're lying low until they've made sure the new regulatory reforms are sufficiently toothless. Not to worry. They'll be fine.

Top Ten Highest Paid Bank/Insurance CEOs, 2010

Bank/Insurance CEO	Yearly Income (millions)	Hourly Income
Jamie Dimon, JPMorgan Chase	$20.0	$9,615
Robert Kelly, Bank of NY Mellon	$19.4	$9,327
John Stumpf, Wells Fargo	$17.6	$8,462
James Cracchiolo, Ameriprise Financial	$16.8	$8,077
Kenneth Chenault, American Express	$16.3	$7,837
John Strangfeld Jr., Prudential Financial	$16.2	$7,788
Richard Davis, US Bankcorp	$16.1	$7,740
James Gorman, Morgan Stanley	$14.9	$7,163
Richard Fairbank, Capital One	$14.9	$7,163
Lloyd Blankfein, Goldman Sachs	$14.1	$6,779
Average	$16.6	**$7,981**

It would take the average family **64 days** to make what the average top banker/ insurance CEO makes in **one hour**!

Source: Equilar. "2010 Executive Compensation." http://www.equilar.com/ceo-compensation/2011/index.php.

LAWYERS

Aren't trial lawyers crippling the economy with their big class-action suits and damage claims? Maybe so, but they're not nearly as well paid as CEOs and the glamour professions.

Top Ten Highest-Paid Lawyers, 2009

Lawyer	Yearly Income (millions)	Hourly Income
Gerald Hosier	$40.0	$19,231
Richard Scruggs	$29.5	$14,183
Fred Baron	$21.0	$10,096

Joseph Jamail	$20.7	$9,952
Ronald Motley	$18.8	$9,038
John O'Quinn	$16.5	$7,933
Joseph Rice	$15.0	$7,212
Michael Ciresi	$14.4	$6,923
Walter Umphrey	$12.5	$6,010
William Gary	$12.1	$5,817
Average	$20.0	**$9,615**

It would take the average family **76 days** to make what the average top lawyer makes in **one hour**!

Source: "Highest Paid Lawyers in the United States." World Law Direct. http://www.worldlawdirect.com/forum/ attorneys-legal-ethics/26541-highest-paid-lawyers-united-states.html.

DOCTORS ET AL.?

We haven't been able to come up with a list of the highest-paid doctors—that seems to be a big secret. Yet we do know that surgeons are the highest-paid doctors. We also know from the New York *Daily News* that Thomas Milhorat, a now-retired brain surgeon at North Shore University Hospital, was the best-paid surgeon in the New York area in 2007—and he earned a mere $7.2 million a year (Evans 2009).

When I was growing up, doctors were at the pinnacle of success and esteem and always lived in the biggest houses. Medical schools were nearly impossible to get into, the training was crushing, and the end result was someone who literally had people's lives in the palm of his or her hand every day. Yet today, doctors have been eclipsed by health insurance executives, pharmaceutical executives, and managed-care CEOs.

You may have noticed the very sturdy glass ceiling in our lists—and not only in the case of celebrities, where Angelina Jolie stands alone. Out of the hundred or so people we've listed, only six are women. The glass is most permeable on the author list, where women may hold four of ten top spots, but J. K. Rowling also famously used her initials so no one would know at first that she was a woman.

You may also have noticed some other gaping holes. For instance, where's Warren Buffett, the "Oracle of Omaha" ($39 billion in wealth)? He's still with us. In fact, America is home to many billionaires we don't list who have accumulated enormous wealth from their companies—such as Bill Gates ($57 billion), the Waltons of Walmart (nearly $100 billion combined), and the Koch brothers ($50 billion combined). They're the richest of the rich, but their yearly incomes are somewhat muted. That's because total wealth (assets minus liabilities) is a different measuring stick from yearly income. Once you have accumulated massive sums of wealth, it never goes away. The people who have it will always have it. If you don't have it, you're not likely to get it (unless you religiously follow our twelve-step guide). Wealth creates a permanent money aristocracy that can bend democracy to the breaking point. It can change a country from a meritocracy to an aristocracy. That's why we have (or had) a sizable inheritance tax—as a nation, we believed that each generation should compete on a more equal playing field.

Billionaires, of course, would love for us to focus on income, instead of on wealth. That way, the country will stay far away from the dreaded wealth taxes that target the accumulated wealth of the very richest among us.

Nevertheless, in this account, we're focusing on income. It provides a clearer view of who is racing up the ladder fastest. Because you're not wealthy, a skyrocketing income is the only way you're likely to make it in our stratified society.

In any case, let's hope we now have a better sense of those glamorous people in the top one-hundredth of 1 percent of the income distribution, including the fifteen thousand families who in 2008 had a declared average income of $27.3 million. Here's what the complete lopsided pyramid looks like:

U.S. Income Distribution, 2008 (includes realized capital gains)

Income Group	Number of Families	Average Income per Group
Top $1/100$ of 1 percent	15,246	$27,342,212
Top $1/10$ of 1 percent	137,216	$3,238,386
Top $1/2$ of 1 percent	609,848	$878,139
Top 1 percent	762,310	$443,102
Top 5 percent	6,098,480	$211,476
Top 10 percent	7,623,100	$127,184
Bottom 90 percent	137,215,800	$31,244

Saez, Emmanuel, and Thomas Piketty. 2003. "Income Inequality in the United States, 1913–1998." *Quarterly Journal of Economics* 118 (1): 1–39. (Longer updated version published as T. Piketty and E. Saez, "Income and Wage Inequality in the United States, 1913–2002," in A. B. Atkinson and T. Piketty, eds., *Top Incomes Over the Twentieth Century: A Contrast Between Continental European and English-Speaking Countries*, New York: Oxford University Press, 2007.) (Data for tables and figures updated to 2008 in Excel format, available from: Alvaredo, Facundo, Anthony B. Atkinson, Thomas Piketty, and Emmanuel Saez. *The World Top Incomes Database*. http://g-mond.parisschoolofeconomics.eu/topincomes, accessed January 17, 2012.

It didn't used to be this way. Between 1945 and 1970, our country went out of its way to turn working-class people into middle-class citizens. The United States taxed the super-rich (people earning more than $3 million in today's dollars) as much as 91 cents on the dollar. Unions were at their peak, and government strictly curbed industries that ranged from telecommunications, trucking, and airlines to Wall Street.

Beginning in the 1970s, however, deregulation and tax cuts for the rich took hold, giving birth to a new era of finance and a widening income gap. Financial sector incomes lost touch with the rest of society.

Here's some good news! To climb to the pinnacle of America's income pyramid, you don't need to be a famous movie star or athlete. You don't need to write best-sellers or defend big criminals or direct blockbuster movies, either. You don't even need to run a big corporation with tens of thousands of employees. All you need to do is lust after money more than anyone else.

In order to make it to the top, though, first you need to know where the top is. Clear your mind of the erroneous assumption that top hedge-fund managers are just like the many other Americans who rake in outrageous sums—entertainers, sports stars, and best-selling authors, not to mention CEOs, doctors, and lawyers. Don't let the glitter confuse you. Don't fall for the line that says just because ridiculously rich people seem to be everywhere, it's no big deal that hedge-fund managers make big money as well.

Repeat after me: I am a big deal. I am the biggest deal!

To become the biggest deal of all, you need to understand that hedge-fund moguls inhabit a parallel universe of riches—a universe so dimly lit that few have any real idea how much hedge-fund moguls make and what they do to make it. Say "hedge fund" to your neighbors, and they're likely to think you're in the garden supply business.

AND WHAT ABOUT HEDGE-FUND MANAGERS?

As you can see from the following chart, the top ten hedge-fund managers receive truly astronomical incomes. The average top hedge-fund honcho earns more than ten times as much as our average top celebrity. It would take more than seventeen years for the average family to earn as much as the average top hedge-fund manager earned in only *one hour*.

The calculation for John Paulson is even more astronomical. For his services, he reaps more than $2.3 million dollars an *hour*. It would take an average family more than 46.5 *years* to earn as much as John Paulson got in *one hour* in 2010. I don't think the human race has seen so much concentrated income since the time of the great pharaohs.

Top Ten Highest-Paid Hedge-Fund Managers, 2010[*]

Hedge-Fund Manager	Yearly Income	Hourly Income
John Paulson	$4.9 billion	$2,355,769
Ray Dalio	$3.1 billion	$1,490,385
Jim Simons	$2.5 billion	$1,201,923
David Tepper	$2.2 billion	$1,057,692
Steve Cohen	$1.3 billion	$625,000
Eddie Lampert	$1.1 billion	$528,846
Carl Icahn	$900 million	$432,692
Bruce Kovner	$640 million	$307,692
George Soros	$450 million	$216,346
Paul Tudor Jones II	$440 million	$211,538
Average	$1.753 billion	**$842,788**

It would take the average family **18 years and 146 days** to make what the average top hedge-fund manager makes in **one hour!**

[*]The list for 2011 shows a significant decline in the average of the top-ten hedge-fund managers' yearly income to "only" $1.191 billion, or $572,596 per *hour*. It's a competitive game. Only four out of the top ten in 2010 made it back onto the top-ten list for 2011 (Dalio, $3.9 billion; Icahn, $2.5 billion; Simons, $2.1 billion; and Cohen, $585 million). Not to worry—the dropouts are not on food stamps.

Source: Taub, Stephen. 2011. "The Rich List." *Absolute Return Alpha*, April 1. 34–38. http://www.absolutereturn-alpha.com/Article/2796749/Search/The-Rich-List.html?Keywords=rich+list.

To see clearly how much these hedge-fund managers stand out from our cavalcade of high earners, let's put together a summary chart of our top-ten stars.

Summary of the Average Income of the Top Tens, 2010

Top Earner	Yearly Income	Hourly Income	Time It Takes Average Family to Make as Much as Average Top Earner
Top Hedge-Fund Managers	$1.753 billion	$842,788	18 years, 146 days
Top Movie Directors/Producers	$126.0 million	$60,577	1 year, 118 days
Top Celebrities	$119.8 million	$57,596	1 year, 94 days
Top Pop Musicians	$87.2 million	$41,923	334 days
Top Corporate CEOs	$47.1 million	$22,644	180 days
Top Athletes	$44.6 million	$21,442	171 days
Top Movie Stars	$44.3 million	$21,298	170 days
Top Authors	$26.9 million	$12,933	103 days
Top Lawyers	$20.0 million	$9,615	76 days
Top Bank/Insurance CEOs	$16.6 million	$7,981	64 days
Average Family	$45,800		

The bottom line is clear: hedge-fund managers are the big winners. You won't be able to justify hedge-fund incomes by hiding behind Will Smith and Tiger Woods. Yes, we have many high-income entertainers and athletes and overpaid big mouths on TV and radio. Yes, we have many wealthy CEOs, and their pay is obscene. Yet hedge-fund managers make a hundred times more than the top bank and insurance CEOs.

However, if you want to earn a million dollars an hour in the hedge-fund business, be careful. The public is likely to ask, "What on earth do hedge-fund managers do to justify making all that money?"

WHAT'S A HEDGE FUND?

It's kind of like a mutual fund exclusively for people with a net worth greater than $1 million, but with one important difference: those rich investors are expecting a higher return than regular Americans do. That higher rate of return is called "alpha"—that's the extra money they extract from investments beyond the average rate of return in the stock and bond markets. Because hedge funds deal only with wealthy "sophisticated investors" and large institutions, they are minimally regulated.

Here's a definition from one of your fellow hedge-fund managers:

> Hedge funds are investment pools that are relatively uncon-strained in what they do. They are relatively unregulated (for now), charge very high fees, will not necessarily give you your money back when you want it, and will gener-ally not tell you what they do. They are supposed to make money all the time, and when they fail at this, their inves-tors redeem and go to someone else who has recently been making money. Every three or four years, they deliver a one-in-a-hundred-year flood. They are generally run for rich people in Geneva, Switzerland, by rich people in Greenwich, Connecticut. (Asness 2004, 8)

Bernie Madoff certainly knows a thing or two about cata-strophic floods. Using his hedge fund as a great reservoir, Bernie sucked in client money but didn't invest any of it at all. Instead, he dribbled out fictitious interest payments and poured the rest of the principal into his own coffers. How did he get away with it for so long? Well, for starters, hedge funds rarely divulge their investment strategies, so it's not easy to spot Ponzi-ing. Second, wealthy investors had little motivation to spot it. They expected to make big bucks, and Bernie gave it to them. He provided a 1 percent return, each and every month. The more he provided, the more people begged him to take their money. Finally, Bernie understood the psychology of hedge-fund investors—exclusivity, greed, and blind faith that as elites they deserve more than everyone else.

Unfortunately, Ponzi schemes and hedge funds often go together. Yet although only a few hedge funds are Ponzis, virtually all Ponzis use the structure of hedge funds as cover. Meanwhile, a more suspicious public has no clue that some of its money also trickles into hedge funds. Institutional investors such as public pension funds, endowments, foundations, sovereign wealth funds, family asset funds, asset managers, insurance companies, and banks find it hard to resist the promise of high returns from hedge funds. About 56 percent of all hedge-fund investment money is now institutional. Public pension funds account for 9 percent of hedge-fund investments. The greatest share of institutional money comes from "funds of funds" or "feeder funds," which, for a sizable piece of the action, move the money into different hedge funds, mostly for wealthy investors. Funds of funds account for 12.3 percent of hedge-fund investments (see the *2011 Preqin Global Investor Report: Hedge Funds*). Supposedly, these funds of funds protect investors from unscrupulous hedge funds. (Well, not quite. Feeder funds dumped billions into Bernie Madoff's coffers: the Tremont Group invested $3.3 billion of its clients' money in Madoff's Ponzi scheme, while Fairfield Sentry dumped in $7.3 billion. So much for due diligence.)

The mutual fund analogy actually is a stretch. Unlike mutual funds, hedge funds can invest money anywhere and everywhere, using every financial device known to the modern world, including equities, bonds, options, futures, commodities, arbitrage, and derivative contracts, as well as illiquid investments such as real estate. Partly as a result, hedge funds are supposed to make you money when the market goes up, goes down, or just stands still. During the crash, hedge funds supposedly didn't crash as deeply as the average mutual fund. Elites just love the idea of investing high above the fray with the help of the coolest, smartest hedge-fund managers. Wealthy people expect higher returns than the rest of us do, and hedge funds aim to fulfill their sense of privilege. Each hedge fund jealously guards its own secret trading theories and techniques. Hedge funds fiercely compete to win the highest returns for their investors and, of course, for themselves.

The definition gets even murkier because, functionally, hedge funds sometimes morph into other kinds of investment funds. Some hedge funds are involved in venture capital—that is, they run around looking for the next fledgling Facebook. Other hedge funds are "activist," meaning that they take large stock positions in underperforming companies and then beat the crap out of management until profits roll in—or else. Then there are hedge funds that invest more as private equity funds do: they buy up companies, take them private, lay off lots of workers, load the companies up with debt, and then sell them back to the public at enormous profits. Some hedge funds even slide back and forth among all of these functions in their quest to garner gargantuan returns. No one knows precisely how many hedge funds do what, but we do know that the vast majority make their money within the realm of high finance—buying and selling financial securities—without worrying about starting new companies, shaking down old companies, or owning anything tangible at all.

The stakes are high for hedge-fund managers (of all persuasions), because they (unlike mutual-fund managers) actually have skin in the game. Typically, managers take 2 percent off the top of all of the money invested in the fund, plus 20 percent of the profits. The super-rich and institutions currently have $2.2 trillion invested in eight thousand to ten thousand different hedge funds (although most of that money goes to the top two hundred hedge funds).

Finally, there are hedge funds nestled within the largest banks that play the same games. When in 2012 JP Morgan Chase lost more than $5 billion making esoteric bet upon bet, it was acting as a hedge fund and losing money to other hedge funds. Nearly all proprietary trading desks at large banks are essentially internal hedge funds. The only difference is that these large banks also are federally insured—and too big to fail.

HOW MUCH IS TOO MUCH?

So, are these mighty hedge funds in tune with how America feels about economic fairness? Two researchers recently tried to find out just how much economic inequality Americans were comfortable with. Michael Norton, of the Harvard Business School, and Dan Ariely, of Duke University, conducted a nationwide poll with more than five thousand respondents to gauge how Americans saw our current level of equality and what level they wanted to see.

The results were startling. First, virtually all Americans greatly underestimated the degree of inequality in our economy today. Second, when asked to construct an ideal distribution of income, 92 percent of Americans preferred radically more equality—on a par with the social democratic state of Sweden! What's more, it didn't matter whether the respondent was a Republican or a Democrat, rich or poor, black or white, male or female. Everyone wanted more economic fairness. Here's how the authors put it:

> First, a large nationally representative sample of Americans seems to prefer to live in a country more like Sweden than like the United States. Americans also construct ideal distributions that are far more equal than they estimated the United States to be—estimates which themselves were far more equal than the actual level of inequality. Second, across groups from different sides of the political spectrum, there was much more consensus than disagreement about this desire for a more equal distribution of wealth, suggesting that Americans may possess a commonly held "normative" standard for the distribution of wealth despite the many

disagreements about policies that affect that distribution, such as taxation and welfare. (Norton and Ariely 2011, 12)

Imagine that! Americans, even Republicans who voted for John McCain, Sarah Palin, Mitt Romney, and Paul Ryan, would rather live in Scandinavia! (At least, when it comes to equality.)

How can this be? Aren't we always hearing that Americans hate European collectivism? Aren't we constantly bombarded with messages about how we need to reward the movers and the shakers? Haven't we internalized the "greed is good" mentality by now? Or can it really be true that we are hard-wired for fairness?

See, it's not easy to make a million an hour without just about everyone wondering whether you're a clear and present danger to society.

———————— DO'S AND DON'TS ————————

- **Don't** worry about being strong, funny, or beautiful. You can be weak, boring, and ugly, and get even richer.

- **Do** keep a low profile. We don't want the masses to know who's really milking the economy.

- **Don't** pay any attention to those who want to turn America's income distribution into Sweden's, even if it's most of the country. Just make your billions, and then buy up IKEA.

STEP 2

Take, Don't Make

In 2009, David Tepper, the head of the Appaloosa hedge fund, earned an astounding $4 billion. Personally. (That's $1,923,076.92 per hour.) The following year, John Paulson of Paulson and Co. broke Tepper's record, hauling in $4.9 billion, or $2,355,769.34 per hour! Each firm reportedly earned around $20 billion. More amazing still is that they earned these enormous incomes during the two most horrific economic years since the Great Depression—and they did it with only a skeleton crew.

So, here's the real puzzle: How did these two hedge funds, which have fewer than fifty employees each, make as much money as Apple Inc., which relies on the hard work of its nearly thirty thousand U.S. employees (and the incredibly hard work of another seven hundred thousand workers and contractors globally)?

Hint: Produce nothing tangible for the real economy. Don't waste your time inventing or manufacturing stuff. In the hedge-fund game, you don't make—you take.

And for good reason. Making things or providing services to large numbers of people is a complicated business. You have to have a marketable idea, probably a brilliant one. You have to hire workers. You have to manage them. (You may even have to deal with a union, God forbid.) You need to build a spirit of cooperation and a culture that values high quality and customer service. And don't forget the R and D you'll need to keep the innovation flowing. Of course, you also have to compete in a crowded global marketplace, create an entirely new niche, or both. It's the kind of work that keeps you up at all hours. The sweat in sweat equity is real. No way do you want to go near this game when you could run a hedge fund instead.

Better to enter the mystical world of money managing, as described by Daniel A. Strachman, who has written several informative books on hedge funds. He believes that hedge-fund managers deserve to make so much with so little labor because they are simply more brilliant than those plebeians who worry about making cute little gadgets. Strachman is absolutely awed by hedge-fund billionaires:

> These individuals are some of the brightest investment managers of all time, possessing unique skill sets that have made them extremely successful at managing money and exploiting market opportunities. Each has a distinct way of considering how investments are valued, made and executed. In essence, they are capable of seeing the markets in ways that most of us simply cannot imagine, and it is this rare vision that allows them to determine whether opportunities have value, thereby creating infinite windows to make money. *That* is what makes them great hedge fund managers. (Strachman 2008, 16)

I have no doubt that these hedge-fund guys are very bright fellows and that the ones who make it to the top possess intelligence, foresight, and obscure knowledge. But really, are these hedge-fund guys so much brighter than those who create and manufacture everything we use? Is their "rare vision" so superior to that of the late Steve Jobs and his associates? And just what *are* those "infinite windows" that "most of us simply cannot imagine"?

You'd better hope that being more brilliant than the most brilliant capitalists is not the only ticket into the million-an-hour club. Because if it is, you're toast.

So, let's take a closer look at how you can avoid providing tangible goods and services to the real economy and still get filthy rich, even if you're not Einstein.

We all know how Apple earns its keep. It invents, manufactures, and markets products that the world voraciously consumes. (It also profits by using regimented workers in China who live in company dorms, wear identical company uniforms, get paid little, and work around the clock whenever Apple needs them.) The iMac, iPod, iTunes store, iPhone, and iPad have driven Apple's net profit from $4.8 billion in 2008 to $8.2 billion in 2009, to $14 billion in 2010, and a stunning $26 billion in 2011.

Meanwhile, Tepper's Appaloosa hedge fund probably took in $20 billion, racking up an incredible 117 percent return for its investors in 2009. Doing what, exactly? Where's *their* iPad?

Here's what the financial website HedgeFundBlogger.com says about how Tepper made his billions:

> [Tepper] did so by *betting* that the recession would not last as long as many analysts and public officials predicted and taking big stakes in struggling firms like Bank of America and Citigroup. Tepper understood that the government would not nationalize these banks and when many were unsure of the two banks' futures his fund was buying up shares which he believed were significantly underpriced. By purchasing these shares and stakes in other smaller banks and financial lending institutions, Appaloosa Management LP was able to turn a $6.5 billion profit in 2009.
>
> "It was crazy," says Tepper, a Pittsburgh native. "In February and early March, people were in a panic." (Italics added.) (Wilson 2010)

If this report is correct, Mr. Tepper made almost as much as Apple by *betting* that we taxpayers would bail out, but not nationalize, Bank of America and Citigroup. And, of course, we did. Citigroup got the Federal Reserve's rock-solid guarantee for more than $300 billion in toxic assets then rotting on the company's balance sheet. Without our bailouts, both banks would have folded— and a slew of other banks and hedge funds would have toppled like dominoes. (These two banks also took advantage of billions of dollars in hidden Federal Reserve loans provided at negligible interest rates.)

Yet Tepper was also shrewdly betting that the government would never play hardball with the big banks. Washington, he sensed, would not nationalize these failing banks, a move that would wipe out its shareholders. No, he saw that the political establishment was too afraid of another Great Depression—and of spooking global markets—to risk letting the big banks fail. Besides, the government's perceived interests had become completely entwined with Wall Street's. The revolving door between Wall Street and Washington was spinning fast, with all of the key economic positions in both the Bush and the Obama administrations held by Wall Streeters. These high finance recidivists temporarily running the government shared the same worldview as their Wall Street colleagues: big banks should not be nationalized. Instead, as Tepper apparently guessed, Treasury Secretary Henry Paulson (under Bush) and then Timothy Geithner (under Obama) would put the power of the government behind those banks so that they could go back to making sizable profits for their shareholders, who would be protected and bailed out.

As Tepper noted, many other investors panicked, either because they did fear nationalization, or because they'd been forced to sell securities to raise cash and cover other losses. Those wary investors dumped their banking securities, creating a delicious buying opportunity for Tepper. He jumped in with both feet.

Ironically, Tepper was betting *against* free market ideology, which preaches that you're rewarded when your investment succeeds and punished when it fails. When investments succeed, shareholders are rewarded with dividends and rising share prices. When they fail, shareholders lose their money.

Citigroup was a financial toxic dump in the fall of 2008, and Bank of America wasn't far behind. Under idealized "free market" capitalism, both banks would have gone under, entirely wiping out shareholders' equity. Bondholders probably would have received pennies on the dollar for their loans. Too bad. To paraphrase the drunken baseball manager played by Tom Hanks in the movie *A League of Their Own*, there's no crying in capitalism.

Tepper's big bets suggest that he knew this quaint form of capitalism was long gone. So, while most investors were fleeing financial stocks in terror, Tepper had the *cojones* to buy them up cheap. *Cojones*—literally. According to the *Wall Street Journal*, Tepper "keeps a brass replica of a pair of testicles in a prominent spot on his desk, a present from former employees. He rubs the gift for luck during the trading day to get a laugh out of colleagues" (Zuckerman 2009).

Tepper reminds me of George Washington Plunkitt of Tammany Hall, who also had *cojones*. Said Plunkitt in 1905:

> There's an honest graft, and I'm an example of how it works. I might sum up the whole thing by sayin': "I seen my opportunities and I took 'em."
>
> Just let me explain by examples. My party's in power in the city, and it's goin' to undertake a lot of public improvements. Well, I'm tipped off, say, that they're going to layout a new park at a certain place. I see my opportunity and I take it. I go to that place and I buy up all the land I can in the neighborhood. Then the board of this or that makes its plan public, and there is a rush to get my land, which nobody cared particular for before.
>
> Ain't it perfectly honest to charge a good price and make a profit on my investment and foresight? Of course, it is. Well, that's honest graft. . . .
>
> It's just like lookin' ahead in Wall Street or in the coffee or cotton market. It's honest graft, and I'm lookin' for it every

day in the year. I will tell you frankly that I've got a good lot of it, too. (Riordon 1905, 9)

Let me make this perfectly clear to any litigators present: I am *not* suggesting that Tepper traded on insider information about impending government moves or that he received any "graft" of any kind. (You're not going to make your next million off me.) I'm only saying that like Plunkitt of Tammany Hall, Tepper knew that business and government were of a piece. So when, on cue, Washington came to Wall Street's rescue, Tepper cashed in on his bet. That's how he alone earned almost as much in one year as Apple and its tens of thousands of employees did.

Does that mean Tepper has our bailout money in his pocket?

Indirectly, yes. By buying shares of Bank of America and Citigroup, Tepper became a part owner. Fine and dandy. But his shares had real value and gained in value only because of the billions in federal cash, the billions in federal asset guarantees, and the billions in cheap federal loans those banks collected from taxpayers. We didn't write a check and put it in Tepper's pocket. We didn't have to. He just "seen [his] opportunities and . . . took 'em."

The key point to remember now is that if Tepper had bet wrong and the Fed hadn't ridden to the rescue, then his hedge fund—and most hedge funds—would have lost billions. In fact, the bailouts saved the entire hedge-fund industry from utter collapse.

. . .

While Tepper set the record for hedge-fund managers in 2009 by correctly reading the political economy, John Paulson would break that record in 2010 by *misreading* it.

Paulson apparently looked at the hundreds of billions of dollars the government had spent to rescue the financial sector and avert a depression—and saw red ink that would turn green in his pocket. Sooner or later, he calculated, all of that stimulus money would overheat the economy, causing inflation to rise. This would drive down the value of the dollar, and the price of gold would skyrocket. So Paulson bought gold. *Lots* of gold.

Paulson had made billions in 2009 betting against the housing bubble (which we will analyze in depth in Step 3). By 2010, the financial community thought that he walked on water. So when Paulson charged into the gold markets, many other investors grabbed onto his illustrious coattails and followed along, pushing up the price of gold. The run-up in gold prices helped net Paulson $4.9 billion in 2010. By 2012, according to *Bloomberg News*, "Paulson & Co. is already the biggest investor in . ... the largest exchange-traded product backed by bullion, with a stake valued at $2.9 billion, a Securities and Exchange Commission filing Feb. 14 showed. Investors have 2,389.7 metric tons [of gold securities], within 0.2 percent of the record reached in December and more than all but four central banks, according to data compiled by Bloomberg" (Larkin 2012).

And yet, if Paulson really did, as reported, bet on gold because he was expecting inflation, he was dead wrong. In 2010, long-term unemployment remained at record post-Depression levels, wages were stagnant, and the economy stayed slack. Prices were not inflated—they were flat overall, as the crucial housing sector continued to crater. Even when the Arab Spring sent oil prices through the roof, the underlying rate of inflation was minuscule. In fact, the Fed was afraid that our anemic economic expansion could stall and die, sending more Americans to the unemployment line. The Fed was actually hoping for some inflation, which would have signaled a robust expansion.

As financial writer Stephen Taub reports, "The inflation Paulson foresaw did not materialize, but his proselytizing of gold as currency no doubt helped the metal soar to new heights as others followed the now-revered trader's move" (Taub 2011).

How amazing is that? Paulson bet the farm on inflation that didn't materialize and became the richest financier on Earth.

Yet not forever. The year 2011 was not kind to Paulson. Is that because his genius dried up? Or because, like anyone else in Vegas, he can't win every hand? It appears that he misunderstood the depth and breadth of the Great Recession. In his quarterly call with investors, Paulson admitted that "we made a mistake." He sure did. His Advantage Plus $18 billion fund is down 47 percent. He seems to be losing his Midas touch as well, according to the *New York Times*:

> Mr. Paulson's gold fund fell 16 percent last month, and it is now only up 1 percent in 2011. The Recovery fund, specifically focused on securities that would benefit from an improving economy, is off 31 percent for the year after losing 14 percent in September. (Ahmed 2011)

Still, if he ends up having to retire early, he can cry himself to sleep at night on cashmere pillows. (Remember, win or lose, he still gets a two percent fee on all the money invested in his fund.) So forget the iPads, the iPhones, and the combined labor of three-quarters of a million workers around the world. Forget the hassle of inventing new products, engineering them, and marketing them all over the world. Forget about the pain and suffering of managing an enormous empire of goods, services, and personnel. Instead, all you have to do to make it big in the hedge-fund world is to *bet big and win*—by reading the economy either correctly or even incorrectly, at least for a while.

· · ·

How is it possible that financial *betting* is as profitable as running one of the most successful consumer businesses in the world? Where, exactly, did Tepper's and Paulson's billions come from? What value did they create for the economy?

We know where Apple got its profits: from the sale of iPhones, iPads, Macs, software, and the like, minus the cost of production (parts and labor and cheap labor in China). Consumers and businesses supplied the money, and Apple supplied the goods: Capitalism 101.

How does money get made over at the billionaire hedge funds, though?

Journalist Sebastian Mallaby argues that the money comes from other hedge funds and investment banks. When a hedge fund makes a bet, said Mallaby, "there has to be someone on both sides of each trade; if a group of hedge funds is betting heavily on a fall in energy prices or the convergence of Latin American interest rates, somebody else must be betting just as heavily on the opposite outcome." In other words, he said, it's a "zero-sum game" (Mallaby 2007, 99).

So, no problem. According to Mallaby, each time Tepper or Paulson makes a billion, someone else loses a billion. In that case, hedge funds are really just playing at a high-stakes poker table where one bunch of rich folks loses to another, and therefore we shouldn't worry about it.

But maybe we should worry just a bit. If Mallaby is right, then hedge funds really are a different kind of economic animal. We wouldn't describe Apple as playing a "zero-sum game." High-tech firms don't win bets against customers who are on the "other side" of its sales. Of course, Apple wants to increase its market share as it competes with other companies, but the market as a whole has been on the rise for several decades. Apple's boat is rising, and so are many other boats in the consumer high-tech sector. Some companies lose out in the competition, but each transaction in the real economy is not simply characterized by winners and losers.

In theory, the financial sector's function is to channel savings into the most productive investments. We put our money into banks, and the banks loan it out. We put our money into mutual funds, and those funds provide capital for corporate investment in goods and services for all of us. Rich people put their savings into hedge funds, and those funds supposedly make productive investments all over the world.

It's Economics 101. These financial functions seem so basic and uninteresting that most economics textbooks virtually ignore them. Finance is just a pump that circulates capital to keep the economy humming along.

Okay, so what kind of pump are hedge funds? An invaluable one, insists Sebastian Mallaby—and unfairly maligned:

Imagine two successful companies. Both are staffed by very smart people, both are innovative, both have an impact far beyond their industry, improving the productivity of the capitalist system as a whole. But the first, based near San Francisco, is the subject of adoring newspaper profiles, whereas the second, based in New York, is usually vilified. (91)

Why do we mistakenly vilify hedge funds? Is it because they make so much money with so few people? Is it because they seem to peddle toxic assets? Is it because they might be engaged in shady practices? No, no, and no, claims Mallaby. We vilify them, he argues, because we don't really understand how important they are to the most vital essence of our economy—productivity.

As any newspaper reader knows technology firms are the leading edge of the U.S. knowledge economy; they made possible the productivity revolution of the past decade. But the same could just as well be said of hedge funds, which allocate the world's capital to the companies, industries and countries that can use it most productively. (91)

So, even though hedge funds employ only a handful of "very smart people," they're just as important to capitalist productivity as Apple, Dell, and Google or Ford, Chrysler, and GM or even Walmart, Boeing, and Nike—companies that employ millions of workers around the world to produce real goods and services.

That's quite a claim. How, exactly, do hedge funds increase capitalist productivity? Mallaby's main arguments are listed (and challenged) in the following sections.

DO HEDGE FUNDS INCREASE ECONOMY-WIDE PRODUCTIVITY BY FOSTERING INNOVATION?

As Mallaby argues in the previous paragraphs, hedge funds help "allocate the world's capital to the companies, industries and countries that can use it most productively," thus benefiting the entire global capitalist system. This is the idealized textbook account of what financial intermediaries do. They deploy savings (capital) to where the money will provide investors with the highest rate of return, given the level of risk each investor wants to bear. The underlying assumption is that the highest return equals the most productive use of capital. Any hedge fund that seeks the best possible return will naturally invest in the most promising industries or ventures, helping them blossom. So, by making our system more efficient, hedge funds are actually fueling the development of great innovations that are changing our lives.

Yet although we have a good idea about how to measure productivity in society, and we're reasonably certain that, for instance, the deployment of computers contributes mightily to it, we really don't have a good handle on how to measure financial productivity and whether hedge funds are contributing to that.

Writing before the 2008 crash, Mallaby assumed that hedge funds should be credited with the creation of wondrous financial innovations that have boosted the productivity of the global economy. We're talking about the likes of synthetic collateralized debt obligations, credit default swaps, and a host of similar products that litter our economy. As we now know, however, these products may not have created real value for our economy. Instead of boosting productivity, they may have harmed it.

Nevertheless, to Mallaby and others, it's obvious that hedge funds create value through the intellectual capital they deploy. They develop a varied array of investment strategies—complicated mixes of stocks, bonds, and derivatives with just the right level of risk, rate of return, and length to suit any rich buyer's personal fancy. Hedge funds can do this, says Mallaby, only because they're "allowed to operate with a great deal of freedom and flexibility, including having the ability to leverage their assets through borrowing and to bet that stocks will fall as well as rise" (93).

This freedom from tough regulations leads to innovation, and innovation leads to productivity. Conversely, argues Mallaby, any benefits that regulations might bring must be "measured against the risk of impeding innovation in the capital markets—an outcome that would be about as desirable as stifling innovation in Silicon Valley" (94).

You've got to have steel *cojones* to make that claim. Mallaby is basically saying that hedge funds earn billions because they are as innovative as Silicon Valley, and that if we do anything to stifle their financial innovation, it would be just as bad as keeping Apple from developing the iPhone.

There's some sleight of hand at work here. We all know that venture capital firms seek out innovative firms and provide them with crucial amounts of seed capital. That's an important connection with the most innovative and vital parts of our economy. We also know that private equity funds seek out troubled firms and try to fix them (although there is considerable debate about whether they make them better or worse). Yet most hedge funds have no interest at all in the well-being of the firms they invest in. They are just looking for a small edge they can leverage, and then they get out as quickly as they can, with as much profit as possible.

Another sleight of hand concerns the role of hedge funds in the stock market. Stock prices give key signals to investors and to our economy. Stocks that rise tend to be successful, and those that don't, fall behind. Yet hedge funds are not needed at all to allow those signals to accurately reflect success or failure. In fact, as we'll see later in this book, hedge funds may be messing up those signals, especially those that engage in high-frequency trading.

In fact, some critics, such as Paul Volcker, contend that there is little or no innovation at all coming from the financial sector.

When the former Fed chairman looks at what hedge funds produce, he doesn't see financial innovation. He sees a giant, unproductive casino. "I wish someone would give me one shred of neutral evidence that financial innovation has led to economic growth—one shred of evidence," Volcker laments. In fact, Volcker says, the only useful product the financial sector has created in the last three decades is the ATM machine.

Clearly, Volcker is not a fan of items such as synthetic collateralized debt obligations (CDOs), an innovation developed by several different hedge funds in cooperation with investment banks.

Before the 2008 crash, CDOs made a lot of money for a few people, but then they turned toxic. First, CDOs pumped up the housing bubble, and then, when the bubble burst, CDOs helped spread the crisis to the entire financial sector.

So, it's a bit of a stretch to argue that CDOs were a productive investment that hugely bolstered the economy. True, for a time they did shower hedge-fund investors and big banks with enormous profits. But then things turned south and cost our economy trillions of dollars and millions of jobs.

Then there's the array of "innovative" financial mortgage products created by Countrywide and Washington Mutual. These items allowed thousands of working-class Americans and speculators to buy homes—homes they couldn't really afford. Those risky mortgages were then sold to Wall Street, where they were sliced, diced, and packaged into securities, given AAA credit ratings, and resold to investors looking to make a killing. They made a killing, alright. The economy was one casualty, the homebuyers were another.

At the time when Mallaby wrote his piece in 2007, it was still fashionable to argue that perhaps exotic securities such as CDOs combined with credit default swaps helped the economy. Yet now we know that they were toxic waste masquerading as AAA-rated securities. Their very existence helped crash our economy. We, the taxpayers, are now the proud owners of many financial Superfund sites. As we will explore in depth in Step 4, hedge funds were key enablers of the housing casino and these wretched securities.

Yet despite all of the damning evidence against these financial "innovations," isn't it still possible that hedge funds contribute to overall capitalist productivity? Maybe their contribution is more subtle and so is hard to locate and measure. In that case, however, Mallaby should temper his outrageous claims. The onus is on Mallaby to precisely and explicitly show how hedge funds are as productive and vital to the economy as the leading high-tech firms are.

He can't do it because it can't be done.

DO HEDGE FUNDS BRING
"LIQUIDITY" TO MARKETS?

One day I ran into a young man who worked as a day trader—a kind of one-man hedge fund. Day traders hop in and out of markets each day, trying to locate small differences in prices between similar investments and betting on which way stocks and bonds will go.

I asked him how a financial transaction tax on trades might affect the kinds of maneuvers he was making. He wasn't happy at all about that idea. He wondered why anyone would want to penalize his useful work by slapping a tax on it. "Look," he said, "we bring money into the markets. We make it easier for everyone to make trades. Bringing liquidity to markets is good for us all."

Hedge-fund cheerleaders love this argument. Mallaby says that "hedge funds are thought to account for a third of the turnover in U.S. equities and an even higher share in more exotic financial instruments" (92). (The FBI's website claims that hedge funds account for 20 to 50 percent of the daily action on the New York Stock Exchange. Those more familiar with high-speed trading say the figure now is nearly 80 percent.)

It's certainly true that bringing money to markets can be a good thing. For example, when distressed mutual funds have to unload stocks and bonds at bargain prices because investors have pulled out, hedge funds snap them up, betting that the securities will regain value. At least some of the time, mutual funds probably get a better price than they otherwise would without these bottom-feeding hedge funds. So hedge-fund liquidity may sometimes moderate wild swings in financial markets.

On the other hand, academics who have dug into this claim about hedge funds rescuing distressed mutual funds found that sometimes hedge funds may actually be siphoning money *away* from those mutual funds through a maneuver called "front-running."

Front-running is betting ahead of the action. For example, if somehow you figured out that a distressed mutual fund soon had to sell a lot of stocks, you could short (bet against) those stocks before the mutual fund dumped them. You'd profit nicely when, as you expected, those stocks declined in value, due to the massive mutual fund fire sale. You can do that legally (if you can actually guess which distressed hedge fund might be dumping what kind of stocks). Or you could do it illegally by obtaining insider information about the impending sale—either from complicit mutual fund employees or from the firms that are handling its trades. (We'll save a fuller exploration of the illegal variety for Step 6.)

Whether legal or illegal, however, this kind of front-running does not serve our economy well. Hedge funds that play this game are not bringing new money into the market. They are selling before the mutual fund dumps its securities, not buying afterward.

Yet how do we even know whether this is really happening, since hedge funds don't have to report their short positions—that is, their bets against securities?

A group of academic experts came up with a way in their paper "Do Hedge Funds Profit from Mutual Fund Distress?":

> Rather than trying to observe hedge funds in the act of front-running itself, we begin our investigation by asking whether, in the time series, hedge funds earn higher returns in those periods when there appear to be more good opportunities for front-running. By analogy, *if one suspected a group of police officers of taking bribes from drug dealers, but was unable to observe the act of bribery directly, it might be informative to ask whether those officers who patrolled the areas with the highest levels of drug activity also owned the most expensive houses and cars.* (Italics added.) (Chen et al. 2007)

An interesting choice of analogies, don't you think?

These esteemed academics aren't saying that hedge-fund managers are like crooked cops, but they *are* saying that hedge funds appear to be engaged in some kind of front-running. If they're right, then hedge funds are not always the great liquidity providers they claim to be.

Some people further argue that hedge funds add liquidity by "deepening the market." What on earth does that mean?

A "deep" financial market is when people are doing lots of buying and selling in every conceivable kind of financial market, so that no one has to worry about finding a buyer for any given stock, bond, future, option, or other derivative. If you have to sell or buy a lot of something, what you want is a really, really deep market. That way, you won't move the market against yourself. You'll just be a small pebble in a very big pond, making a tiny ripple.

It's always safest to buy and sell in very deep markets. And because the United States has the deepest markets on the planet, most of the world's investment money flows through the United States.

So, thank heavens for hedge funds, say Mallaby and company, which contribute $2.2 trillion toward "deepening" U.S. markets. Hedge funds and their banking cousins make our markets hum, which is why they're the envy of the world.

Yet if hedge funds deepen and liquefy markets so much, how come they didn't prevent the massive freeze-up of nearly all financial markets during the Great Recession? Where was that much-vaunted liquidity and depth when we needed it most? It dried up in a matter of hours as the crisis deepened. Suddenly, everyone was selling into down markets, which pushed them down further. In many markets, there were no takers. Entire markets, including money-market funds, had to be totally guaranteed by the federal government before they could even function again. It seems that although hedge funds can indeed bring massive liquidity to markets, they can also dry up in the space of minutes, contributing to economic catastrophe.

I have a different question, though. When hedge funds actually *are* providing liquidity to the market, who benefits? Those of us with modest investment funds trade infrequently. Our pension funds aren't frequent traders, either, so liquidity isn't such a big deal for us. Is it possible that hedge-fund traders are mainly deepening markets *for one another*? That all of this liquidity is mainly benefiting the high-frequency trading strategies of hedge funds and the proprietary trading desks at banks? If so, we need to reconsider the claim that hedge-fund liquidity is a boon to mankind.

Let's try a thought experiment: What would happen if hedge funds didn't exist at all? Where would all that liquidity go? Would rich investors, pension funds, and endowments suddenly hide money under their mattresses? Or would that money still seek out investments? Of course it would. Some investors would invest on their own. Others would use mutual funds. Some might leave more in bank CDs and government bonds. Yet one thing is certain: the stock markets would not be starved for funds.

What would be missing is the *extra leverage*—the borrowed money that accompanies hedge-fund investments. We'd also be missing the billions of high-speed trades that might be destabilizing markets and moving prices away from reflecting their true worth. (More on that in the following pages and in the step on high-frequency trading.)

Perhaps the best way to view hedge-fund liquidity is as a form of high-speed amplification—the leverage, plus the rapid turnover of trades, dramatically increases the volume on stock exchanges. Yet it's highly questionable whether that produces any real value for the economy. It does, however, have an important function: it siphons off investor wealth into the pockets of crafty traders.

Do Hedge Funds Make Market Prices More Accurate and Efficient?

This takes us to the heart of what many hedge funds do. Like my friendly day trader, they scour the world looking for inconsistencies in the prices of similar financial products. For example, the hedge-fund trader Keith McCullough, who wrote (with Rich Blake) *Diary of a Hedge Fund Manager*, specialized in searching stock markets in emerging nations looking for similar companies with similar prospects but that had different stock prices. Once he was sure he had found a pair, he would bet that their prices would converge. He shorted (sold) the one with the higher price and went long on (bought) the one with the lower price. As the prices converged, he'd make a tidy sum on both sides of the deal.

Theoretically, at least, capital will be invested better if those price discrepancies don't exist. This "arbitrage" investment strategy ends up creating a truer price, the argument goes, and the more accurate the price, the better the allocation of capital all over the world. The closer the price is to its "real" value, the better our overall deployment of capital.

Because hedge funds and banks deploy hundreds of billions of dollars in search of these price discrepancies, markets all over the world are becoming more price-efficient. So many hedge funds know how to do arbitrage now that it's actually getting harder to make big bucks at it. We're told that some hedge funds have hired all manner of mathematicians and physicists to mine the data in mysterious ways, trying to uncover shadowy pricing patterns that others can't see.

Yet how, exactly, does this kind of "price efficiency" benefit the general public? Is it really a massive waste of resources if prices of similar securities in the same industry are a bit off? What difference would it make, really, if these minor price differences existed for a few more minutes? (Of course, hedge-fund managers don't care whether price efficiency benefits everyone. In fact, a horribly inefficient market could be a hedge-fund bonanza: the more price anomalies, the more profits.)

To my knowledge, no one has measured what that slight wobble might cost us. That's because it's not worth the effort. Investors will always notice the difference and move the prices by buying and selling until the differences go away.

Arbitrage has been going on for centuries, but now highly sophisticated hedge funds with enormous bankrolls, leverage, and sophisticated computer technologies are able to exploit those differences in a nanosecond, instead of a few days. My question is: So what? How is extracting those profits good for society, because the price discrepancies would have closed anyway—at whatever speed?

High-speed trading does have real consequences in other ways, though. As we'll see in Step 7, high-speed trading makes it easier for hedge funds to engage in destructive trading. Hedge-fund managers, with their ultrafast computers, can often sense price movements more quickly than anyone else—including you, if you're the average investor. So they jump ahead of your trade, making money by buying the security before you do and selling it back to you at a slightly higher price. It's as if a hedge fund got to see the end of the race before everyone else. They know immediately who is going to win, and they bet accordingly.

Again, we have no evidence to suggest that hedge funds make prices more efficient. Meanwhile, there's considerable data emerging that they are moving prices away from their true worth. There is every reason to think that if hedge funds didn't exist at all, prices would still find their proper level and perhaps do it even better than when battered about by hedge-fund traders. What would be missing, of course, are the vast profits that get siphoned into the pockets of hedge-fund managers. Remember that hedge-fund managers don't care about finding the "right" price. They only care about cashing in before you do.

Do Hedge Funds Absorb and Reduce Financial Risk?

Okay, so maybe hedge-fund managers are a bit greedy, and maybe hedge-fund trading can be a bit disruptive, but don't hedge funds ultimately reduce overall risk in the system? With all of those hedge funds inventing unique trading moves, aren't we dispersing risk? Mallaby puts it this way:

Moreover, hedge funds collectively do not so much create risk as absorb it. The funds can be viewed as quasi insurers; by shouldering risks that others wish to avoid, they remove a potential obstacle to business. For example, banks have to limit their lending for fear that borrowers might default. But hedge funds are willing to buy credit derivatives that transfer the default risk from the banks to themselves—freeing the banks to finance more economic activity. (97)

Why didn't this help us during the Great Recession of 2008? I suppose it could be argued that it would have, if there had been more hedge funds and fewer big banks.

To understand Mallaby's claim, however, we need to understand what he's really talking about: the $26 trillion market for credit default swaps. This invention allows investors and speculators to bet that a given company or financial security will or will not fail. It's basically financial insurance, but it's not called insurance, in order to avoid strict insurance industry regulations. Those who want to insure a given security against default pay quarterly premiums to those who are giving out the insurance.

In theory, this moves risk from those who don't want it to those willing to take it on. Mallaby suggests that the hedge-fund buccaneers are the prime insurers—they're willing to take the risk from banks and others in exchange for the flow of premiums. This, in turn, makes our banking system less risky.

In the real world, it's a different game.

Before the economic crash, the big financial insurer was AIG. It bet nearly half a trillion dollars by insuring all kinds of mortgage-related securities against default. (Think of it as AIG providing mortgage insurance for tens of thousands of homes at the same time.) Because these credit default swaps weren't regulated, AIG didn't have to put aside reserves as a real insurance company does. So when the market crashed, and the company had to pay up, it couldn't. The American taxpayer then poured more than $170 billion into AIG to keep it from taking down a major part of the economy. If hedge funds were acting as "quasi insurers" during the crash, they were two-bit players compared to AIG. In fact, as we'll see in Step 4, several key hedge funds actually bet against the housing market, using synthetic CDOs. These hedge funds were acting as the insured, not as the insurers.

Let's think about what being "the insured" really means. It means that hedge funds would profit from instability, from the insolvency of firms, from the crash of securities, and from general economic mayhem. This kind of insurance allows hedge funds to rig bets by designing securities that will quickly fail so that they can bet against them using financial insurance (credit default swaps). In short, the more financial instability, the more opportunities for arbitrage and bet rigging.

Back in the real world (instead of in Mallaby's), what are hedge funds the cure for? Not much at all. They are money-making companies, not welfare institutions. When they trade in risky instruments, the risk does not magically disperse. It's still in our system. That's not theory. It happened before, and it can happen again.

As we will see in Step 4, during the crisis, hedge funds were major players in wrecking the economy, not saving it. The credit default swap insurance game did not disperse risk—it amplified it and contaminated the entire financial system. So when the house of cards came down, the pain also traveled far and wide. Hedge funds interconnect many parts of the global financial system. As a result, it's now hard to contain economic shocks in one sector or one corner of the world. Instead, the shock spreads everywhere and rapidly. This kind of efficiency comes with an enormous price—increasing instability.

Unless you're Rip Van Winkle and slept through the Great Recession, you won't have any trouble seeing through a few more of Mallaby's hedge fund apologias.

- Hedge funds are supposed to *"reduce the danger that economies will over-respond to shocks"* (97). So, where were they when markets were collapsing? They were destabilizing Lehman Brothers, GM, AIG, and any other company they could find to bet against.

- Hedge funds *"reduce the chances that markets will rise to unsustainable levels in the first place"* (97). But somehow they missed the biggest housing bubble in history?
- Hedge funds *"actually diminish the risk of the nightmare scenario"* (100). Whoops.

In sum, industry cheerleaders can't come near to answering our initial question: what value do hedge-fund elites create in exchange for their million an hour?

———— Do's and Don'ts ————

- **Don't** ever get into the business of making things. Your job is to take money away from people who make things.

- **Do** claim to bring liquidity to markets. It sounds profound, even if you take it away when it's most needed.

- **Don't** tell Paul Volcker what you do for a living, unless you meet at an ATM.

STEP 3

Rip Off Entire Countries Because That's Where the Money Is

If you want to make a million per hour, you can't worry about democracy or national sovereignty or even the welfare of millions of people. You can't worry about the needs of widows and orphans, and you can't worry about whether you bankrupt a country. Sometimes you just have to suck it up and rob a national treasury. And please don't worry about getting bad press, because there are plenty of hedge-fund cheerleaders around to justify your every move.

With pompoms in hand, they'll be quick to claim that hedge-fund gamblers can actually protect citizens from irrational government policies. So you can rob a country blind and then claim to be helping its citizens. Perfect!

You see weak-kneed politicians buckle under special interests and their own selfish and short-sighted political aspirations. Yet hedge-fund managers can rise above the fray, acting as grand enforcers. They're the go-to guys who can compel governments to do the right thing, the same way they ostensibly compel corporate executives to do the right thing.

We can see how speculators can discipline wayward governments by examining one of the iconic hedge-fund trades of all
time: George Soros versus the Bank of England. How did this top
hedge-fund manager use his wealth and power to influence government policy? And was that influence benign or helpful?

Here's the *Cliffs Notes* version of this Soros saga: After the fall
of the Berlin Wall in 1989, the former West Germany spared no
expense to swiftly integrate the former East Germany into a unified country and economy. Yet Germany's leaders feared that the
enormous costs of absorbing the East would also trigger inflation (which the German people have deeply feared ever since
the hyper-inflation of the Weimar Republic). So the central bank
raised interest rates to cool down the economy and contain any
hint of rising prices.

Although that move made good sense to the Germans, it created
turmoil elsewhere. At the time, European and British currencies were hooked together in a negotiated system—the European
Exchange Rate Mechanism (ERM)—that aimed to limit currency fluctuations within narrow target ranges. Each nation in the
ERM agreed to contain currency movements by having the country's central bank buy up its own currency when the value dipped
too low and selling its reserves when the value got too high. This
agreement was an important step toward a united Europe based
on a common currency—the euro.

When Germany raised its interest rates to prevent inflation
and protect the value of the mark, however, traders of all kinds
flocked to the scene. They began selling other European currencies and buying up the mark, taking advantage of the spike in
Germany's interest rate.

This put England in a difficult quandary. Under ERM rules, it
was supposed to keep the value of the pound sterling within the
agreed-on range. Yet with traders everywhere selling their pounds
to buy German marks, the Bank of England was obliged to protect the pound's value. It had several options: It could hold to the
ERM standards, either by buying pounds itself or by raising its
own interest rates so that others would want to buy pounds, or

it could blow off the ERM agreement and announce that it was devaluing the pound, dropping out of the ERM range.

Raising interest rates was an unhappy option, because most English home mortgages came with adjustable rates pegged to the interest rate set by the Bank of England. So if the central bank hiked interest rates, homeowners all over England would suffer. What's more, the country's economy was stalled at the time, and higher interest rates would further slow economic activity—not a winning political strategy for the conservative government of John Major.

Yet England's quandary was George Soros's big moment. He and his skilled lieutenants Stan Druckenmiller and Rob Johnson bet the farm against the pound (they "shorted" it). Soros sold pounds at the current price and agreed to buy them back in the future, when he predicted that the price would be much cheaper. If the pound did indeed drop in value, Soros would pocket the difference. If it increased in value, Soros would lose. He believed, however, that all of the signs were pointing to a decrease in the pound's value.

In fact, Soros knew his bet was "asymmetrical," which is a hedge-fund manager's nirvana. *Asymmetrical* means that it was quite possible that he'd win big, but not very likely that he'd *lose* big. Yes, it was possible that the British pound might go up, but probably not by much. After all, the Bank of England's only aim was to keep the pound within the agreed-on range. It had no desire to see the pound burst through the roof. Yet it was far more likely that the pound's value would crash. If it did, Soros's short bet would net a fortune.

Soros sold a whopping $10 billion worth of pounds—and other hedge funds piled on as well. The collective sell-off pushed down the value of the pound and put enormous pressure on the Bank of England, which didn't have enough reserves to outlast the assault. In a last-minute defense of the pound, the Bank of England increased interest rates by 2 percent. It didn't work. The downward pressure (more selling and shorting of pounds) continued until the Bank of England gave up on the ERM range and allowed for a devaluation of the pound.

This spelled victory for Soros, to the tune of $1 billion—the biggest hedge-fund killing ever, to date. (In 1992, Soros did it again, more quietly this time, when he successfully pressured Sweden to devalue its currency. The yield on this bet: another billion.)

This brief sketch of Soros's remarkable trade and the complex political issues surrounding it brings us to the main question: Did Soros protect citizens from irrational government policies? Or did he fleece them? Who won and who lost in this deal?

Once again we turn to Sebastian Mallaby, who in *More Money Than God: Hedge Funds and the Making of a New Elite*, admits part of the truth: The losers were the lowly British citizens, the taxpayers. The winners were a few already fabulously rich individuals.

> Britain was presiding over a vast financial transfer from its long-suffering taxpayers to a global army of traders. . . . Of the almost $4 billion loss to British taxpayers, an estimated $300 million flowed to Bruce Kovner, the senior member of the Commodities Corporation trio [another large hedge fund], and $250 million to Paul Jones [the head of the Tudor Investment hedge fund]; the top seven currency desks at U.S. banks were said to have bagged $800 million among them. But Soros Fund Management's profits on the sterling bet came to over $1 billion. (Mallaby 2010, 166–167)

Yet as we'll soon see, Mallaby came to praise Soros, not to bury him.

• • •

Before you try your hand at becoming the next George Soros, you might want to ask yourself two questions: Is there any way to justify this transfer of wealth from the people of England to a tiny handful of speculators? Is there any redeeming social value to this transaction?

Mallaby again suggests answers that exonerate hedge funds. He claims that the entire concept of currency "pegs"—the ERM's goal of keeping currencies within a narrow range of value—was a bad idea. Hedge funds basically destroyed such currency pegs, and Mallaby says good riddance:

> In committing to the exchange-rate mechanism, European governments had made a promise that they lacked the ability to keep. They had bottled up currency movements until a power greater than themselves had blown the cork into their faces. (Mallaby 2010, 169)

Mallaby goes even further: Yes, the nation maybe was fleeced, he says—not by hedge-fund speculators, but by the duly elected government of England. Here's a passage designed to stave off any twinges of guilt that hedge-fund speculators might suffer:

> To be sure, [Soros's and] Druckenmiller's trading had upended the economic policy of the British government, but this was not necessarily bad. The high interest rates accompanying German unification had created a situation in which sterling needed to exit the exchange-rate mechanism. Britain's rulers had failed to recognize this truth until Druckenmiller had recognized it for them. The fact that John Major had transferred $1 billion plus of taxpayers' money to the Soros funds was not entirely Druckenmiller's fault. If somebody had fleeced the country blind, it was the prime minister not the speculator. (Mallaby 2010, 171)

Better yet, Mallaby claims we should view hedge-fund managers not as economic vandals but as "liberators":

> By betting against the pound and helping to destroy the ERM, Soros ended up making money not by economic vandalism but by liberating Britons from their leaders'

unsustainable choices. As the economists Melvyn Krauss and
the former hedge fund manager Michael Simoff have written, hedge funds may be a disruptive force—but they disrupt
what needs disrupting. (Mallaby 2007, 96)

Yet what, exactly, needs disrupting? Well, it certainly is possible to argue that by forcing the Bank of England to devalue the
pound sterling, British interest rates could come down, thereby
helping to counter a slack economy that was harming the British
people. In that way, the British people would be the ultimate ben-
eficiaries of a sounder monetary policy, even if it transferred billions of dollars into the pockets of currency speculators. Maybe it
would be worth the price?

It's not as if Soros and company were hired as consultants
to help straighten out Europe or the British economy, though.
The collapse of interest rates was purely coincidental to what
the speculators hoped to achieve. They were shorting the pound
and wanted to collect on that bet. "Liberation" of the British
people was the furthest thing from their minds. After all, Soros
was representing no one but himself. He was protecting his
money, not the people of England. If his maneuver did anything
good at all, it was entirely accidental. No one elected Soros to
serve as the financial William the Conqueror. Is it really possible, as Mallaby does, to justify robbing from the poor to give to
the rich?

Well, when in doubt, you can fall back on economic theology:
that markets when left to themselves always achieve the best
results, and that government interference always creates need-
less inefficiencies. Free-market theologians, therefore, would
argue that Soros was simply carrying out the work of the omni-
scient invisible hand that prevented the governments of Europe
from further screwing up currency markets and their own
economies.

And doesn't this story have a happy ending? Didn't Soros's
trade accelerate the move by Europe toward adopting a common
currency—which is where it wanted and needed to go?

As a child of the Holocaust, Soros certainly wanted to see a new common currency, which he believed would mitigate the risk of another European conflagration. In fact, Soros reportedly said that a common currency wasn't in his personal financial interest, but he wanted it anyway. A single European currency, he said, "would put speculators like me out of business, but I would be delighted to make that sacrifice" (Madrick 1992, 427). (You might, too, after you make your first billion.)

Part of Soros's wish came true on January 1, 2002, when continental Europe (but not England and Scandinavia) adopted the euro as a common currency. The ERM ended, and so did speculation on the European currencies that no longer existed. But alas, Soros was wrong: hedge-fund speculators were not put out of business. They just moved on to other arenas ripe for their "disruptive liberation"—particularly, sovereign debt and banks that hold it. Today, these speculators are contributing to dangerous runs on the debt of the PIIGS—Portugal, Ireland, Italy, Greece, and Spain.

The ironies abound. The PIIGS debt crisis stems directly from the 2008 Wall Street–created crash. Private banks in these nations had invested heavily in mortgage-backed securities that came with AAA ratings from the U.S. rating agencies but turned out to be toxic trash. When Wall Street crashed, so did many of these European banks. The PIIGS governments were forced to bail out their largest banks, assuming massive debts in the process. The bailouts, combined with the economic slowdown, deepened government deficits and increased the risk that these countries would default on their national debts. This drove up the interest rates that the nations would have to pay to refinance their debts—making deficit reduction even harder. The higher rates and spending cutbacks weakened the economies of the PIIGS, further increasing their debt burdens.

Powerhouse hedge funds, whose speculation had helped drive Wall Street over the edge in the first place, are now hard at work "liberating" Europe once again. These bond vigilantes want their bonds fully repaid, and they want the PIIGS to cut government spending dramatically before banks and hedge funds loan these governments any more money. To get the job done, bond vigilantes are pressing to "liberate" European workers from their social safety nets so that PIIGS government deficits are reduced. As of this writing, we are witnessing draconian cutbacks in social programs of every shape and kind, especially in Greece. Once again, the average citizen will have to make do with less so that these very rich speculators can profit more.

The battle over Greek debt again pitted hedge funds against nation-states. This time, the nation-state was all of Europe, in the form of the European Union and its central bank. The hedge-fund game was to buy up discounted Greek bonds and then insure them at full value by buying credit default swaps (mostly from the European banks). If Greece suffered a "credit event," then the insurance would kick in, and the hedge funds would make a killing. If Greek debt was restructured "voluntarily," then hedge funds would earn less or maybe even take a loss, depending on the price they paid for the discounted bonds. Europe did not want the bailout money for Greece to end up in the hedge-fund coffers, especially while Europe was insisting on such draconian cuts in Greek wages, benefits, and public services. To achieve a modicum of fairness, Greece, with full backing from the EU, threatened to rewrite the terms of any bonds held by hedge funds that refused to accept the "voluntary" agreement.

Not so fast. Hedge funds threatened to go to court—and not just any court. They were headed to the European Court of Human Rights, of all places, claiming that their economic rights would be usurped if the bond rules were changed by Greece. To settle the matter, Europe once again made a major concession to hedge funds, while still allowing for an orderly default. The restructuring of Greek debt successfully reduced the real value of the bonds to about 26 cents on the dollar, thereby saving Greece tens of billions of dollars in interest payments. Nevertheless, a "credit event" was declared by the International Swaps & Derivatives Association (ISDA), the private bankers' group in charge of triggering the credit default swap insurance claims. The net result was the transfer of $2.5 billion into the hedge-fund coffers, most of it coming from subsidized European banks.

Here's another irony. The common currency, which Soros believed would be far superior to the ERM system, now is serving as a straitjacket that prevents fiscally distressed European countries from climbing out of recession. If these nations still had their individual currencies, they could devalue them by printing more money. Not only would this reduce the real value of their public debts, but this action would also lower the prices on their exports, making their industries more competitive. Rising exports, in turn, would help propel them out of their economic doldrums. Yet that's not an option for the countries using the euro as the common currency.

When the whole story finally emerges about the role of speculators during the most recent European debt crisis, someone will almost surely claim that the hedge funds were simply "disrupting what needs disrupting." Already, there is talk about why the common European currency may not be sustainable. (By the time you read this, the entire euro project may be in shambles.)

It seems that speculators not only didn't like currency pegs, but don't much care for a unified currency, either. So, what do they really want?

Money, money, and more money! For hedge funds, it's always about making as much money as fast as they can. It's certainly not about contributing to the common good or supporting just policies—or "liberating" anyone from anything. Hedge funds do not "disrupt what needs disrupting," but they're certainly happy to disrupt anything and everything, so long as it provides a heftier bottom line.

Is it really only about money, though? Of course, but colossal egos are also in play. It's one thing for a hedge fund to take on a corporation and beat it into submission. It's quite another to garner the resources to make England buckle, one of the wealthiest countries in the world—and a nuclear power, no less. Just think of the royal satisfaction of bringing a royal kingdom to its knees. It harks back to the days when European kings were beholden to wealthy moneylenders to fund their perpetual wars and profligate lifestyles. Yet there is one enormous difference: During the feudal era, if a king felt too squeezed, he had the power to confiscate the money and the property of any moneylender who pushed too hard for repayment. The sovereign could even put the financier to death. With today's international mobility of capital, hedge funds fear no significant reprisals. They can and do attack sovereign nations at will.

Finally, we need to step back to admire Soros's astonishing innovation. Not only did he take on the British state by betting on its failure, but he also did all he could to make it so. By betting so large and so forcefully, he pushed the Bank of England beyond its resources. It laid down its sword after it could no longer withstand the assault on its financial ramparts. Hedge funds got the message. From that point on, they embraced that innovation. Not only would hedge funds bet on the failure of companies, currencies, and entire countries, but they would also encourage the very failures they needed to win their bets. It didn't take long (as we will see in Step 5) to develop an entirely new business—the business of designing securities that were certain to fail so that hedge funds could bet against them—and win big, even bigger than Soros.

. . .

For all of you would-be hedge-fund billionaires (and cheerleaders), you're damn lucky you didn't live in the wake of World War II. Back then, Allied leaders had no tolerance at all for speculators. The soon-to-be-victorious leaders of the war were determined to put currency speculators out of business as they met at Bretton Woods in 1944 to shape a new global financial system.

Virtually every Allied representative believed that the awful turbulence of the Great Depression had been greatly exacerbated by currency speculators. In fact, U.S. Treasury secretary Henry Morgenthau told the Bretton Woods delegates, their global agreements needed to "drive the usurious moneylenders from the temple of international finance" (Reill and Szelényi 2011, 243).

They also believed that the Depression was deepened by nations that had adopted a "beggar-thy-neighbor" approach to trade—using restricted trading zones and currency manipulation to push their own exports at the expense of other nations.

So as World War II came to a close, the major capitalist powers wanted stable exchange rates that would encourage free trade, instead of debilitating trade wars that could eventually lead to the real thing—as they had in the previous two world wars. They also wanted to design a system that would allow each nation to institute progressive social welfare programs and full employment policies without fear of capital flight. As part of the drive for stable currencies, governments sought to limit the way private corporations, banks, and investors moved money around the globe. Hence, the Bretton Woods agreement adopted capital controls to put sharp limits on speculation.

The United States was already leading the way by enacting national policies to severely restrict finance in other ways—again, with the aim of preventing a repeat of the Great Depression. U.S. policymakers had reached a profound consensus about what had caused the catastrophic stock market bubble of the late 1920s: unrestrained speculative fervor. They believed that only strict government controls on the financial sector would prevent such bubbles and busts in the future. Lawmakers passed New Deal legislation enabling the government to police the stock market and tightly control the private banking system. They also erected a high wall between investment banks and commercial banks so that federally insured consumer deposits could not be used to bankroll financial gambling (the Glass-Steagall Act). As a result of these controls, Wall Street's compensation was reduced to something more on a par with similarly educated workers in other sectors of the economy. All in all, these draconian controls turned Wall Street into a fairly boring place to work—which was precisely the point.

More important, the net effect was to protect the public from financial chaos. The combination of international monetary controls, controls on capital, restrictions on speculation, and tight controls on Wall Street all contributed to the longest period of financial stability and economic growth since the dawn of the Industrial Revolution. From the launching of the Bretton Woods agreements at the close of World War II up through the early 1970s, financial crises virtually disappeared. (There was only one of note: Brazil, 1964.) Yet since the 1970s, when the U.S. government began easing Wall Street controls, the world has experienced dozens of financial crashes.

Here's how Carmen Reinhart and Kenneth Rogoff, who have compiled comprehensive data on financial crises dating back eight hundred years, described the financial calm between the late 1940s and the early 1970s:

> This calm may be partly explained by booming world growth, but perhaps more so by the repression of the domestic financial markets (in varying degrees) and the heavy-handed use of capital controls that followed for many years after World War II. (We are not necessarily implying that such repression and controls are the right approach to dealing with the risk of financial crises.)
>
> *Since the early 1970s, financial and international capital account liberalization took root worldwide. So, too, have banking crises.* [Italics in the original.] (Reinhart and Rogoff 2008, 6–7)

What Reinhart and Rogoff are saying in polite terms is that the deregulatory wave that swept through America and most of the Western world after the 1970s again turned financial markets into boom-and-bust casinos. Hedge funds began popping up everywhere just as government took its foot off Wall Street's neck. A modern Henry Morgenthau might suggest that hedge-fund speculation helped trigger the many financial crises we've weathered since deregulation. (We'll return to this topic in Step 4.)

You can be virtually certain, however, that there would be no million-dollars-an-hour club if hedge funds had to submit to New Deal limits on finance and Bretton Woods controls on exchange rates and capital mobility.

Lucky for you that President Nixon put an end to the Bretton Woods agreements in 1970 by taking the dollar off the gold standard. This allowed all currencies to "float" in value against one another.

Hallelujah! Speculators were back in the "liberation" business.

Do's and Don'ts

- **Do** remember that any and all regulations on capital mobility are evil and must be destroyed.

- **Do** remind people that taking away their money teaches them important life lessons.

- **Don't** put your money in a foreign bank when George Soros is visiting.

- **Do** visit Greece before a hedge fund buys it (or after, if you're the buyer).

STEP 4

Use Other People's Money

With the end of the Bretton Woods accords, speculators such as George Soros could target currencies with the hope of making a quick killing at the expense of the average citizen. Let's not pick on Soros, though—he didn't make these lax rules. Soros is what happens when you decontrol currencies.

Yet Soros and company won big not just because the rules had changed or because they seemed to be smarter than everyone else in reading the complexities of Europe's political economy. Their great success also depended on *having billions of dollars to bet*. Where on earth do these massive sums of investment capital come from? How did the wealthy investors and the large institutions get their hands on all of that capital? Soros could not become Soros without having billions of dollars to play with.

There are two massive sources of capital that we need to wrap our arms around. The first comes from the changing nature of the U.S. income distribution. We need to explore how the gains in U.S. productivity were transferred from working people to the top 1 percent of our population.

The second major source of betting money is less obvious but even more astounding. Hedge funds are able to spike up their bets with vast quantities of borrowed money (both real and fictitious). Thanks to the debt boom created by the Federal Reserve and financial deregulation, hedge funds could leverage their bets to the hilt. Wall Street "financial engineers" offered hedge funds exotic new ways to magnify their bets, which in turn created more debt capital. Fantasy finance was able to create new betting money out of thin air.

Between rich people's skyrocketing incomes and increased access to enormous leverage, hedge funds had the money to bet big.

To make your first million an hour, you'll need to latch onto these two gravy trains. Let's look more closely at each.

PRODUCTIVITY GROWTH AND WAGE GAINS BREAK APART

If there is only one graph or chart in this book that you need to remember, Figure 4.1 is it. It's key to understanding how hedge funds found so much money to play with and why the rest of us are at their mercy.

Figure 4.1   U.S. Nonsupervisory Weekly Wages (in 2012 Dollars) and Productivity

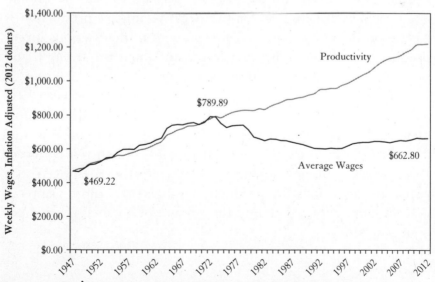

Source: Author's calculations based on Bureau of Labor Statistics data.

Take a close look at the top line, which charts productivity since World War II. Productivity is a crude measure of a nation's economic prowess. It is derived by taking the total value of everything we produce in the private sector and dividing by the number of hours worked to produce it. Wages are not part of this statistic. We only want to know how many working hours it takes to produce all of our private-sector goods and services. Then we index that number so that we can measure the year-to-year percentage change in our output per hour. As you can see, productivity has gone up dramatically since World War II. (The productivity index number rose from 32.2 in 1947 to 152.5 by January 2012.) Remarkably, the productivity index rose in sixty of the last sixty-five years.

Although it's a very rough measure, productivity does tell us a great deal about our economy because it indicates the overall level of knowledge, organization, effort, and skills of our entire workforce. It also reflects the extent to which technology (from manufacturing hardware to office software) has increased our output. The more a society can produce per hour, the more advanced its workers' skills and overall productive capacity.

To be sure, there are major flaws in this statistic. Here's a big one: it leaves out many things that don't have a price in the marketplace. For instance, it doesn't fully account for our health and our overall well-being or for the negative impact production is having on the environment. Yet even within these serious limits, productivity tells us something important about the strength and capacity of our economy and society.

Figure 4.1 has two basic time periods. The first, between 1947 and 1973, depicts the years of our post–World War II economic miracle. During those years, our economy experienced a sustained rise in productivity, year after year (with the exception of 1956, where it dipped slightly). These were the Bretton Woods years, during which the productivity index rose more than 128 percent—more than doubling the amount of goods produced per hour of labor.

The bottom line of Figure 4.1—average weekly wages minus inflation—shows that during that same period, the fruits of our productivity, our bounteous output of goods and services, were shared by the vast majority of Americans. As productivity increased, so did our real wages and our overall standard of living. As you can see, during that post–World War II boom, *the two lines danced their way up together*. Wages, after taking out the impact of inflation, went up by 68 percent.

I saw it in my family and all around us in working-class New Jersey. My mother was a bookkeeper at a furniture company, and my father worked in a factory as a wiring technician. We were not particularly well off, but by the late 1950s, my parents could afford to buy a modest home in a middle-class suburban community with a strong school system. As the economic boom continued, their wages increased slowly but surely, so that by the mid-1960s, they could afford to send me to a private college (with the help of some scholarship money and student loans). By the end of the 1960s, they even earned enough to take a short vacation abroad, instead of to the Catskills.

We were not alone in our modest but growing prosperity. The vast majority of working people—the group called nonsupervisory production workers, about 80 percent of the workforce—saw a similar rise in income and wealth. As the bottom line shows, from 1947 to 1973 this group's average real wages jumped from $470 to $790 (in 2012 dollars), mirroring the nation's productivity gains. Although racism and the legacy of slavery continued to keep African Americans at the bottom of the pay scale during this period, black workers also made great economic gains during the postwar era, and many black families rose out of poverty, thanks especially to good-paying industrial jobs.

Not only was this rising prosperity good for American families, but it also gave the United States enormous leverage during the Cold War. The United States could proudly proclaim that we were the real workers' state, not the USSR or China. In fact, our standard of living became the envy of the world. This was part and parcel of combating the specter of spreading communism, which spurred the United States and European nations (with the enormous help of the Marshall Plan) to adopt social policies to defuse movements toward communism. To do battle with USSR- and China-style socialism, the Cold War encouraged the United States to constrain its elites and boost working-class prosperity.

The productivity rise and the way the bounty was shared were not accidental. America was helping to rebuild a war-torn world and benefited greatly from serving as the world's factory. New Deal controls on the financial sector and the Bretton Woods agreements created a remarkably stable financial system. The government also used steeply progressive income taxes to keep our income distribution relatively tight, so that America could win the bragging rights against world communism.

There was a cost: the rich had to pay significant taxes to support this remarkable prosperity. The marginal tax rates on the wealthy—people making $3 million or more in today's dollars—reached 91 percent during the conservative Eisenhower administration. (That is, for the next dollar of income you earned over $3 million, you paid 91 cents in federal taxes.) Even counting all of the loopholes, the effective tax rate was still 42 percent in 1961 for the four hundred richest families (Johnston 2009, 1375–1377; see also Johnston 2010). By 2008, it had dropped to only 16 percent.

Workers themselves deserve much of the credit for their economic gains: during the postwar era, they organized. By the mid-1950s, one in three workers in the private sector belonged to a union, and their rapidly rising wages benefited everyone, as wage standards rose for union and nonunion workers alike. Even as union density started its long slide downward, the upward pressure on wages continued for decades. Government, labor, and business developed a de facto partnership to protect American-style free enterprise, both at home and abroad. People viewed unions as woven into the fabric of American life.

All of this—rising productivity, government regulations, steep income taxes on the rich, unionization, and booming markets, both at home and overseas—created the foundation for a vibrant middle-class economy. It was the new American reality, not just the American dream.

Then something happened, and you can see it in Figure 4.1. Notice how the two lines pull apart beginning in the mid-1970s.

What happened? A great deal. In fact, so much happened that we can only wave at some of it here. For starters, Germany and Japan got on their feet again and began cutting into the United States' economic dominance. Our economy was overheating, in large part because of unfunded military expenditures on the Vietnam War. The world was also flooded with our Cold War dollars, not only from the war but from the hundreds of military bases the United States maintained as part of the effort to "contain" communism.

By 1970, it became obvious that these dollars could no longer be converted into gold, as specified by Bretton Woods. So Nixon ended the agreement and let the dollar float—which led to its immediate devaluation. The Middle Eastern oil-producing nations that had founded OPEC used the 1973 Arab-Israeli conflict as a perfect excuse to quadruple their oil prices (which were denominated in dollars), in part to make up for the dollar's decline. Dramatically rising commodity prices sent U.S. prices spiraling upward. All of this colluded to create a new condition called stagflation—high inflation, coupled with flat economic growth and high unemployment—something that economists had theorized could never happen. Yet there it was.

Meanwhile, social tensions shattered the cohesion that had characterized the postwar period. In the 1960s, students led a national movement against the Vietnam War. Women were demanding their rights. Blacks were fighting for equality. Cities were in flames. And JFK, RFK, and MLK were assassinated. For the first time since World War II, trust in government declined. After Watergate, it plummeted.

This new economic and social turmoil helped turn the intellectual tide against the New Deal and the Great Society. Those who had always distrusted government and unions found an audience for their extreme economic ideas. In fact, the right-wing economic

Industry (year deregulated)	Was Industry Regulated?		% of U.S. Economy Regulated (1999 GDP)	
	1975	2001	1975	2006
Oil and Gas Extraction (1980)	Yes	No	.89%	.00%
Railroads (1976, 1980)	Yes	No	.25%	.00%
Airlines (1978)	Yes	No	1.02%	.00%
Trucking (1980)	Yes	No	1.25%	.00%
Pipelines (1978, 1985)	Yes	Yes	.07%	.07%
Electricity (1992)	Yes	Yes	1.19%	1.19%
Telecom (1984, 1996)	Yes	Partially	2.10%	.70%
Radio/TV (1985, 1987)	Yes	Partially	.70%	.23%
Finance (1978, 1980, 1982, 1987, 1989, 1994, 1996, 1998, 2001, 2003)	Yes	No	3.28%	.00%
Insurance	Yes	Yes	.77%	.77%
Totals			**11.52%**	**2.96%**

Source: Crandall, Robert W. (2007). "Extending Deregulation: Make the U.S. Economy More Efficient." Opportunity 08, a project of the Brookings Institution. http://www.brookings.edu/~/media/Files/Projects/Opportunity08/PB_Deregulation_Crandall.pdf.

theories then growing in popularity weren't new. The laissez-faire ideology that preceded the Great Depression had also called for removing the government from the economy and letting free markets reign supreme. Now, much of the focus was on full-scale deregulation, massive tax cuts, and radically reducing union power.

The charge was led by Milton Friedman, the well-respected University of Chicago libertarian, who not only wanted to unleash capital from government constraints, but also opposed the draft and supported the legalization of drugs. While young people were challenging corporate and individual greed, economists such as Friedman made the case that greed was good for all of us. He and many others argued that corporations should stop worrying about "social responsibility," because they could best serve society by maximizing profits for their shareholders and themselves. The pursuit of profits, they argued, would lead to the best allocation of resources for the entire society.

Friedman and company had a lot of dismantling to do. We tend to forget that during the post–World War II boom, our version of capitalism was heavily regulated. Government regulators oversaw everything from railroads, trucking, and airlines to telecom, utilities, radio and TV, and finance. In fact, in 1975, government controls covered more than 11.5 percent of the entire private sector. Yet by 2006—after three decades of the new economics (now called neoliberalism)—government oversight dwindled to less than 3 percent of the private sector.

For neoliberals, deregulating the financial system was a top priority. They argued that the financial industry needed the freedom to "innovate." It was time to get rid of outmoded New Deal controls that hobbled the United States' ability to compete in an increasingly global economy. This, combined with radically cutting taxes on the wealthy, would produce a mammoth investment boom, the neoliberals said. All American boats would rise.

President Jimmy Carter kicked off the deregulation frenzy by allowing credit card interest rates to rise at will. Then came President Ronald Reagan, who declared open season on unions by crushing the air traffic controllers union (PATCO). He also unleashed the savings and loan industry, which quickly turned into a massive deregulated criminal enterprise. (By the time the crisis ended, more than a thousand S&L executives had been convicted.) Under Bill Clinton, Congress gutted Glass-Steagall, the law that separated investment banking from commercial banking (to prevent banks from gambling with government-insured consumer deposits). Congress also prohibited regulations on the fast-growing derivatives markets. And when George W. Bush arrived, the money spigot gushed upward as he bestowed billions in tax cuts on the super-rich (which also set the stage for a budget crisis).

Yet rather than making all boats rise, these new economic policies promptly ended the post–World War II boom for working people. Take another look at our productivity and wage chart (Figure 4.1): Although U.S. productivity continued to climb, most working people stopped getting their share of the bounty. Average weekly wages, after accounting for inflation, actually declined from their highs in the early 1970s.

So What, Exactly, Happened to the Trillions of Dollars in Real Output Each Year That Stopped Going to Working People?

No secret here. As productivity continued and as wages stalled, the billions represented by the space between the two lines went to the richest Americans, especially those in the financial sector. The charts that follow will demonstrate why financial elites can make a million an hour.

The first chart (Figure 4.2) shows the dramatic change in income distribution in the United States. Before the Great Depression, in the days of laissez-faire economics, the top 1 percent of income earners garnered nearly 24 percent of all income. Under New Deal and post–World War II policies, that number dropped to 8.9 percent by 1976. With the rise of massive deregulation, tax cuts, and union busting, however, the share of wealth going to the super-rich returned to near record highs—23.5 percent by 2007, just before the crash. Is there a strong correlation among financial deregulation, extreme income distribution, and financial crashes?

Now the second chart (Figure 4.3) really should make hedge-fund wannabes drool. Take a look at the average total compensation in the financial sector, compared to average compensation in the rest of the nonagricultural economy. (Remember, *average* means everyone employed from top to bottom, financial secretaries, janitors, and potentates all jumbled together.) Now look back at our productivity/wages chart (Figure 4.1). It's no coincidence that the shape of the two graphs is virtually identical. There's a

Figure 4.2 Change in U.S. Income Distribution in the Last Hundred Years

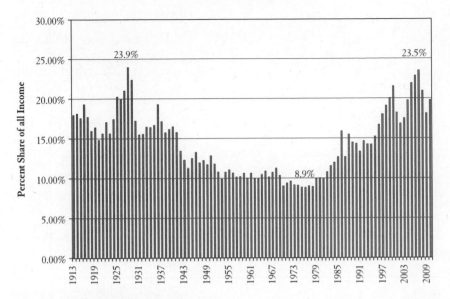

Sources: Saez, Emmanuel, and Thomas Piketty. 2003. "Income Inequality in the United States, 1913–1998." *Quarterly Journal of Economics* 118 (1): 1–39. (Longer updated version published as T. Piketty and E. Saez, "Income and Wage Inequality in the United States, 1913–2002," in A. B. Atkinson and T. Piketty, eds., *Top Incomes Over the Twentieth Century: A Contrast Between Continental European and English-Speaking Countries* [New York: Oxford University Press, 2007].) (Data for tables and figures updated to 2008 in Excel format, available from: Alvaredo, Facundo, Anthony B. Atkinson, Thomas Piketty, and Emmanuel Saez, *The World Top Incomes Database*, http://g-mond.parisschoolofeconomics.eu/topincomes, accessed January 17, 2012.

powerful correlation between the rise of Wall Street bankers and the stalling of middle-class incomes. It's also no wonder you want to get out of that bottom line and into the top!

In short, the "free-market" economics revolution, which tossed out New Deal and Bretton Woods restrictions, helped create a virtual wall of money at the top of the income scale. Not surprisingly, we became a more stratified nation as a result. Yet this vast pool of money also allowed for the proliferation of hedge funds and proprietary trading desks at the big banks. After all, you can't fit that much money under a mattress.

**Figure 4.3   Financial Sector vs. Nonfinancial Sector
Yearly Compensation (in 2010 Dollars)**

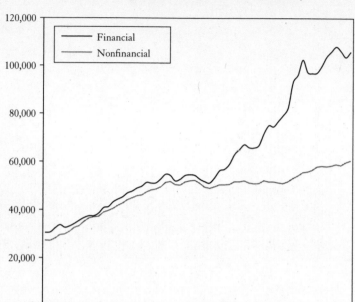

Sources: Data compiled by the author from the Bureau of Economic Analysis, "National Income and Product Accounts Tables, Section 6—Income and Employment by Industry," available at http://www.bea.gov/iTable/iTable .cfm?ReqID=9&step=1, accessed March 28, 2012. Average compensation of employees adjusted for inflation using the Bureau of Labor Statistics CPI Inflation Calculator, available at http://www.bls.gov/data/inflation_calculator.htm.

Ah, so that's where Soros and others got the cash they needed to out-duel the Bank of England: from the American people. And that's where you might find the moolah to bet your way into the million-an-hour club. But there's more to be found.

BORROWED MONEY

It's nice to have lots of money to invest, but you'll never make it big in the hedge-fund racket unless you can leverage that money many times over by borrowing other people's money—or by creating money out of thin air.

Let's start with a straightforward example. Let's say you buy a stock at $100, and it goes up to $101. You sell and net 1 percent. But what if you bought the stock with only $1 of your own money and borrowed the rest? You would make a 100 percent profit and double your money (minus the costs of financing your deal). So if you want big returns, you really need to juice up your bet with borrowed money. Of course, you can also rack up big losses, because a one-dollar drop in the price of that stock would wipe out your equity.

Okay, but where does this borrowed money come from? Does it come from banks that loan out our savings? Banks can lend our money because they know we all won't need it back at one time. By law, bankers can lend out about eight times what people have deposited. The Federal Reserve can affect how much gets lent out by adjusting the interest rate on federal funds. The Fed can also adjust how much capital banks are required to hold.

That's only for regular banks, though. There's also a vast "shadow" banking system. This includes investment banks, money market funds, hedge funds, and other players who all find ingenious ways to loan money to one another. These entities engineer ways to hold much less capital behind their loans—creating vast sums for leveraging investments. While regular banks can't leverage beyond a ratio of eight dollars for every dollar on deposit, many investment banks, before the 2008 crash, were leveraging loans at ratios of up to twenty or thirty to one. One hedge fund, Long-Term Capital Management, hit one hundred to one before it burst in 1998. Commercial banks also learned to play this game by using off-the-books "Special Purpose Vehicles" to hide loans.

The Federal Reserve, under Alan Greenspan and Ben Bernanke, greased the wheels by setting interest rates low, making money extra cheap. Most important, however, they turned a blind eye to the various tricks banks used to hide their loans and leverage their bets. Greenspan, in particular, believed with all of his heart and soul that the financial free markets would police themselves!

In the real world, however, the free market went wild on debt. Even before the 2008 crash, economist Nouriel Roubini warned all who would listen that the financial sector—including hedge funds—was built on a mountain of debt:

> Just to clarify this credit pyramid that looks like a Ponzi Game: you start with 20,000 euros invested by some investors into a hedge fund of funds; this is all equity. Then, this fund of funds borrows—at a leverage ratio of three—and invests the initial capital and the borrowed funds into a hedge fund. Then this hedge fund takes this fund of funds investment and borrows—at a leverage ratio of two—and invests the raised capital and the borrowed funds into a deeply subordinated tranches of Collateralized Debt Obligations (that are themselves highly levered instruments with a leverage ratio of nine). So the final investment of 1 million has behind it 20,000 of equity capital and 980,000 of debt. So, if the value/price of the final investment falls by only 2% the entire capital behind it is wiped out. This is a credit house of cards where a dollar of capital is turned into 49 dollars of additional debt to finance an investment of 50. The systemic dangers/risks of this fragile credit house of cards are complicated to assess as they depend on how much of this debt/credit accumulation is concentrated or spread among many financial intermediaries. But, at face value, this kind of leverage ratios looks scary. (Roubini 2007)

So now we have a reasonably good account of how hedge funds bankroll their outsize bets. The money comes from (1) wages Americans didn't get that ended up in the hands of wealthy investors; and (2) vast leverage.

No wonder the top two hundred or so hedge funds have billions to play with.

THE SHIFTING BALANCE BETWEEN
DEMOCRACY AND FINANCE

With so much money sloshing around in investment funds, the balance between democracy and finance has shifted. The super-rich, along with their hedge funds and investment banks, have become hugely potent political forces, undermining the average citizen's power to affect government policy.

Back in 1832, President Andrew Jackson saw this problem coming. He brought down the Second National Bank (which was a government-chartered banking monopoly), because he saw that such a bank operated by some of the richest citizens in the land would have too much influence over public policy. Such an institution, he argued, could hold the country hostage:

> Is there no danger to our liberty and independence in a bank that in its nature has so little to bind it to our country? The president of the bank has told us that most of the State banks exist by its forbearance. . . . Their power would be great whenever they might choose to exert it; but if this monopoly were regularly renewed every fifteen or twenty years on terms proposed by themselves, they might seldom in peace put forth their strength to influence elections or control the affairs of the nation. But if any private citizen or public functionary should interpose to curtail its powers or prevent a renewal of its privileges, it can not be doubted that he would be made to feel its influence.

> It is to be regretted that the rich and powerful too often bend the acts of government to their selfish purposes. Distinctions in society will always exist under every just government. Equality of talents, of education, or of wealth can not be produced by human institutions. In the full enjoyment of the gifts of Heaven and the fruits of superior industry, economy, and virtue, every man is equally entitled to

protection by law; but when the laws undertake to add to these natural and just advantages artificial distinctions, to grant titles, gratuities, and exclusive privileges, to make the rich richer and the potent more powerful, the humble members of society, the farmers, mechanics, and laborers who have neither the time nor the means of securing like favors to themselves, have a right to complain of the injustice of their Government. ("President Jackson's Veto Message," 1832)

What Jackson feared has come to pass as we become a billionaire-bailout society. The largest banks and hedge funds are now too big to fail and too powerful to regulate. And "the humble members of society"—the 99 percent—"have a right to complain of the injustice of their Government."

So, if you want to join this million-an-hour club, better not let another Andrew Jackson ride in on his high horse.

—————————— Do's and Don'ts ——————————

- **Do** complain vociferously about government debt, while you borrow as much as you can or create debt out of thin air.

- **Don't** worry if wealth gushes to the top. That's just more money for your casinos.

- **Do** stop worrying about "social responsibility." Just maximize profits and proclaim that they benefit everyone.

- **Don't** sell high horses to politicians. Better to own both.

STEP 5

Create Something You Can Pretend Is Low Risk and High Return

Believe it or not, a set of hedge-fund trades known as the Greatest Trade Ever (GTE) was even more lucrative than Soros's Bank of England heist. This group of enormous bets against the housing bubble earned hedge-fund bettors billions upon billions of dollars. Don't you wish you'd gotten a piece of that action?

Well, maybe next time. So, to get you ready, let's figure out who won and who got left holding the bag.

Fortunately, there's no shortage of information and little argument about how the GTE unfolded. Two popular books and many articles examine this set of trades, and there was also an SEC case concerning it, now settled. We know the kind of securities involved (synthetic CDOs), and we know, more or less, who made how much.

Strangely, what no one has analyzed—yet—is what effect, positive or negative, the GTE had on the rest of us.

I became engrossed with synthetic CDOs while researching my last book, *The Looting of America*. It turns out that five school districts (right next to where my in-laws live in Wisconsin) had invested $200 million in these exotic securities. Unfortunately, the securities were not only exotic but toxic, and the Wisconsin schools lost nearly their entire investment in a matter of months. For them, these CDOs proved to be the Greatest Trade Ever—for somebody else. The schools are engaged in litigation to get restitution from the banks and the brokers who bamboozled them into buying the damaged goods. (In August 2011, the SEC sued the brokers who did the bamboozling.) So I was fascinated to learn about the GTE, which involved the same financial instruments but seemed to have created nothing but joy for hedge funds and admiration from their cheerleaders.

That got me wondering: Is there a darker side to the Greatest Trade Ever?

. . .

The popular lore about the Greatest Trade Ever comes largely from the book of that name written by Gregory Zuckerman, a writer for the *Wall Street Journal*. Zuckerman sees the story as a near-biblical David-versus-Goliath fable, in which a few "unsung investors" outsmarted powerful financial insiders and made off with the booty (Zuckerman 2009, 10).

In Zuckerman's version, we have on one side the Goliaths: the big, klutzy, unimaginative banks and investment houses that pumped up the housing bubble to outlandish proportions during the 1990s and early 2000s, yet were somehow blind to the possibility that it would collapse. And on the other side, we have the Davids: a small group of prescient and fearless hedge-fund managers, including the wily John Paulson, who spotted the housing bubble, correctly guessed that it was about to burst, and then bet against the housing market, thereby making billions—hence the greatest trade ever.

You've got to hand it to Zuckerman: it's an awfully appealing story line. How refreshing and satisfying to think that a handful of quirky outsiders could outwit the financial sharks at Goldman Sachs and JP Morgan Chase. For many Americans, that alone would count as an enormous public service. If that were the case, then Paulson and a few others may really deserve their mountain of booty because, after all, they took it from the bad guys who were asleep at the switch. Shouldn't we celebrate their ability to humiliate the same monster banks that we taxpayers later had to bail out? Thank goodness, someone was smart enough to stick it to them. We all know that Washington didn't have the nerve.

Such a gratifying story—except it's not true.

The real narrative runs more like this: Imagine what would happen if David and Goliath decided to collaborate, instead of fight. Yep. That's precisely what happened.

For starters, the big boys at the big banks *did* know the housing market was crumbling. By 2006, the largest investment banks, including JP Morgan Chase and Goldman Sachs, believed that the housing market was peaking, and just as the hedge funds did, the big banks began betting big against it. Even more telling, far from battling the Goliath Goldman Sachs, hedge-fund manager John Paulson, for example, worked hand-in-glove with that investment house to pull off a deal that netted him a cool billion. Unfortunately, Goldman Sachs got caught by the SEC for misleading its investors, who were on the other side of Paulson's bets. That cost Goldman Sachs $550 million in penalties, but Paulson got off scot-free with a billion dollars in his pocket.

Meanwhile, as Pulitzer Prize–winning journalists Jesse Eisinger and Jake Bernstein have documented, JP Morgan Chase had a similar cozy relationship with the hedge fund Magnetar. (We'll go over their findings in the next step.)

So, at least on Wall Street, David and Goliath never bothered with the rock-throwing contest. Instead, they formed a highly profitable partnership to milk investors dry. By working in tandem, they and other such partnerships first prolonged the housing bubble and then made its collapse even more severe.

It's hard to find any real Davids at all in this story. As you'll see, the bankers and the big hedge funds were both Goliaths, and they were up to no good.

INTRODUCING MY COUSIN NORMAN

Before we dive further into fantasy finance, allow me to introduce you to my cousin Norman, who has been pestering me with annoying questions about synthetic CDOs ever since he first read drafts of *The Looting of America*.

Cousin Norman is not only an avid fisherman—and I mean maniacally avid—but he has earned enough money from real estate development to support his fishing addiction. (Full disclosure: he often takes me fishing with him and graciously picks up the tab, but although well off, he does not make a million an hour.) Cousin Norman never plays the markets. He doesn't buy stocks or bonds or derivatives. He has made his millions by building affordable condos for middle-class retirees. So although he doesn't gamble on Wall Street, he knows a thing or two about deal making.

After reading drafts of my book, Cousin Norman could not understand the economics of synthetic CDOs, which I thought I had brilliantly detailed (and will do so again briefly in this chapter). In those deals, one side bets that a group of loans or mortgages will fail, while the other side bets they won't fail. Norman just could not understand why someone would pay good money to bet that a financial security would fail. Sure, they might go down in value, but aren't these mortgage-backed securities designed to return principal and interest?

For example, when Cousin Norman read what I wrote about the Wisconsin school debacle, he couldn't fathom why the Royal Bank of Canada (RBC) (which would make money only if the securities in question failed) was, in effect, paying insurance premiums to the Wisconsin schools. After all, the financial securities in question were synthetic—meaning they were just bets. Neither party owned anything tangible like a loan or a mortgage.

Because these securities were rated AA and AAA (which means they are unlikely ever to go bust), why did the Royal Bank of Canada waste money on those insurance premiums, asked Cousin Norman?

I danced around the question for quite a while but really couldn't give him a convincing answer. Maybe the Canadian bank wanted the insurance so it could sleep better? Maybe it wanted to hedge its loan portfolio? But Cousin Norman didn't buy my answers and rightfully so. I sensed he had found a little kink in my otherwise rock-solid explanations.

Well, I finally have an answer for my dear Cousin Norman. It turns out that both of us were far too naive and trusting. We never, not even for a moment, considered the possibility that the entire synthetic CDO deal *was created and designed to fail* from the get-go. Maybe the banks that had bet against those securities designed them to fail so that they would be able to collect big on their insurance policies. We never considered the possibility that the Wisconsin schools may have been suckered into a $200 million rigged bet.

It's not hard to understand why my astute cousin never considered that possibility. In his forty years in the business world, few people had ever overtly cheated Cousin Norman. They couldn't afford to, because that would endanger their long-term prospects for keeping his business. Norman's senior-citizen developments took years to construct and sell. They depended on many relationships of trust. Norman trusted the construction companies that he repeatedly used. He trusted his sales staff. He also relied on long-term relationships with his partners and financing institutions. So the idea that someone would design a business product—such as a condo—to fail was simply outside his business experience. It was preposterous that anyone ever would build a condo to collapse on the heads of the elderly, so that the developer could collect the insurance. That's not the capitalism he knows and loves.

But guess what? If you want to make a million an hour, you have to be willing to design financial products that fail and fail miserably. You will have to build a financial condo that will kill everyone in it so that you can collect the insurance. I know, I know. That sounds totally over the top. Yet we now know for dead certain that Goldman Sachs and JP Morgan Chase designed synthetic CDOs to fail miserably. (In the fall of 2011, Citigroup also paid more than $250 million in SEC fines to settle similar charges.)

Although we don't yet know the full story in Wisconsin, we do know this: Almost as soon as those school districts closed their deal in 2006, they began to suffer enormous losses. Within a single year, their $200 million investment was worth less than a million. The Royal Bank of Canada allegedly collected all of that money as insurance. Either that was a rigged bet, or those Canadians are lottery lucky. We'll soon find out, as that case moves through the Wisconsin courts. As of this writing, the Royal Bank of Canada isn't talking. (This just in: Stifel Nichols, the investment company that brokered the deal to the five school districts, has settled out of court to forgive the $154 million in loans taken out by the school districts to put into the shoddy investment. The brokerage firm has also agreed to pay the school districts $22.5 million and work with them to sue for damages against the Royal Bank of Canada.)

Lots of people are now talking about similar rigged bets. Unfortunately, to understand them requires a headlong plunge into the insane world of fantasy finance. Only then can you really appreciate how to design financial products to self-destruct.

Typically, when you make an investment, you expect a risk to come with a high return, and safety to come with a low return. You've probably seen this with your retirement account, as young people are encouraged to put their money in the stock market for the higher return (and a greater potential for short-term losses), and older people are encouraged to put their money into something with a guaranteed smaller return.

If you can convince people you've invented something with a high rate of return at a low risk, you've found the goose that lays the golden eggs. As long as it's not illegal, it doesn't matter if those eggs later turn out to be rotten.

FANTASY FINANCE 101: HOW TO CREATE
A HOUSING BUBBLE AND BUST

First, we need a basic understanding of the housing bubble assembly line—how high-risk mortgages became risky derivatives and toxic mortgage-related securities that were sold all over the world. Maybe you've already gotten a good whiff of this business from all of the financial stories of the last several years. Let's walk through this drama once again, though, so that we don't get confused later on.

Act One: Sell Predatory Mortgages to Homebuyers

Companies such as Countrywide and Washington Mutual (WaMu) cooked up a smorgasbord of high-risk mortgage products and peddled them to the public with reckless abandon, turning predatory lending into a fine art. These mortgages were high-risk because the homebuyers didn't really have the income to cover the payments. Even worse, they often came with affordable teaser rates that reset after two years, and homebuyers were told they would be able to refinance again, so not to worry. The riskier the loan, the greater the fees earned by the mortgage company.

You can find all of the gory details in a bipartisan congressional report—*Wall Street and the Financial Crisis: Anatomy of a Financial Collapse*—compiled by the Senate Permanent Subcommittee on Investigations. Here we get a detailed description of the plethora of dangerous mortgages that WaMu, the nation's largest savings bank, used to foist on unsuspecting homebuyers. Your blood pressure will climb when you read how the bank used focus groups to help its mortgage brokers find better ways to sucker customers into risky mortgages—even though the applicants qualified for and wanted safer fixed-rate mortgages. The report also details outright fraud. Brokers forged documents, made phony loans, and stole money, then were rewarded repeatedly for their high sales figures—even after they were caught! Nobody cared because the loans were quickly sold to Wall Street. (See Act Two.)

Act Two: Sell the Loans to Wall Street

The major banks and investment houses developed a voracious appetite for high-risk loans. Why? Because they came with higher interest rates, meaning that when the banks packaged the mortgages together into securities (Act Three), those securities could offer a higher rate of return. Investors flocked to the scene, and the big banks and the investment houses made a mint.

Act Three: Create Mortgage-Backed Securities

Through the marvels of financial alchemy, Wall Street banks and investment houses turned large pools of junk mortgages into supposedly safe and secure AAA-rated securities. You've probably heard about how they put together a thousand or so mortgages and used the returned principal and interest on those mortgages to create interest payments for "tranches"—slices of the pooled mortgages. The game was glorious. The top 80 percent or so— the senior tranches—would get first dibs on the income from the underlying pool of mortgages. Supposedly, there would *always* be enough money in the mortgage pool to pay off those investing in the top tranches. So they got a decent rate of return and very little risk—so little that the rating agencies (for a nice fat fee) declared these senior slices AAA.

The mezzanine slices were next in line to be paid from the mortgage interest payments collecting in the pool. These slices were riskier and received a lower rating, because defaults were more likely, and too many defaults could cut down on investors' interest payments. Happily, though, the mezzanine slices offered a higher rate of return, and they still got decent ratings.

The bottom slice—called the *equity* tranche—was the gamblers' slice. It was the first to get wiped out if defaults rose in the underlying pool of mortgages. Yet it also came with deliciously high interest rates—sometimes as high as 20 to 30 percent—and it was designed to pay off quickly. These slices were unrated because the risk was so obvious.

The entire deal hinged on finding buyers for the equity slice. They were often treated as the deal's "sponsors."

Act Four: Sell the Securities and Create Collateralized Debt Obligations

Only the large institutions had the personnel who could sell this shady stuff, but the sales were made easier by all of the excess capital floating around the world at the time. Plenty of people were ready to invest in supposedly safe triple A–rated products that came with a higher rate of return than stodgy old investments such as government securities and corporate bonds. Investors were also excited about the mezzanine slices, especially during the boom's early years. Yes, there was a little more risk, but the rate of return was so seductive.

Yet here's an important clue to understanding how this crisis happened: After the housing market stalled in 2005–2006, it got harder and harder for banks to sell the middle mezzanine tranches. Investors didn't want to take on the risk. So, what did the banks do?

This might seem hard to believe, but they gathered up all of the pieces of unsellable mezzanine tranches from a wide variety of mortgage-backed securities and created a new, bigger pool. Instead of a thousand mortgages, those combined mezzanine tranches might now represent ten thousand or more underlying mortgages. The new pool was tranched again, just as the previous pools had been, except that each tranche now represented many more mortgages. This new security was called a collateralized debt obligation, or CDO.

Lo and behold, a miracle happened. After the ingenious bankers had stacked it up and sliced it again, the ratings agencies took a look at this scary pool of securities and declared that 70 to 80 percent of them deserved a triple-A rating. The bankers had packaged together securities representing tens of thousands of underlying high-risk mortgages and were now selling them as if they were as sound as U.S. Treasury bonds. Remember, these were the mezzanine slices that bankers were having trouble selling on their own. We're looking at a medieval alchemist's dream—turning dung into gold!

What followed was a Ponzi-like insanity. Just as before, the banks' sales force had no trouble selling the AAA-rated top CDO slices. They even sold some, but not all, of the mezzanine slices. But what to do with those unsold mezzanine CDO leftovers? I'm sure you've guessed by now: throw them into new CDOs. Yep, they used those unsold mezzanine slices to stir up an entirely new mega-security called a CDO squared and then tranched it up all over again and got AAA ratings for the top slices. Who would know the difference? It was like expanding your hamburger meat by throwing in seasoned sawdust.

Any mezzanine slices that still couldn't be sold would either get warehoused on the bank's balance sheet or get stuffed once again into a new CDO or CDO squared.

The banks then turned this process into a hidden, high-level Ponzi scheme: *The unsold pieces packaged by Bank A got shipped to a CDO in Bank B. And when Bank B couldn't sell all of the mezzanine pieces, it would send them over to Bank C, which would launder the mess into a fresh new CDO. Then Bank C might pass its unsold bits back to Bank A, which would start the Ponzi cycle all over again.*

Each time a mortgage-backed security or CDO or CDO squared was created and sold, the bank earned enormous fees. In fact, when the dust settles, I suspect we'll find that this was the most lucrative business in the history of Wall Street. What a machine!

Act Four Continued: Sell the Equity Tranche

This dog won't hunt without buyers for the bottom slice. You've got to find someone to scoop up that junky equity tranche in each and every mortgage-backed security, CDO, and CDO squared (and even in every CDO cubed—yes, they're rumored to exist). Who in their right mind would buy such a risky portion of the pool—even if it did come with a sumptuous rate of return?

Sadly, some of that junk was dumped onto pension funds, endowments, and charities that foolishly trusted their brokers and bankers. According to a *Bloomberg News* report titled "Poisons in Your Pensions," the now-defunct global investment company Bear Stearns made a concerted effort to sell about 20 percent of its equity tranches to those gullible pension-fund managers who actually trusted the company. To make the deal look a little safer, banks and investment houses sometimes held on to some of the equity slices themselves. Out of a billion-dollar deal, however, the bank might put only $10 million or so of its own money at risk.

So that's what the Goliath banks were up to. But what about the hedge-fund Davids? Granted, these hedge funds were often very clever. Some hedge-fund managers found an inventive way to literally hedge their bets: They gobbled up the equity tranches, while betting against the mezzanine tranches. This was called a "correlation trade," because the prices of the two would go up and down together. If the CDO crashed, the hedge fund's equity tranche would get wiped out, but the hedge fund would make even more money from shorting the mezzanine tranche. If the CDO didn't crash, then the hedge fund would keep getting those fat returns from the toxic waste tranche. (This correlation trade was possible only because during the bubble mania, you could cheaply bet against the mezzanine tranche.)

The hedge fund Magnetar, as we'll see shortly, bought up as many equity tranches as it could find and used the high returns, while they lasted, to finance enormous bets against the housing market. In effect, Magnetar used its profits from housing bubble securities to bet that the bubble would burst. Very clever, indeed!

Obviously, hedge funds played a major role in pumping up the housing bubble. If hedge funds hadn't snapped up those equity tranches, there would have been no CDOs, and CDOs were a big part of the problem. We don't want to lay *all* of the blame for the housing bubble and bust on hedge funds, but how could anyone keep a straight face while arguing that hedge funds helped keep the system honest? Not only did hedge funds help puff up the bubble and keep it going, they helped accelerate the bubble's collapse in ways that damaged our financial system and the economy.

But wait, aren't reckless homeowners and their government backers really to blame? Many of you might be thinking that I've got it all backward. Hedge funds didn't drive this CDO machine—homeowners did. Didn't this whole thing get started because of those hapless, irresponsible homebuyers who took out mortgages they couldn't afford? And weren't they abetted by the government, which pressured the banks and the mortgage brokers to make risky loans to unqualified (read "minority") buyers?

This narrative is spreading because of two deeply ingrained ideas in our culture. First, our focus on individual responsibility. You sign a mortgage, and you're responsible, whether or not you were duped. No one forced you to buy a home you had no way of paying for. Second, there's the pervasive belief that government is to blame for most societal problems—especially when it comes to "social engineering" aimed at helping people of color. Those two ideas combine to create an easy-to-grasp story that virtually exonerates Wall Street and hedge funds, while blaming government and dumb consumers whose eyes are bigger than their wallets.

Here's how one very wealthy hedge-fund manager puts it:

> The one major problem with democratic society is the ability to vote yourself a share of your neighbor's wallet. It is a virus that hurts the most productive in the short-term, but especially damages the most in need in the long term. The recent subprime debacle is a textbook example, whereby Fannie Mae and Freddie Mac approved loans based on a political mandate to broaden home ownership. (Drobny 2011, 250)

Many in this camp like to point the finger at the federal Community Readjustment Act, which attempts to prevent banks from red-lining minority communities. These critics also blame the government-backed lending agencies Fannie and Freddie for playing the CDO game (although these far from angelic agencies actually entered that particular casino long after the housing bubble had peaked).

Yet this antigovernment, personal-responsibility narrative defies the facts. We were pushed into the crisis by too little regulation, not too much. People with CRA mortgages are not in more distress than the rest of the population is. They received standard mortgages for which they qualified, not high-risk loans. Yes, many people of all colors and incomes took on mortgages they really couldn't afford, but that could easily have been prevented had the regulators lifted a finger to stop predatory lending. Predatory lending was not a necessary step in increasing home ownership (a goal that the business-oriented Bush administration was pushing, with the blessing of Wall Street).

Imagine if a coffee shop had a ten-cent-coffee day, and later it turned out that the coffee contained tainted water the shop had been paid a handsome sum to dispose of. Sure, you could say we should have known better than to think we could all get coffee for ten cents, but don't you think there'd be a bit more blame spread around?

We were not voting ourselves a share of our neighbor's wallet. Wall Street was picking ours.

In truth, the entire CDO machine was driven from the top of Wall Street down, not from the bottom up. Nomi Prins, the brilliant former Goldman Sachs managing director, doesn't mince words on this subject (or on any other, for that matter):

> Wall Street pushed lenders. Lenders pushed borrowers. That's how it worked. Don't let anyone tell you otherwise. If you can borrow at 1 percent and lend it out at 6 or 8 or 13 percent, you can make money. Even the squirrels in my backyard can make money at that play. (Prins 2009, 7)

• • •

Maybe squirrels also created the credit default swap (CDS)—the next level of financial insanity you'll need to master on your way to the million-an-hour club.

By 2005–2006, Wall Street's appetite for junk mortgages to package up and slice was so huge that it was running out of product. Despite the mythology about government pressure to increase homeownership, there just weren't enough homebuyers willing to take the plunge on a high-risk mortgage.

This lack of supply was slowing down the whole beautiful money-making machine, and time was running out. By 2006, all of the big banking boys, not just hedge funds such as Paulson and Magnetar, saw that housing prices were stalling. This made it even riskier for the big banks to assemble all of those juicy mortgage-backed securities. It took time to create the CDOs, which meant those mortgages had to be warehoused on the banks' balance sheets—and that was getting scary. Banks had to scurry to repackage the garbage, hoping to limit their exposure to those raw mortgages at a time when the housing market was looking shaky. At any moment, the value of their warehoused mortgages and unsold CDO slices could come crashing down.

Those squirrels are quite inventive, though. For just when it was most needed, a fresh financial innovation rode to the banks' rescue: the credit default swap. It turned out to be another wonderfully profitable collaboration between hedge funds and big banks. Unfortunately, it also made the bubble and the bust much, much worse for the rest of us.

So, what is a credit default swap? It's basically a financial insurance policy. When you take out an insurance policy on your home, you pay premiums in exchange for protection if something bad happens—fire, flood, theft. With a credit default swap, you're taking out insurance to protect against a credit failure in a corporate bond or some other financial security. You pay premiums to an insurer that will make you whole should something bad happen to the security you're insuring—such as a bond default, a drop in the bond's credit rating, or the bankruptcy of the company involved.

Yet credit default swap insurance differs from normal insurance in two important ways. First, you don't have to own what you're insuring. You actually can buy insurance on a GM bond or a mortgage security tranche that you don't even own. It's a pure bet that the security will go bad, and if it does, you will receive much more money back than the cost of your insurance. In home insurance, insuring a property that doesn't belong to you is a no-no. Regular insurance companies figured out long ago that if you take out insurance on someone else's house, for example, you have an incentive to torch it (or at least to encourage your neighbor to store your old newspapers and oily rags in his attic). So you have to have what's called an *insurable inter-est* to get life, home, or car insurance from a regular insurance company. Yet you don't need an insurable interest to buy what is called a "naked" credit default swap.

A credit default swap also differs from regular insurance in that it's not heavily regulated. Normal insurance companies are required to hold real assets in reserve to make sure they have suf-ficient money to cover all claims. Houses do burn down. People do die. Cars do crash. Without regulations requiring a certain level of assets, insurance companies might be tempted to sell lots of insurance, pocket the premiums, and then go bankrupt when too many people make claims. They could simply go out of busi-ness and run away with the money. That's why we have stringent insurance regulations.

Yet there are no such rules for credit default swaps. You just work out a contract with a counterparty that agrees to make you whole. The contract might require the counterparty to hold a certain amount of collateral, just in case, but no government agency is making sure that the counterparty will pay up. So, what if they can't?

Think AIG, the giant insurer that went belly-up in 2008. The company had insured $450 billion in credit default swaps on mortgage-related securities. When the crash came, AIG didn't have the money to pay up. Tough luck for those who bought that financial insurance? No. It was tough luck for the taxpayers, who were forced to come to the rescue.

Credit default swaps have become a global best-seller. Some $600 trillion worth of CDS credit insurance is out in the world now. That's thirty times the size of the entire U.S. economy.

Why did these unregulated insurance contracts grow so pop-ular? For starters, they give the buyers the illusion that they are totally protected from risk. You can buy a bond or a slice of a CDO and then hedge your risk by buying insurance. Back in the late 2000s, when the financial sector boomed and began to engulf the rest of the economy, the demand for this financial insurance boomed, too.

Back then, most people believed that America would never again face a financial crisis such as the Great Depression. So, okay, CDSs weren't regulated, but the odds were really low that a bank or a hedge fund offering this financial insurance would ever have to pay out. Meanwhile, there were handsome up-front fees and quarterly payments to collect—all for doing nothing. It was like minting money without having to put up any of your own. Plus, you could still collect the income from any collateral you'd posted as part of the deal. As long as the economy was steaming ahead, you were in the money.

More than that, though, the credit default swap market has become an enormous and highly lucrative global casino. Using a "naked CDS," you can bet on anything, anywhere, anytime, because neither the insurer nor the purchaser of insurance needs to own the product being insured.

A PACT WITH THE DEVIL?

CDSs and CDOs were a match made in heaven—or hell, depending on your position in the market during the housing boom and bust. The partnership solved two big problems for Wall Street during the housing boom. First, it helped supply Wall Street with a substitute for the risky mortgages it craved. Recall that CDOs are created by assembling slices of mortgage-backed securities, each containing thousands of mortgages. The securities actually do include those high-risk mortgages. A credit default swap can be designed to mimic those CDO slices *without* owning the actual underlying mortgages. So banks could create CDOs that were made up entirely of bets on securities they didn't own. It's exactly like playing fantasy baseball, except instead of pretending to own major league players, you pretend to own crap mortgage slices. Because this kind of security is only a series of bets, not a collection of real mortgages, it's called a *synthetic* CDO.

Voila! Wall Street had a new product to slice, dice, and sell, collecting all of its fees and payments—but one that didn't require a steady supply of actual crappy mortgages. (To see how these financial shenanigans played out in Wisconsin, please read the first chapter of *The Looting of America*, which can be found for free on Alternet.org.)

The unholy marriage between CDOs and CDSs also helped Wall Street solve another vexing problem: how to bet *against* the housing bubble. By 2006, the smart money—including within the large investment banks—was counting on a housing bust. The bankers knew that homebuyers were beginning to default on their high-risk mortgages, and that the defaults would mount as the teaser rates on these mortgages expired.

So they wanted to bet against the housing market but couldn't find a way to do it on a large (and therefore highly profitable) scale. Not until Wall Street wizards figured out how to marry CDSs and CDOs.

Talk about a fantasy wedding. Here's how it works. There are two sides of the bet: long and short. The "long" betters are buying the synthetic security, thinking that the slice they bought will continue to provide them with solid interest payments, just as any other bond would. Sure, the bond might go up or down a bit, depending on overall interest rates, but very few of these buyers ever dreamed that the entire security—both principal and interest—could vaporize into nothing.

Yet the synthetic CDO contained enormous hidden risks for the "long" buyers. The money from the long investors doesn't really buy anything tangible, such as a mortgage, because there are only bets involved. Instead, the money from the long investors usually winds up in a special purpose fund set up in the Cayman Islands. The money is then invested in short-term government and corporate notes and pays out interest.

Meanwhile, the short sellers, those who are betting on failure, pay their premiums into the Cayman Islands fund, which then becomes part of the interest received by the long buyers. So there's really no there, there. The long investors' money basically sits offshore as an insurance pool, waiting and ready to give to the short sellers should failure occur.

The short sellers, of course, are betting that the referenced mortgages in the synthetic CDO will crash in value. If that happens, the short sellers get to pocket the Cayman Islands funds.

So, one investor bets that the mortgage slices will go bad—the short side. Another investor bets on the long side—that those slices will continue to pay interest for the duration of the security (four years or so) and then also return the original investment. The long-side investor has the comfort of knowing that the top 75 to 80 percent of the synthetic CDO slices are rated AAA. What's the big deal?

Here's where it gets really nasty. Put yourself in the shoes of the short seller. You are putting up good money in the form of "insurance" payments on a bet that some slice of mortgage-backed securities somewhere or another will go bad. As the securities in question begin to fail, the value of your short bet rises. So, what's your best winning strategy as a short seller? Here's your chance to ask yourself, "What would George Soros do?"

If you answered, "Make absolutely certain the securities you bet against will fail," you get an A. In fact, you get an AAA.

The only winning strategy is to make sure that the security in question fails. The best way is to construct a security that references the very worst mortgages in the country—the ones most likely to go belly-up in a hurry. In short, *as a short-seller you have every incentive in the world to rig the bet so that you can't possibly lose!*

Sure, you could insure your neighbor's house and have him make it a fire hazard. But what if it never burns? The smarter play is to build a whole house out of cardboard and oily rags, take out insurance on it, and light the match.

This is no joke. As you'll see in the next step, hedge funds and large banks colluded to create mortgage-related securities that were designed specifically and precisely to go belly-up. That's the toxic game that wins you a million an hour.

———— Do's and Don'ts ————

- **Don't** bet on a horse until you know how the race ends.

- **Don't** fight a financial Goliath if you're David. Better to team up with him and split the cash.

- **Do** make absolutely certain that the securities you bet against will fail.

- **Don't** let them outlaw synthetic CDOs. Financial Alzheimer's is sure to set in and then you can start up this lucrative casino again.

STEP 6

Rig Your Bets

Whenever there's a great upheaval, our instinct is to look for someone to blame. Who's the bad guy in this story? If you want to be a high-roller, you want it to be you. Ideally, if you made out big on a bubble—or on a bubble popping—you want to be the force that blew it up and popped it. Why surf, unless you make your own waves? Why gamble, unless you're the house?

In our current financial melodrama, Goldman Sachs claimed the role (so far) of chief villain. It even has a sinister new nickname: Vampire Squid. Since journalist Matt Taibbi came up with that description in his infamous *Rolling Stone* piece, Goldman Sachs has wasted millions on PR trying to erase those bloodthirsty tentacles from our minds. No such luck. Goldman Sachs CEO Lloyd Blankfein didn't help matters any when he told the *New York Times* that he "was doing God's work."

The Securities and Exchange Commission further tarnished Goldman Sachs's image when it slapped the bank with a $550 million fine for misleading its investors. Meanwhile, in its report, which used Goldman Sachs as a core case study, the Senate

Permanent Subcommittee on Investigations all but accused the bank's top officials of committing perjury.

Yet this game of cops and robbers won't take us very far. When you have a systemic meltdown, it's best to look for systemic causes. It doubtful that Goldman Sachs was the only bad guy and those other banks were saints.

For a long while, some people thought maybe JP Morgan Chase was the good guy in this crime flick. Jamie Dimon, its CEO, was known as Obama's favorite banker. The word among media mavens was that JP Morgan Chase took bailout loans only because it was asked to do so by the Treasury Department, in order to give cover to the other banks and help the government set up its controversial TARP program in 2008. But really, they claimed, Dimon and company didn't need that money—they'd been smart enough to avoid the gambling spree that took down the economy. (Yet not smart enough by 2012 to avoid losing more than $5 billion on another gambling spree?)

How noble that this one bank stood above the fray, while all of its competitors were building bigger and bigger casinos and walking away with unbelievable cash until it all crashed.

Yet like the fluffed-up David-and-Goliath version of the Greatest Trade Ever, JP Morgan Chase is not the King Solomon of our story. No one is.

Jesse Eisinger and Jake Bernstein of *ProPublica* (and *Naked Capitalism* blogger Yves Smith before them) were certainly suspicious. Their investigations revealed that JP Morgan Chase was actually playing the same game as Goldman Sachs. What's more, that other supposed tribe of good guys—the hedge-fund industry—was playing the game, too. Case in point: the Magnetar trade—another deal that features David teaming up with Goliath.

FANTASY FINANCE 101:
HOW TO CHEAT THE MARKETS

Magnetar, a suburban Chicago multibillion-dollar hedge fund, was named after the super-magnetic field generated by a dying star. In 2006, this hedge fund was seeking the super-profits generated

in a dying housing market. By then, it was clear that the key mortgage companies had flooded the market with unsustainable loans,
many with teaser interest rates that would swamp homeowners
after two years. Magnetar (along with other hedge funds) knew
that the mortgage pools of 2005 and 2006 were soon likely to fail.

Magnetar helped turn the stellar housing market into a profitable black hole through a secretive set of trades that escaped
media and regulatory scrutiny until very recently. In more than
thirty deals, this hedge fund fleeced the markets. In failed deal
after failed deal, investors swallowed at least $40 billion in losses,
while Magnetar managers took away billions in profits. Magnetar
denies the deals were designed to fail, but the *ProPublica* investi-
gatory reporters believe otherwise.

> An independent analysis commissioned by *ProPublica* shows
> that these deals defaulted faster and at a higher rate com-
> pared to other similar CDOs. According to the analysis, 96
> percent of the Magnetar deals were in default by the end of
> 2008, compared with 68 percent for comparable CDOs. The
> study was conducted by PF2 Securities Evaluations, a CDO
> valuation firm. (Magnetar says defaults don't necessarily
> indicate the quality of the underlying CDO assets.) (Eisinger
> and Bernstein 2010)

These deals created the template for how to cheat the markets.
How did Magnetar do it?

Act One: Find a Friendly Bank to Play Ball

No problem. There were plenty hungry for the action—including
our "good bank," JP Morgan Chase:

> At least nine banks helped Magnetar hatch deals. Merrill
> Lynch, Citigroup and UBS all did multiple deals with
> Magnetar. JP Morgan Chase, often lauded for hav-
> ing avoided the worst of the CDO craze, actually ended
> up doing one of the riskiest deals with Magnetar, in May
> 2007, nearly a year after housing prices started to decline.

According to marketing material and prospectuses, the banks didn't disclose to CDO investors the role Magnetar played. (Eisinger and Bernstein 2010)

Act Two: Select the Worst Mortgage Slices for Your CDO
Put the absolute lousiest mortgage slices into your synthetic CDO. Remember, because it's synthetic you don't actually have to buy the high-risk mortgages or mezzanine slices from brokers and banks. You can just reference CDO slices that already exist. (This is simply the finance version of fantasy baseball. Your team can hinge on Derek Jeter even if he doesn't know you from Adam. In this case, however, you're looking to load up your team with the worst baseball players to ever have played the game, so that you can bet against them.) You're looking for mortgage pools that have lots of mortgages in areas where housing prices are inflated, such as the "sand" states (Nevada, Arizona, California, and Florida). Try to find pools that were put together by the most predatory companies—for example, Countrywide and WaMu. Remember, you don't want any mortgages that might turn out okay.

Act Three: Connive to Get a AAA Rating
After assembling this explosive mix, you need to structure and slice it up so that the ratings agencies will give 80 percent of this toxic brew a AAA rating. And hopefully give the next 18 percent (the mezzanine slice) a decent rating as well. (This was a snap, because the ratings agencies turn tricks for cash and relied on the banks' own models to cook up their ratings.)

Act Four: Collude with a Hedge Fund to Screw Your Investors
Normally, the next step is to find buyers who are willing to gamble on the bottom unrated and risky "equity" slice in exchange for a very high interest rate, but that was getting tricky. By this time, mortgage defaults were increasing, which meant that the equity slice could soon get wiped out. Very few investors were willing to take a chance and it was getting hard to find more pension funds and school districts to dupe. Yet those who were willing to gobble

up the equity tranches were treated royally by the banks that helped structure the deals.

Magnetar made a shrewd move: it bought up the equity slices, which made Magnetar the "sponsor" of these deals—and in the process gained a great deal of leverage over how the deals were structured.

By buying up the bottom tranche, Magnetar also made the deal look sound. Because a big hedge fund *seemed* to be betting on the synthetic CDO to succeed (going long), other investors took heart and bought the higher-rated slices. After all, whoever owned the equity tranche had skin in the game—they would suffer the first losses if the mortgages referenced in the synthetic CDO stopped paying. (Then again, the entire equity tranche is not that large— maybe $10 to $20 million out of a billion-dollar synthetic CDO.)

So, what was Magnetar's real play? The hedge fund bought the high-return, high-risk equity slices to give it the income to fund big bets *against* the value of the mezzanine tranches in the deals it created. In other words, Magnetar used the high income from the most toxic slice (while it lasted) to keep paying insurance premiums on its short bets against the major parts of the synthetic CDOs. Magnetar could afford to pay for insurance on the mezzanine tranches *because it had designed the deal to profit even from a crash.* (Remember Cousin Norman!) And when it did, Magnetar's short positions would pay off big.

Why should we care if Magnetar wins big and some other investors lose big? Why does that matter to average Americans who have no connection whatsoever to any of this?

Unfortunately, we *do* have a connection. Those deals were much more than simple bets among sophisticated consenting adults. They didn't just net billions for a few lucky investors; they also sucked billions away from the rest of us.

It's important to remember that pooling mortgages and then slicing and dicing them into securities for sale to investors started out as a good idea. It drew more money into the mortgage markets and allowed banks to make room for more mortgage making. The Government National Mortgage Association (Ginnie Mae) had successfully bundled and sliced traditional mortgages since the 1970s without incident. Yet the game changed when the bundling and betting were based on crap mortgages and done on a scale that could distort and then harm much of the economy.

The Magnetar deals were huge, exerting a powerful gravitational pull on the mortgage-backed security galaxy, perhaps accounting for up to 60 percent of the demand for subprime bonds. They contributed mightily to puffing up the housing bubble and extending its life. That made the crash that much bigger and more costly. In fact, a good case could be made that this one hedge fund—Magnetar— helped precipitate the crash and the trillions of dollars of bailouts and guarantees that we taxpayers have had to shoulder.

To back up that claim, let's return to Yves Smith, whom I met in 2010 through a mutual friend. At the time I hadn't yet read her book *ECONned*. Over a couple of drinks and the din of a noisy New York café, I remember her getting quite exercised about Magnetar. "I mean, why isn't the media going after Magnetar? Why are all the postmortems ignoring it? They're at the heart of the crash. I just can't believe that no one is on to them." And so on, until I literally got a headache.

Until that conversation, I'd been feeling pretty good about how I nailed the CDO scam in *The Looting of America*. I was also getting a fair amount of kudos for it. Yet in truth, I had missed the Magnetar story entirely, which is not something a loud-mouthed critic of synthetic CDOs wants to do—hence the headache.

What was Yves Smith so agitated about? She'd figured out that the Magnetar deals (each one named after a different constellation, of course) were so large that they had literally kept the housing bubble afloat. As Smith wrote in *ECONned*,

Industry sources believe that Magnetar drove the demand for at least 35%, perhaps as much as 60%, of the subprime bonds issued in 2006. And Magnetar had imitators including the proprietary trading desks at the major dealers; thus their strategy is arguably the most important influence on subprime bond issuance in 2006–2007. (Smith 2010, 287)

Recall that in 2006–2007, the housing market had started to stall. By generating the demand for 35 percent to 60 percent of the subprime bonds issued, Magnetar, through its clever deals, kept much of the subprime game alive. If that's not puffing up the bubble, nothing is.

How is that possible? How could one hedge fund exert so much force on a trillion-dollar mortgage market? The answer, once again, is leverage. These securities contained so many levels of imbedded leverage that they became large enough to push the mortgage market. According to Smith, every dollar Magnetar had invested in the equity tranche of these deals "created $533 dollars of subprime demand. . . . Is it any wonder that anyone in the United States who had a pulse could get a mortgage?" (Smith 2010, 288). (And a few without pulses as well.)

There's more. Not only did Magnetar create an enormous demand for junk mortgages, it spread the AIG disease far and wide.

As discussed earlier, AIG wrote $450 billion in credit default swap insurance, but it wrote insurance only on the top slices of AAA mortgage-backed securities. At a certain point, even AIG could see that the housing market was turning and that writing more insurance was a bad bet. So by 2006, AIG wouldn't even insure AAA tranches. In fact, it totally stopped writing credit default insurance on all mortgage-related securities.

Uh-oh! That's a big problem. Without AIG and some of the other bond insurers, who was going to keep the big, profitable subprime synthetic CDO machine running? Who would write the insurance that Magnetar needed for its bets? You can't go short in a synthetic CDO unless someone else is willing to write you a CDS and bet that the referenced mortgage slices will continue to perform. Because if the smart money wouldn't go near it, who would?

Dumb money!

The answer takes us back to Wisconsin (and a lot of other places around the world, including the town of Narvik, Norway, which lost much of its revenue after getting suckered into the synthetic CDO scam). Instead of relying on sophisticated institutions such as AIG to serve as the insurers, banks went hunting for dupes. The banks partnering with Magnetar needed to find investors—that is, customers who would buy the mezzanine tranches of the synthetic CDOs *without realizing that they were actually serving as pint-size insurers.* The big banks scoured the world to find these unsuspecting marks.

The Wisconsin school districts' trusted broker told them they were buying AA- and AAA-rated securities, kind of like a basket of corporate bonds. Even the broker didn't seem to know that there was nothing real in that basket. It was just a receptacle to store the school boards' money—plus the premiums from those who were betting the security would fail. (The security referenced but didn't actually own the junk debt held by the Royal Bank of Canada.)

When that referenced debt turned to excrement in a matter of months, the receptacle holding the school boards' money was emptied to pay off the insurance claims to the Royal Bank of Canada. Presto! The school boards' investment fell from $200 million to less than $1 million, and the Royal Bank of Canada was made whole. The school boards had been unknowing insurers and now had to pay off the claims.

This isn't just third-hand reporting. I watched videos of the broker pitching those synthetic CDOs to the Wisconsin school-board finance committee. In my opinion, no one in that room, including the broker, had any idea that the schools would be serving as a financial insurance company. It was the blind leading the blind—just the way the big banks and their hedge-fund partners wanted it. Dumb and dumber money galore!

Similar traps were set for public entities around the globe. No one yet has tallied how many such entities, including pension funds, were conned into playing this role.

Most of the deals were snapped up by large banks, however, especially those in Europe and Asia, where faith in the U.S. rating agencies remained high. They trusted our fabled rating agencies! Tough luck, guys.

It was too bad for the rest of us, too. Because when the crash came, all kinds of mortgage-backed securities turned out to be worth next to nothing. Profiteering by Magnetar, in collusion with big banks, helped generate thousands of junk securities. Now the public is paying a heavy price.

Yet Magnetar was not the only hedge fund fattening at this trough.

The Amazing Abacus Deal

Gregory Zuckerman turned hedge-fund manager John Paulson into a folk hero, Wall Street–style. In Zuckerman's book *The Greatest Trade Ever*, Paulson is a courageous outsider with a terrific sense of smell. He sniffs out that the subprime mortgage boom is a fraud. He's baffled that the Wall Street dons don't see the collapse coming but pleased at the opportunity this presents. He'll find a way to bet against this mania and make a buck. He might even do all of us a great service by helping to puncture the bubble so that it won't do as much damage on the way down. He's the good guy, the smart guy. And come on, wouldn't you like to be as smart as him and earn millions of dollars an *hour*? It's a feel-good story of doing well by doing good.

The deal we know the most about, Abacus, "earned" Paulson $1 billion. All told, his firm reportedly made $20 billion from its bets against the housing market. This tiny band of brothers called Paulson and Company—with fewer than fifty employees— out-earned Apple Corp. during the worst economic year since the Great Depression. Bravo!

The reason we know so much about Abacus is that it was the subject of both an SEC investigation and a detailed case study in a report of the Senate Permanent Committee on Investigations.

For me, the Senate report is like a racy novel in the hands of a curious teenager. I can't get enough of it. For someone who is spending way too much time trying to figure out how these financial elites are doing "it," this report is a steamy thriller.

The report finds that Abacus and similar deals were based on a slew of shoddy practices:

> Those practices included at times constructing RMBS [residential mortgage-backed securities] or CDOs with assets that senior employees within the investment banks knew were of poor quality; underwriting securitizations for lenders known within the industry for issuing high risk, poor quality mortgages or RMBS securities; selling RMBS or CDO securities without full disclosure of the investment bank's own adverse interests; and causing investors to whom they sold the securities to incur substantial losses. . . .
>
> Goldman marketed a CDO known as Abacus 2007-AC1 to clients without disclosing that it had allowed the sole short party in the CDO, a hedge fund, to play a major role in selecting the assets. The Abacus securities quickly lost value, and the three long investors together lost $1 billion, while the hedge fund profited by about the same amount. (Senate Permanent Committee on Investigations, 319)

And which devilish hedge fund was this? None other than our shining knights at Paulson and Company.

Goldman Sachs, the Senate investigators report, had billions of dollars' worth of risky mortgage-related securities on its balance sheet and wanted to dump them as fast as possible without suffering major losses. If Goldman could stuff them into CDOs, the bank could actually make a lot of money off these suckers. So Goldman designed a series of deals, including several under the name of Abacus, that allowed the bank to sell off its inventory and bet against the housing market.

So much for the myth that Paulson and other hedge-fund geniuses saw the housing crash coming, while the big bad banks were blind to the upcoming disaster. Goldman Sachs was every bit as much a player on the short side as Paulson was—and then some.

The last Abacus deal was the most unusual, because for the first time Goldman Sachs allowed a client to become a virtual partner.

Abacus 2007-AC1 was the first and only Abacus transaction in which Goldman allowed a third party client to essentially "rent" its CDO structure and play a direct, principal role in the selection of the assets. Goldman did not itself intend to invest in the CDO. Instead, it functioned primarily as an agent, earning fees for its roles in structuring, underwriting, and administering the CDO. . . .

Goldman originated Abacus 2007-AC1 in response to a request by Paulson & Co. Inc. ("Paulson"), a hedge fund that was among Goldman's largest customers for subprime mortgage related assets. Paulson had a very negative view of the mortgage market, which was publicly known, and wanted Goldman's assistance in structuring a transaction that would allow it to take a short position on a portfolio of subprime mortgage assets that it believed were likely to perform poorly or fail. Goldman allowed Paulson to use the Abacus CDO for that purpose. (395–396)

That's one sure path to the million-an-hour club.

There's little doubt that Paulson helped pick the referenced assets for the Abacus deal, according to the Senate report. And there's little doubt that Paulson's objective was to pick the worst of the worst.

Documents show that Paulson proposed, substituted, rejected, and approved assets for the reference portfolio. Goldman was aware of Paulson's investment objective, the role it played in the selection of the reference assets, and the fact that the selection process yielded a set of poor quality assets. (396)

Yet Goldman and Paulson had one little problem. By this time, even the dimmest investors knew that Paulson always bet *against* the housing market. So if it became public knowledge that Paulson was selecting the assets for this deal, no one would bet against him.

ACA Management, however, believed that Paulson and Goldman Sachs wanted the security to succeed. The misdirection play was so convincing that ACA bought a big chunk of the billion-dollar deal.

> ACA Management LLC, the company hired by Goldman to serve as the portfolio selection agent, told the Subcommittee that, while it knew Paulson was involved, it was unaware of Paulson's true economic interest in the CDO. The ACA Managing Director who worked on the Abacus transaction stated that ACA believed that Paulson was going to invest in the equity tranche of the CDO, thus aligning its interests with those of ACA and other investors. ACA and its parent company both acquired long positions in the Abacus CDO as did a third investor. The Abacus securities lost value soon after purchase. The three long investors together lost more than $1 billion, while Paulson, the sole short investor, recorded a corresponding profit of about $1 billion. Today, the Abacus securities are worthless. (396–397)

Not only did the investors get screwed by this rigged race, they also got screwed out of the full insurance premium payments that Paulson should have been paying. Remember that in the synthetic CDO, the interest payments that the long investors receive (for as long as the CDO is solvent) come in part from the premiums that short investors are supposed to pay into the CDO. So, how much Paulson paid in insurance premiums was vitally important to the investors, even in a bad deal.

Yet Goldman Sachs and Paulson had a better idea: let's screw the investors out of some of their premiums and split the extra booty.

> In addition to not disclosing the asset selection role and investment objective of the Paulson hedge fund, Goldman

did not disclose to investors how its own economic interest was aligned with Paulson. In addition to accepting a sizable placement fee paid by Paulson for marketing the CDO securities, Goldman had entered into a side arrangement with the hedge fund in which it would receive additional fees from Paulson for arranging CDS contracts tied to the Abacus CDO that included low premium payments falling within a specified range. While those lower premium payments would benefit Paulson by lowering its costs, and benefit Goldman by providing it with additional fees, they would also reduce the amount of cash being paid into the CDO, disadvantaging the very investors to whom Goldman was marketing the Abacus securities. (397)

So to recap: Goldman and Paulson set up a billion-dollar deal designed to fail. Paulson picks the worst securities he can find for the deal to ensure that it will go under. Yet investors are misled into thinking that Paulson is actually risking all in favor of the deal by going "long" and buying the equity tranche. Then Paulson and Goldman pick over the carcass some more to cut Paulson's costs in betting against the deal. In the end, the investors lose a billion dollars, and Paulson makes a billion. Goldman Sachs makes fees up and down the line for the role it plays in packaging the deal. Goldman also profits because Paulson will use the bank's services in the future.

Ahh, but wait—there's a legal and economic dénouement to this seamy, steamy tale.

On the legal side, the SEC went after Goldman Sachs for failing to disclose Paulson's role. Here's the SEC's press release about the settlement:

Securities and Exchange Commission today announced that Goldman, Sachs & Co. will pay $550 million and reform its business practices to settle SEC charges that Goldman misled investors in a subprime mortgage product just as the U.S. housing market was starting to collapse.

In agreeing to the SEC's largest-ever penalty paid by a Wall Street firm, Goldman also acknowledged that its marketing materials for the subprime product contained incomplete information. . . .

In settlement papers submitted to the U.S. District Court for the Southern District of New York, Goldman made the following acknowledgment:

Goldman acknowledges that the marketing materials for the ABACUS 2007-AC1 transaction contained incomplete information. In particular, it was a mistake for the Goldman marketing materials to state that the reference portfolio was "selected by" ACA Management LLC without disclosing the role of Paulson & Co. Inc. in the portfolio selection process and that Paulson's economic interests were adverse to CDO investors. Goldman regrets that the marketing materials did not contain that disclosure.

Moments after this July 15, 2010, SEC release, Goldman Sachs shares jumped nearly 5 percent. Apparently, the markets were greatly relieved that the penalties weren't higher. No one was indicted, no individual was fined. Goldman Sachs didn't have its property seized under racketeering statutes. Goldman simply had to pay back some of the money that it had already made on its housing bets.

Paulson got to keep his cool billion, too. Like the Magnetar deals, this gigantic bad bet contributed mightily to the economic mess we're now in.

Many of the players in this game had hedged their bets by taking credit default insurance from AIG. When AIG couldn't pay out, Uncle Sam stepped in and poured $175 billion into the company. Then AIG turned around and paid out more than $60 billion to the largest banks in the world at 100 cents on the dollar.

Goldman Sachs received $12 billion of U.S. taxpayer money via the AIG bailout. No wonder investors got excited when they learned that Goldman would have to pay only a half billion plus, despite cheating—I mean, misleading—its customers and helping to trigger the crisis.

It's true, Paulson and Magnetar didn't do it by themselves. They had plenty of help from Goldman Sachs, JP Morgan Chase, and the rest of the banking establishment, both dead and alive—as well as from ratings agencies and regulators. Yet history will show that hedge funds were more than complicit in the economic crisis. These horrific deals couldn't have been closed without hedge funds. Synthetic CDOs couldn't have taken off without hedge funds. Without hedge funds to slobber over the equity tranches, "structured" finance would have stayed in a small corner of the financial community, instead of metastasizing throughout our economy.

As Yves Smith put it, the "much celebrated subprime shorts were one of the primary causes of the financial crisis. Their use of credit default swaps greatly inflated the level of subprime exposures, and the eventual losses, well above what they would have been otherwise" (Smith 2010, 289).

Meanwhile, the suckers who were turned into unknowing insurance companies "suffered or will suffer terminal losses; the survivors owe their existence to massive taxpayer bailouts, central bank subsidies, and regulator forbearance" (290).

So, help me out here. Can anyone find one redeeming virtue in the role that Paulson or Magnetar played in this so-called Greatest Trade Ever?

Yes, there is one, and one only. This trade gets you into the million-dollars-an-hour club. Welcome aboard.

———— DO'S AND DON'TS ————

- **Do** remember that you can always fool some of your investors some of the time, and you can still make billions by betting against the crap you sell them all of the time.

- **Do** fight against creeping socialism, except when it means millions for your firm.

- **Don't** hold your financial compass near a Magnetar. It will always point to your wallet.

STEP 7

Don't Say Anything Remotely Truthful

Now that you're more familiar with rigged bets, you may be asking, "Do you really have to cheat in order to make it into the million-an-hour club?" Well, it depends on what you mean by *cheat* and *have to*.

You absolutely don't have to—no, no, no, hedge-fund supporters assure us. There are only a few rotten apples in the hedge-fund barrel, writes the ever optimistic Sebastian Mallaby:

An industry of around 9,000 hedge funds is indeed bound to harbor some criminals. But insider trading is already illegal, and prosecutors have the tools to go after offenders in hedge funds without new regulations. The number of fraud cases suggests that regulators are not shy about using these powers, and hedge funds regularly experience inquiries from the SEC when they happen to trade heavily in a stock ahead of a

price-moving announcement. Moreover, some of what politicians and journalists label "hedge-fund abuses" involve leaks
of inside information from investment banks rather than
from hedge funds, making the hedge-fund managers who
receive the leaks accomplices rather than the chief offenders.
(Mallaby 2007, 95)

You've got to admire how far Mallaby will go to exonerate
hedge funds—golly, they're not really bad crooks. They're not
the "chief offenders." They only drive the getaway cars! But how
many getaway drivers are there? How does Mallaby or anyone
else know that hedge-fund cheating is not widespread? And how,
for that matter, would we prove the opposing view—that foul
play is endemic in the hedge-fund industry? In fact, until a lot of
"accomplices" are wiretapped or tell all, it's virtually impossible
for outsiders to really know the extent of the cheating.

We need to hear from an informed insider, someone who has
run a major hedge fund, someone who hasn't been nabbed and
isn't just talking to cop a plea. Yet what hedge-fund manager in
his right mind would dare to tell all about the lawless world of
hedge funds?

Enter Jim Cramer, the frenetic star of the highly successful
CNBC show *Mad Money*. Before he became a TV star, Cramer
made tens of millions of dollars running his own hedge fund, one
of the most successful ever. After a decade in the business, Cramer
knows a thing or two about hedge funds. Yet unlike others in this
famously mysterious field, Cramer talks about it in his entertain-
ing autobiography, *Confessions of a Street Addict*.

In 2002, Cramer drew a gory picture of the cutthroat tactics
required for hedge-fund survival. Five years later, in an interview
on TheStreet.com (a website he cofounded and still co-owns),
Cramer admitted that the industry actually pushes people, including himself, out to the ethical edge—and beyond.

• • •

James Cramer, a good Jewish boy from a middle-class home in Philadelphia, grew up smart and quirky. While other kids pored over baseball cards, young Jim was obsessed with stock market quotes. He tried to keep up with as many companies as possible and engineered make-believe trades. Fantasy market-playing became part of his peppery persona long before fantasy baseball came along.

As he plowed his way through Harvard (where he was president of the *Harvard Crimson*) and then Harvard Law School, Cramer continued to feed his obsession with the stock market. He started picking and investing in stocks as a student, and when he graduated, he began to manage money for one of his professors, Marty Peretz, the publisher of the *New Republic*.

Instead of a summer internship with a law firm, Cramer nailed a job at Goldman Sachs and then put in four years on its sales force. With his energy and charm, he was a budding star with a knack for landing big accounts. Yet his real passion was still playing the markets himself. He soon found the means to set up a hedge fund with his wife, Karen—aka "The Trading Goddess." During the late 1980s and the 1990s, he traded like a wild man—and became exceedingly rich in the process.

In his *Confessions*, Cramer shows all the signs of the "good Jewish boy" genetic program (believe me, I know): he presents himself as a walking disaster. In contrast, his wife, Karen, is shrewd, brilliant, and always right. She never makes a bad trade or a bad hire. Meanwhile, poor Jim combines bad judgment with a psychosis Woody Allen would be proud of, as he stumbles his way toward riches. After their kids are born, Karen becomes the calm, caring stay-at-home mom, while Jim is consumed by work, blowing off family and school events left and right. When things go awry, Jim panics, screams and yells, and generally acts like someone who desperately needs to be scolded by a good Jewish mother, which, of course, Karen is.

Jim Cramer was a man possessed and obsessed, outworking everyone, all of the time. And he absolutely detested losing money. In an industry of alpha males reaping alpha profits, he had to have A-pluses on all of his report cards. He drove himself to make the highest returns, year after year, beating all of the biggest names every time. He was ablaze with energy:

I simply couldn't stay asleep past three. No matter what I did, no matter how late I went to bed, no matter what I took, Sominex, cabernet, Bombay and tonic, didn't matter, I would sit up, eerily awake every night at 3:00 am, sweat pouring from every pore. Jeez it's dark at that hour. And nobody to talk to at all. Once up, all I could do was lie there and be paralyzed by the poor trades I had made the day before or the potential for great trades I could make the next day. I would roll on my stomach, press my head to the pillow, and think about the money I had lost if I had traded poorly, or the positions that had gone against me even if I had traded well. What good would it do to go over the good trades? That couldn't make you money.

Eventually, after a ritual hour of bogus attempts to fall back asleep, at 4:20 am I would give up and find myself on the treadmill in the basement. Bleak existence. (Cramer 2002, 103)

Then someone invented the Internet—and made it go live on Wall Street—so that Jim could work even harder:

Now I knew what to do when I couldn't sleep. I would get up and read and enter message boards, go to the Web sites of all of the newspapers around the world, and plan what our Web site would look like. I would spend from 3:30 until dawn working on designs for what would be TheStreet.com and then shift to my day job of trading until 4:00 pm, when I would once again start working online, taking a break for dinner before reimmersing myself in a night of e-mail and planning. (103)

On his way to work from suburban New Jersey (in his chauffeured Mercedes 500), he would read hundreds of reports, write blogs, and talk to his key traders and the press.

Cramer clearly wanted us to understand that he made his millions by working harder than everyone else in the universe—and millions he made. For a full decade starting in 1987, Cramer and Company (later renamed Cramer-Berkowitz) averaged a 23 percent return *per year*. That means, if you invested $1 million with Cramer, in ten years it would be worth $6.4 million. (Would that our 401k's followed that trajectory.) In one good year, the value of Cramer's hedge fund went from $300 million to $400 million. While Cramer took 1 percent of the assets as his administrative fee (staff salaries and such), he and his wife took 20 percent of the profits, too. That's a tidy $20 million in one year—in addition to the $4 million Cramer was paid to run the office. (Today, most hedge-fund managers continue to skim 20 percent of the profits, while administrative costs are usually 2 percent or more of the assets under management.)

Yet there's a catch: You get your 20 percent only when your returns take the fund over what's called the "high-water mark." If you lose money, then you won't collect another 20 percent until you make up those losses and bring your fund back past the last high-water mark. So you can never afford to lose money.

Then there are those dreaded redemptions. That's when the fund's investors decide to take their money and run. Each year, hedge funds offer investors a window of time—perhaps a few days, two or three times a year—when they can take out some or all of their funds. If your fund is losing money, your investors may run for the hills, which makes it nearly impossible to get back to your high-water mark. You risk going into a rapid death spiral, as more and more investors flee. Suddenly, you're toast. It's not uncommon, and it can happen very quickly.

Jim Cramer was desperate to avoid such a dismal outcome. At stake was not only his huge hedge fund, but also his growing media presence, including his regular appearances on shows such as CNBC's *Squawk Box*. Jim did a lot of squawking, offering controversial, rapid-fire opinions on all things financial. He loved to let it rip on the air. His cachet and credibility were entirely built on his day-to-day life as a top kick-ass hedge-fund manager—the ultimate insider (and the only hedge-fund honcho who regularly shared his thinking with the everyday investor). If his hedge fund failed, his entire media persona would crumble as well. He had more to lose than money.

In his book, Cramer does a masterful job of setting us up for a fall. We know it's coming, we just don't know when or how.

• • •

The year was 1998. That's when Long-Term Capital Management (LTCM) (a hedge fund run by Nobel laureates that was leveraged 100 to 1) nearly took down the entire economy, forcing the New York Federal Reserve to engineer a private bailout. LTCM's collapse tore the heart out of many hedge funds, because so many of them had mimicked its strategies.

Cramer began the year with what he calls "hubris." Going into 1998, he said,

I could recite the litany of my greatness in my sleep: Never had a down year. In cash for the crash of '87. Made money in the minicrash of '89. Weathered 1990 and 1994 better than most; two years that closed lots of funds for awful performance. Coined money on national TV in the Asian contagion. By 1998 I figured I had the money making process down pat. I knew that if I came to work every day with just my wits, made my calls, looked at my stocks, looked at the tape, the procession of stocks crossing the ticker, checked in with my sources and my analysts, I could make $400,000 in 12 hours. I could beat my trends line. Everybody would love me no matter what, even if I had an off period because I had been so darned good.

What a dope I was. (183)

Then came the crisis at Long-Term Capital Management, and Cramer learned some facts of life about hedge-fund capitalism:

This is money we are talking about, not love and not a home sports team. Money's fungible and molten. It flows to wherever the hottest hand might be and it departs cold hands as quickly as someone might change the channel on a boring television show. There's no loyalty with money, even after years of outperformance. Which is why 1998 leaves the most bitter taste in my mouth even now, four years after the debacle. (183–184)

Cramer's hedge fund lost 10, 20, 30 percent of its value in a matter of days. In the middle of it all, the fund entered an unexpected redemption period. According to Cramer, it happened because his good friend Eliot Spitzer, an investor, needed to take his money out so that he could run for New York State Attorney General. Cramer had made a pledge that if he let one person pull money from the fund, he'd let everyone do it. So Cramer opened up the fund just at the peak of the LTCM crash. Many of his dearest friends took their money and ran.

In three excruciating chapters, Cramer shares his pain. We feel his anger and disappointment at those who fled his fund. We feel his despair, his loss, his failure. He has us sweating along with him, as everything he tries fails and every move he makes backfires.

I've read many accounts of how hedge funds fail, and Cramer's strikes me as remarkably realistic. Because of the fund's loss of value and lack of cash, Cramer had to borrow tens of millions to pay off the investors who were leaving. Eventually, he even had to break margin rules to borrow more than he was allowed to, hoping against hope that his broker bank, Goldman Sachs, wouldn't catch him and liquidate his collateral. Cramer was on the verge of losing his shirt, along with his entire wardrobe.

It got so bad that his beloved Trading Goddess found a babysitter for the kids so she could focus on scoring a few trades that might keep the fund from folding.

Meanwhile, word was spreading among reporters and talk show hosts. Jim Cramer was in trouble. Cramer had to go on TV and admit that times were tough—though the hedge fund, he insisted, was not about to go belly-up.

That didn't keep other hedge-fund sharks from circling in for the kill, betting against Cramer's positions to force him to liquidate. (Remember, this is a key part of the million-an-hour strategy: if you think something could die, bet it will die, and then kill it.) Cramer desperately defended his key positions by buying more and bluffing. It was a battle of wills and money. Somehow Cramer managed to keep the sharks at bay, at least for a few days.

Then things got really grim. Cramer's good friend Larry took his money out of the fund and called Cramer a loser. Cramer hit bottom:

> For someone whose only security came from finishing first, the words stung so deeply I might as well have been told to kill myself. For a moment I thought, that's why those people jumped in '29. They jumped because they *should* have jumped. They jumped because they had just lost a lot of money and were losers delivering loser performances, and people wanted that money back. They jumped because it was rational. Because it was right. Because it was, yeah, the honorable thing to do. Because it was quicker than hiding or disappearing. (215)

Cramer still had the Trading Goddess, though. She just happened to be running the trading desk at the moment when the market finally bottomed out. There were only hours to go before the Cramer fund had to pay out the redemption requests and close its doors for good.

> "How can you be so sure it is the bottom?" I said, trying to divine what she saw as I stood watching the markets rise on eight screens in front of us at the top of the trading desk. "What makes you so certain? How do you know this bottom will hold? How do you know you will be right?"

"Simple." She bent down and whispered to me so that others in the room could not hear. "Because at the bottom even the coolest, most hard-bitten pros blink. At the bottom, there is final capitulation." She waited until it dawned on me who she was talking about. "At the bottom, Jimmy, you capitulated. At the bottom you gave up. That's how I know it's the bottom." (245)

Then, by chance, at the eleventh hour, the Cramers were saved: Fed chair Alan Greenspan slashed interest rates, and the markets bounced back.

For the last quarter of the year, the Cramer fund made up all of its losses and then some. The Cramers again went back to presiding over a booming hedge fund, and maybe Jim Cramer matured a bit. After a few more years, he decided to quit the firm to save his health. He became a full-time writer and media personality.

Despite its title, Cramer's book is not his real confession. Yet he is brutally honest about a number of things—especially the trauma of failure. He doesn't even pretend that the hedge-fund industry is socially useful or that hedge-fund managers such as him are really worth all that they earn. He admits that he only cares about winning because he was someone "whose only security came from finishing first."

Cramer's real confession came in his truly remarkable interview for TheStreet.com years later, in 2007.

· · ·

"It's just fiction and fiction and fiction," says Jim Cramer.

When Jim Cramer's interview with Aaron Task of TheStreet .com spread to YouTube in March 2007, it kicked up such a storm that the website pulled the piece and told everyone else to pull it as well. (As of this writing, however, you can still find the interview on YouTube and transcripts on Antisocialmedia.net.) Note that all extracts quoting the transcript in this chapter are from Antisocialmedia.net.

TheStreet.com was not exactly hostile territory for Cramer, because he'd cofounded it with Marty Peretz. When the site went public, Cramer's shares were worth millions.

The last thing Aaron Task wanted to do was to score a block-buster incriminating interview with a man who was essentially his boss. He just wanted Cramer to talk about recent market gyra-tions. Yet Cramer seized on Task's first innocuous question to boast about how he had cheated:

> Cramer: A lot of times, when I was short at my hedge fund and I was positioned short, meaning I needed it down, I would create a level of activity beforehand that could drive the futures. It doesn't take much money. Or if I were long and I would want to make things a little bit rosy, I would go in and take a bunch of stocks and make sure that they're higher, maybe commit $5 million in capital to do it, and I could affect it.

This is not exactly what they teach you in business school. Hedge funds are supposedly betting on the movement of markets, not manipulating those movements to ensure a winning hand. Yet Cramer was confessing that when he was betting against stocks—going short—he temporarily drove the market down, and when he was long, he drove the market up. After this brief manipulation, Cramer collected on his bet, scoring a nice a profit, and got out.

> Cramer: But it's a fun game and it's a lucrative game. You can move it up and then fade it. That often creates a very negative feel. So let's say you take a longer-term view intra-day and you say, "Listen I'm gonna boost the futures, and then when the real sellers come in, when the real market comes in they're gonna knock it down and it's gonna create a negative view."
>
> That's a strategy very worth doing when you're evaluat-ing on a day-to-day basis. I would encourage anyone who's in a hedge fund to do it, because it's legal.

It's a very quick way to make money, and very satisfying.

By the way, no one else in the world would ever admit that, but I don't care.

After this startling confession from his subject, Aaron Task was dumbfounded. Apparently hoping to give his boss time to pull his pants back on, Task quickly changed the subject by asking how the growth in hedge funds affected hedge-fund strategies.

Cramer blithely ignored Task, however, and continued the exposé himself. He explained that the goal of his market manipulation was to ensure that by the end of each quarter, his fund was up—"because that's your payday." For Cramer, the pressure not to fail is overwhelming. You just can't afford to let your guard down for a minute.

Cramer explained that his eye was always glued to the key stocks, including Apple and Research in Motion (RIM), the maker of the BlackBerry, because when they move, they take the entire market with them (or so they did in 2007). According to Cramer, if you're betting short, you've got to take matters into your own hands.

> Cramer: You really gotta control the market. You can't let it lift. When you get a Research in Motion, it's really important to use a lot of your firepower to knock that down 'cause it's the fulcrum of the market today.

Aaron Task stumbled to keep up as Cramer took complete control of the interview.

> Cramer: So let's say I were short. What I would do is I would hit a lot of guys with RIM. Now you can't foment. That's a violation of . . .
> Task: Ferment?
> Cramer: Yeah, you can't foment—
> Task: Foment.
> Cramer: You can't create yourself an impression that a stock's down. But you do it anyway 'cause the SEC doesn't

understand it. That's the only sense that I would say this is illegal. But a hedge fund that's not up a lot really has to do a lot now to save itself. This is different from what I was talking about at the beginning [when he was using his money to buy certain instruments that would eventually move down the price of RIM].

And what makes it so different?

Cramer: This is just actually blatantly illegal. But when you have six days and your company may be in doubt because you're down, I think it's really important to foment, if I were one of these guys. Foment an impression that Research in Motion isn't any good, because Research in Motion is the key.

Listen carefully to Cramer's words: "when your company may be in doubt"; and "if I were one of these guys."

Cramer's company *was* in doubt. He *was* one of those guys. So, was Cramer himself doing those things he described as "blatantly illegal"?

And what exactly did he mean by "illegal fomenting"?

Apparently, he meant manipulating the press, spreading rumors—and breaking the law.

So, what's the law? According to the Securities and Exchange Commission, rumormongering is defined as "the intentional spread of false information intended to manipulate securities prices." The prosecution would have to show that "first, the rumor was inaccurate; second, the market was impacted by the rumor; and third, the defendant knew or should have known that the rumor was inaccurate" (Marshall 2009).

Did Cramer go too far?

Cramer: Again, when your company's in survival mode it's really important to defeat Research in Motion. You get the Pisanis of the world and the people talking about it as if there's something wrong with RIM.

Cramer was admitting that he fed bogus information on Research in Motion to financial reporters such as CNBC's Bob Pisani. Quite an admission—especially since Cramer actually worked for CNBC at the time. Pisani was a colleague. Yet Cramer was *using him to gain personal profits*.

> Cramer: Then you would call the [*Wall Street*] *Journal* and you get the bozo reporter on Research in Motion, and you would feed that Palm's got a killer it's gonna give away. [PalmPilot was then a key BlackBerry rival.]
> These are all the things you must do on a day like today. And if you're not, maybe you shouldn't be in the game.

Say that again? According to Jim Cramer, if you don't engage in illegal rumormongering to manipulate the market, *then you shouldn't be running a hedge fund*. Maybe Cramer was simply justifying his own behavior by using that classic children's defense "But everyone else is doing it!" Or maybe he was accurately describing the cutthroat game as it really is played, with stakes in the tens of millions of dollars.

Back to the interview, though, and poor Aaron Task, who was still trying to change the subject by asking what role Apple plays in the markets. Cramer ignored the obvious lifeline and proceeded to offer a tutorial on how to illegally beat down Apple's share price!

> Cramer: Apple's very important to spread the rumor that both Verizon and ATT have decided they don't like the phone [iPhone]. It's a very easy one to do because it's also you want to spread the rumor that it's [the iPhone] is not gonna be ready for Macworld [the big trade conference]. This is very easy because the people who write about Apple want that story, and you can claim that it's credible because you spoke to someone at Apple. . . .
> Task: They're not gonna comment [meaning that Apple never comments on rumors so you can get away with starting one].

Just in case we didn't understand how to manipulate Apple, Cramer ran through it again:

Cramer: Again, if I were short Apple, I would be working very hard today to get that. The way you would do that is you pick up the phone and you call six trading desks and say, "Listen, I just got off the phone with my contact at Verizon and he has already said, Listen, we're a Lucky G house [LG phones]. We're a Samsung house. We're a Motorola house. There's no room for Apple. They want too much. We're not gonna let them in. We're not gonna let them do what they did to music." I think that's a very effective way to keep a stock down. . . . You kind of create an image that there's gonna be news next week, and that's gonna frighten everybody. . . .

Then they call Pisani again. You have to use those guys and say, "Listen, I see a big buyer of puts [a financial instrument that protects a hedge fund if the price goes down] and I'm told that it's SAC [a very large hedge fund with lots of buying power]." You would do that, too. These are all what's really going on under that market that you don't see.

You bet you don't see it. If you did (and if Cramer was right), all of the top hedge funds would be under investigation.

Flat-out *lying*, Cramer went on to say, is the only way to win. And you've got to win, because otherwise you face the trauma of failure, the fear of seeing investors leave your fund:

Cramer: But what's important when you're in that hedge fund mode is to not do a thing remotely truthful because the truth is so against your view that it's important to create a new truth—to develop a fiction. The fiction is developed by almost anybody who's down 2 percent, up 6 percent a year. You can't take any chances. You can't have the market up more than it is if you're up six because starting Jan 2 you'll have all your money come out.

And here comes the indirect admission that when he was in big trouble in 1998, he cheated:

Cramer: What would you do if you were in that situation and you felt like you're desperate? You would do these actions.

Aaron Task scrambled to frame Cramer's bald admission of lawbreaking into a perfectly normal conversation about "market mechanics" and "fundamentals," but Cramer would have none of it:

Cramer: Who cares about fundamentals! . . .
   But look what people can do. I mean that's a fabulous thing. The great thing about the market is it has nothing to do with the actual stocks. Now, look, over maybe two weeks from now the buyers will come to their senses and realize that everything they heard was a lie. . . .
   It's just fiction and fiction and fiction. I think it's important for people to recognize that the way that the market really works is to have that nexus hit the brokerage houses with a series of orders that can push it down, and we get to the press and get it on CNBC. That's very important. Then ya have kind of a vicious cycle down. It's a pretty good game and it can be played—it can pay for a percent or two.

Task tried to yank Cramer away from the confessional once again by asking him about investing in the cell phone market. And once again, Cramer ignored the safe haven and went on to describe yet another classic illegal maneuver—price fixing:

Cramer: The problem with the cell phone market, frankly, is that these guys are all killing each other. Someone has to take a dive. Motorola and Nokia have to get in the room and just fix price. They've been reluctant to do that because of the various justice departments.

Task, however, pointed out that price fixing is illegal. Cramer snapped back, "Well, that hasn't stopped a lot of other companies."

Task then finally succeeded in getting Cramer to talk about something that wouldn't incriminate him—some chitchat about Fed policy and Ford versus GM.

But Cramer had the last word, and it was a whopper. After just explaining with crystal clarity that you've got to lie to the media about stock prospects to make a profit on your short bets, he emphasized that it was absolutely imperative for hedge funds to bring down Research in Motion before the quarter ended, even though the company was doing really well and should be going up in market price:

Cramer: It's Friday. You [hedge funds] have five more days to make your quarter. Can you really risk having them [Research in Motion] up this much? I don't think you can.

• • •

What do we make of Cramer's confessions? Are they credible? After all, the guy has just boasted that when you're in "hedge fund mode," you've got to be sure "not to do a thing that is remotely truthful." So how can we trust him when he tells us that this time he is telling the truth?

In *Confessions of a Street Addict*, Cramer never mentions any form of stock manipulation. (I'm sure his lawyers made sure of that.) He never hints that he illegally used the media—including his own colleagues at CNBC—to twist the truth. Yet five years later, in the interview with Task, Cramer argues that if your hedge fund isn't manipulating markets, "maybe you shouldn't be in the game."

To know for sure whether Cramer cheated, the SEC would have to go back through his records to look for signs of "fomenting": was Cramer really able to affect the prices of the stocks he was playing? But that investigation won't happen because Cramer has been out of the business for more than a decade.

Unless Cramer is schizophrenic, on top of being a charming nut, the odds are that Cramer's two confessions are deeply linked. You can't read *Confessions of a Street Addict* without sensing the emotional upheaval Cramer experienced when his fund came within minutes of going under. It's the heart of his book and maybe the main reason he wrote it. To me, it feels as if he needed to exorcise the demons of failure. I believe him when he said that his entire identity was based on winning and the adoration that came with it. You don't make it to the top of Harvard Law School and Goldman Sachs unless you are competitive to your core. Smart is not good enough.

Then, in Cramer's second confession, he kept returning to how unbearable it felt when there were only a few days to go till the quarter ended, and when you knew that if you didn't post good numbers, your investors would walk out on you. *"What would you do if you were in that situation and you feel like you're desperate? You would do these actions."*

In his *Hedge Fund Fraud Casebook*, author Bruce Johnson compiles one hundred hedge-fund fraud cases and tries to understand what conditions and structures were most likely to produce fraud. (If you have lots of money and are into psychotropic drugs, you might want to drop $95 on this book. Its flow charts and spinning diagrams are like Woodstock for Wall Street.)

Hedge-fund fraud doesn't usually happen because certain evil people consciously set up a Ponzi scheme to cheat investors, Johnson concludes. Instead, hedge funds usually resort to fraud only when they're in danger of collapse—precisely the predicament Cramer faced in 1998.

It's no mystery what happens when a hedge fund "blows up"—say, when a rogue trader makes a billion-dollar blunder or when someone's Ponzi scheme is outed: the fund goes on immediate life support and usually shuts its doors in a matter of weeks, at most.

Yet when a hedge fund's survival—and the manager's performance fees—are at risk for less spectacular reasons, things get complicated. If there's still room and time to maneuver, the hedge-fund manager has options—and might just try them all.

With the aid of his psychedelic diagrams, Johnson describes these "mortality calculations." They include "cutting over-heads and drawing upon retained earnings or other partnership resources." Or a manager might "shift to higher volatility strat-egies or increase leverage" to improve the odds of getting a per-formance fee. Another, "darker practice," he says, is to "obtain illiquid assets where the value can more easily be overstated" (Johnson 2010, 24).

The most serious cases of fraud, however, come when all of these maneuvers fail. That's when hedge-fund managers begin to consider more powerful forms of cheating.

> [A] substantial proportion of frauds and perhaps those most dangerous to investors begin as legitimate businesses. These "funds gone bad" have likely had managers that made simi-lar fund mortality calculations. But they did not limit their choices to the business alternatives outlined thus far and allowed themselves to consider unconventional solutions that included criminal behavior. (25–26)

Bernie Madoff's "success" is criminal from the get-go. Simon Lack, in his book *The Hedge Fund Mirage*, describes a meet-ing he had with Fairfield Greenwich, a large feeder fund that provided billions of investor money to Madoff. Lack was trying to understand how Madoff made such "remarkably consistent" high returns (Lack 2012, 133). He reports being told that Madoff operated two businesses—a brokerage that executed trades for clients and a hedge fund that executed its own trades. The mes-sage was clear. Fairfield Greenwich was implying that Madoff made lots of money by using information he gleaned from mak-ing trades for his brokerage clients and then would illegally front-run those trades with his hedge-fund money. Lack wrote,

Although the Fairfield marketers never used the term *front-running* and didn't suggest anything illegal was taking place, it occurred to me that this was probably what they themselves believed was supporting the consistently successful results of Madoff's hedge fund. Madoff's investors, including those brought in by Fairfield Greenwich, were profiting at the expense of the brokerage clients. The further attraction of such a scheme to a hedge fund investor could be that they'd be the passive beneficiary of such activity, with no liability for doing anything illegal yet still able to profit from it. (133)

So, some very savvy investors probably suspected that Madoff was doing something illegal, but of a kind that was palatable. That was fine with all concerned, *as long as the returns kept coming*. What's a little front-running among friends? Yet when it turned out that Madoff was running a classic Ponzi scheme, all bets were off, because the returns could not and did not keep coming.

How many rotten apples are there in a hedge-fund barrel? Johnson tries to give us an estimate in his hedge-fund-fraud casebook:

In its most simple terms . . . an investor with a hypothetical portfolio of 100 hedge funds might be likely to experience one fraud per year. A more realistic hedge fund, or fund-of-funds portfolio of 20 funds, could be expected to encounter a fraud about once in five years. (Johnson 2010, 253)

So, for every hundred hedge-fund apples, Johnson's careful and cautious account claims that at a bare minimum, one hedge fund is rotten enough to get caught.

• • •

Is there a connection between Type A+ personalities and widespread hedge-fund cheating? Because such highly competitive personalities populate nearly all of the hedge-fund industry, is cheating endemic as well—despite Johnson's one-in-a-hundred estimate?

Lynn Stout, the Paul Hastings Professor of Corporate and Securities Law at the UCLA School of Law, wrote an extremely provocative blog post in the *Harvard Business Review* in December 2010 titled "How Hedge Funds Create Criminals."

The recent hedge-fund scandals, she claims, "raise suspicion that some hedge fund trades may have succeeded at beating the market not through careful research and original analysis but allegedly by breaking the law." She goes on to ask this carefully parsed question: "Why does a portion of the hedge fund industry stand accused of succumbing to illegal behavior?"

Stout's answer is a slap in the face to the hedge-fund industry: "from a behavioral perspective," she wrote, "my research suggests that hedge funds are 'criminogenic' environments." (And she didn't invent that word.)

Professor Stout isn't claiming that *all* people are naturally poised "to break the law or exploit others when it serves their material interests." She maintains that behavioral science has conclusively *disproved* this claim. In truth, she says, "people often act 'prosocially'—unselfishly sacrificing opportunities for personal gain to help others or to follow the rules. Few people steal their neighbor's newspapers or shake down kindergartners for lunch money."

It's all about the circumstances, Stout posits: some circumstances promote prosocial behavior, others don't—such as hedge funds. Stout says that hedge funds, "both individually and as a group, can send at least three powerful social signals that have been repeatedly shown in formal experiments to suppress prosocial behavior." They are:

Signal 1: Authority Doesn't Care about Ethics. Since the days of Stanley Milgram's notorious electric shock experiments, science has shown that people do what they are instructed to do. Hedge-fund traders are routinely instructed by their managers and investors to focus on maximizing portfolio returns. Thus, it should come as no surprise that not all hedge-fund traders put obeying federal securities laws at the top of their to-do lists.

Signal 2: Other Traders Aren't Acting Ethically. Behavioral experiments also routinely find that people are most likely to "follow their conscience" when they think others are also acting prosocially. Yet in the hedge-fund environment, traders are more likely to brag about their superior results than [about] their willingness to sacrifice those results to preserve their ethics.

Signal 3: Unethical Behavior Isn't Harmful. Finally, experiments show that people act less selfishly when they understand how their selfishness harms others. This poses special problems for enforcing laws against insider trading, which is often perceived as a "victimless" crime that may even contribute to social welfare by producing more accurate market prices. Of course, insider trading isn't really victimless: for every trader who reaps a gain using insider information, some investor on the other side of the trade must lose. But because the losing investor is distant and anonymous, it's easy to mistakenly feel that insider trading isn't really doing harm. (Stout 2010)

All three signals are flashing away in Jim Cramer's confessional:

1. Cramer definitely does not think that hedge funds "put obeying federal securities laws at the top of their to-do lists," as Stout puts it. Cramer openly disdains authority, in the form of the SEC. He "foments" with impunity, even though he knows it's illegal: "You do it anyway 'cause the SEC doesn't understand it."
2. Cramer is quite certain that other traders aren't acting ethically. In fact, he believes that any trader who *does* act ethically (by not "fomenting") "shouldn't be in the game."

3. Cramer clearly doesn't think that his rule breaking hurts others. In his view, if you *don't* play fast and loose with the rules, you're hurting yourself, suffering the most humiliating defeat possible.

A blogging colleague who works in the financial industry has come up with his own one-word description of the ultra-competitive world of hedge funds: "Sociopathic."

Do's and Don'ts

- **Don't** ever admit to the media that you manipulated the media for fun and profit.

- **Do** remember to move markets up and down whenever you need to. "It's a fun game and it's a lucrative game."

- **Do** understand that you can always move the ethical edge out a little further.

- **Do** look your criminogenic best when they take your mug shot.

STEP 8

Have the Right People Whispering in Your Ear

Raj Rajaratnam sits slightly slumped and rumpled in his chair next to his tallish, white-haired, high-priced defense attorney. The man next to me in the overflowing courtroom gallery says, "It sure looks like he had a restless night."

He will have many more.

The Raj, as he likes to be called, is a barrel-shaped fifty-four-year-old man with a very round face and a very dark complexion. He's nearly six feet tall and well over 200 pounds. He also is, or at least was, a big man in finance. *Forbes* reported that in 2009, when Raj headed the Galleon hedge fund, he was the 236th richest person in America, with an estimated net worth (total assets minus liabilities) of $1.8 billion. That's more than twenty-three thousand times the median U.S. family's net worth (which was $77,300 in 2010, down from $126,400 in 2007) (Appelbaum 2012).

The Raj shows no facial or emotional affect at all as the bow-tied Judge Richard Holwell carefully reads out the sentence—eleven years in federal prison in Butner, North Carolina, the current home of Bernie Madoff. The Raj must also cough up $10 million in fines and forfeit $53.8 million in ill-gotten gains. With good behavior, he gets out in nine years. The money is chump change.

You wonder what the Raj must be thinking as the judge accuses him of befouling our financial markets, scaring away investors, and putting jobs in danger. Only a few short years ago, the Raj was worshipped as a great American hero, an icon of finance, and a philanthropist who cared deeply about helping those less fortunate. He was precisely what every business school graduate wanted to become. His billions were proof positive of his genius and of his value to society. Back then, his aggressiveness to secure "privileged" information was more a badge of financial acumen—the kind of take-no-prisoners behavior that investors expected of the very best hedge-fund chieftains. He was an important face (albeit a brown one, originally from Sri Lanka) of the new American capitalism—a capitalism built on an ever-widening role for high finance. He was our future.

When our future nearly succumbed to financial follies, however, sacrificial lambs were needed to appease the populist gods. The rotund Raj looked good on the spit. How easy it is to turn this dark-skinned financier from the epitome of capitalism into a scoundrel. His crime of insider trading, according to the judge, is nothing less than an "assault on the free markets that are a fundamental element of our democratic society." The judge continues,

> There may not be readily identifiable victims, but when the playing field is not level, the integrity of the marketplace is called into question and the public suffers. This is not to say that the defendant's insider trading is the cause of the economic dislocations that our society now faces. That would be too easy an answer. But his crimes and the scope of his crimes reflect a virus in our business culture that needs to be eradicated. (*United States v. Raj Rajaratnam* 2011, 30)

The disease is so endemic to hedge funds, Judge Holwell opines, that the stiff sentence, the longest ever given for this offense, is needed to "deter other fund managers, traders, and brokers from engaging in insider trading."

The prosecution wants the sentence doubled because of the enormity of the crimes and the ways in which the Raj tried to conceal them and because of his lack of remorse. Prosecutor Reed M. Brodsky believes a stronger message must be sent to the financial elites. He wants a sentence that

> [P]unishes him for his extensive crimes, reflects the seriousness and brazenness of those crimes, and sends a clear and unmistakable message to money managers and hedge funds that insider trading must stop and if you get caught, no matter how powerful, no matter how rich, no matter what your position is in the securities industry, you will be punished accordingly. (24)

Yet Judge Holwell takes into account two mitigating circumstances. First, the judge believes that the Raj actually is a significant philanthropist whose "responsiveness to and care for the less privileged goes considerably beyond the norm and can be seen in the scores of letters I received detailing his efforts to help tsunami victims in . . . Sri Lanka, earthquake victims in Pakistan, a homeless shelter here in New York and 9/11 victims as well." Second, the judge reveals from previously sealed documents that the Raj has advanced diabetes and liver failure and that he will probably need a transplant. Prison time "is a more intense experience for people with serious health conditions," he says. So this humane judge believes eleven years (nine actually served) plus two years' probation is enough (32–33).

(Maybe the sentence should be calibrated to how long it would take the Raj to count all of his money. If he counted by ones and did so sixteen hours a day, seven days a week, he would be counting for more than sixty-four years before reaching $1.8 billion.)

Unlike major drug dealers, the Raj gets forty-five extra days of freedom before reporting to prison. So, we don't get to see this billionaire do a perp walk out of the courtroom. There are no handcuffs, no leg shackles, no shuffling through the courtroom doors into hell. Instead, after the trial we witness the Raj and his very muscular security guard slowly, but very forcefully, mow down a mob of professional photographers outside the Worth Street entrance to the federal courthouse in lower Manhattan as they escape into their black SUV. The Raj then heads to his upscale duplex apartment on Sutton Place, confined to quarters for the next forty-five days. Boy, will he miss that apartment.

The federal trial of Raj Rajaratnam exposed what the government claims is a ubiquitous hedge-fund practice. The prosecution successfully argued that the Raj had accumulated ill-gotten gains of more than $70 million by cashing in on tips from informants whom he'd paid under the table. If this game really is widespread among hedge funds, as both the prosecution and the judge believe is proven beyond a shadow of doubt, then cheating indeed may be a major source of hedge-fund "alpha" profits.

Understanding how widespread lying, cheating, stealing, and general corner cutting are, is important to figuring out how millions can be made. After all, hedge funds are supposed to be good for America, pushing markets and investments in the direction of innovation and efficiency. If hedge funds are mostly just capitalizing on investments already moving in the right direction or even raking in profits from pushing markets in the wrong direction, well, it certainly makes the path to millions a lot simpler. You don't have to understand what no one else understands. You just have to be willing to do what no one else is willing to do.

I was going to title this step "Don't Get Caught." But you know that. Instead, let's describe exactly what you don't want to get caught doing.

• • •

Let's go back to September 2008. All hell had just broken loose in the financial markets as mortgage-backed securities crashed, taking some major financial institutions down with them. On September 15, Lehman Brothers declared bankruptcy, as hedge funds were shorting it to death. The next day, the government took over AIG and soon infused it with $175 billion in cash, to prevent its collapse as well.

On September 2, the Dow Jones Industrial Average had stood at 11,516. By September 17, though, it had lost more than 900 points, to close at 10,609. Financial markets were paralyzed as hundreds of billions of dollars of toxic waste assets plummeted in value. The ratings agencies were flipping thousands of their AAA ratings into junk status. No one knew which institutions had how much poison on their books, so no one wanted to lend to anyone else.

By March 9, 2009, the stock market hit rock bottom at 6,547. Within months, nearly eight million workers had lost their jobs. This was, and still is, the Great Recession.

Times were tough, even for hedge funds. Many had levered way up during the good times, investing heavily in mortgage-related securities with borrowed money, and now the losses were piling up. Hedge-fund investors were clamoring to get their capital back. For many hedge funds faced with both losses and redemptions, it was starting to look like the end. Only a handful of hedge funds, especially those that had shorted (bet against) the bubble, escaped the panic. All of the other funds were desperately searching for a way to profit from the turbulent markets—or else face certain ruin.

Yet during good times and bad, the Raj had an edge to ensure his continued prosperity: a network of highly placed insiders ready to supply invaluable and illegal information. (Note to Mallaby: He wasn't just the "accomplice" driving the getaway car.) Among them: Rajat Gupta, a Harvard MBA and the former head of McKinsey and Company, the global consulting firm. After retiring as McKinsey's CEO in 2007, Gupta joined many corporate boards, including Goldman Sachs and Procter & Gamble.

From his ring-side seat on Goldman Sachs's board, Gupta, the prosecution contends, provided the Raj with very lucrative insider tips during this volatile period. Yet Gupta had other plans. He wanted to leave Goldman for a much higher-paying position at KKR, the giant private equity firm. Rajaratnam understood Gupta's core ambitions—that he wanted to climb up the grand pecking order of high finance and approach the Raj's own lofty heights. (The Raj was perched even higher than the top Goldman Sachs executives.) According to federal wiretaps, Rajaratnam said, "I think he wants to be in that circle. That's a billionaire circle, right? Goldman is like the hundreds of millions circle, right?" (Lattman and Sorkin 2011). But the Raj couldn't bear the thought of losing one of his best-placed sources.

Fortunately for the Raj, Goldman Sachs CEO Lloyd Blankfein persuaded Gupta to hold off on his resignation. Blankfein feared investors might bolt if one of the directors resigned in the midst of the market turmoil.

So, while others were succumbing to the crash, Gupta allegedly continued to serve as one of the Raj's cash cows. Here's some of the milk he produced:

- After Blankfein told Gupta that the 2008 second-quarter returns for Goldman Sachs would be better than Wall Street analysts had expected, Gupta called the Raj, who promptly bought options for more than 350,000 Goldman Sachs shares. A few days later, he sold them—at a $6.6 million profit.
- Then, in the middle of the fall 2008 crisis, Blankfein informed Gupta that Goldman's fourth-quarter earnings would actually drop $2 a share, rather than gain $2.50 as predicted. This was startling news because Goldman Sachs had never before experienced a losing quarter. Within twenty-three seconds of this revelation from Goldman's CEO, Gupta was on the line with the Raj, according to federal prosecutors. Rajaratnam immediately sold his Goldman shares, saving himself a $3 million loss.
- On September 22, 2008, only a week after the collapse of Lehman Brothers, Blankfein asked the board's permission to convert Goldman Sachs into a bank holding company, which would give the company access to Federal Reserve

emergency loans and other governmental financial good-
ies. Gupta immediately called the Raj, who then purchased
eighty thousand shares of Goldman stock.

- One day later, at 3:54 p.m. on September 23, 2008, Blankfein
  initiated a board conference call to share some really good
  news: Warren Buffett, the "Oracle of Omaha," was investing $5 billion in Goldman Sachs. This seal of approval by
  the nation's most beloved investor, which would be made
  public after U.S. markets closed for the day—that is, six
  minutes later—would greatly calm nervous Goldman investors. And that really mattered, because both Wall Street
  analysts and government officials—including Treasury
  Secretary Timothy Geithner—thought Goldman Sachs was
  in real danger of going under.

- Gupta must have had the Raj on speed-dial, because four
  minutes after that board conference call began—at 3:58
  p.m.—Raj Rajaratnam bought 175,000 shares of Goldman
  Sachs with just two minutes to spare before markets closed.

- At 4:00 p.m. on September 23, Goldman shares closed at
  $125.05. The next morning, after the Buffett announcement
  was officially released, they opened at $133.20, gaining $8.15.
  The Raj sold his new shares for a $900,000 profit.

Federal prosecutors claim that Gupta's insider information
alone netted the Raj a total $13.6 million. (On June 15, 2012,
Gupta was convicted on three counts of securities fraud and one
count of conspiracy.)

During the two-month trial, the prosecution played forty-
six wiretap recordings on which Rajaratnam secured insider tips
from a cadre of elite sources. The tapes also caught the Raj coach-
ing others on how to set up secret accounts to conceal their bribes
and hide their incriminating e-mails and phone records from pry-
ing authorities.

The overwhelming evidence convinced the jury to find
Rajaratnam guilty on all fourteen counts. The Raj isn't going
down alone. As of May 2012, the FBI's "Perfect Hedge" strike

force has arrested sixty-six financiers on insider-trading charges, fifty-nine of whom have been convicted or have pleaded guilty. The FBI claims to have a five-year backlog of cases, and the Bureau wants more. To drum up business, it is commissioning public service announcements featuring none other than Michael Douglas, who played the infamous Gordon "Greed is good" Gekko in the movie *Wall Street*.

So beware all members of the million-an-hour club. If you're going to cheat, you'd better not talk about it on the phone or through e-mail, or you'll end up like Gekko—in jail (and then out and rich again in the sequel?).

As the arrests spread, it's impossible to tell whether the barrel is half full or half empty of rotten apples. The Feds obviously see a very big problem. Preet Bharara, the U.S. Attorney for the Southern District of New York, said that insider trading is "everywhere you look" (Packer 2011). In fact, the Raj investigation has spilled over onto one of the largest and most prestigious hedge funds in the world, SAC Capital Advisors, headed by Steven A. Cohen. SAC is often cited in hedge-fund books as the very exemplar of high "alpha" production. To date, several former employees have been nabbed, but not Cohen, who in 2011 was the fourth-highest hedge-fund earner, at $585,000,000.

Despite Bharara's statement of pervasive hedge-fund crimes, neither he nor anyone else has gone after the big-time perpetrators of the actual transactions that led to the financial crisis, who, so far, have gotten off scot-free.

• • •

On the scale of financial high crimes and misdemeanors, Rajaratnam's are perhaps relatively innocuous. Illegal and punishable, to be sure, but the Raj and his inside informants did not spew forth those awful mortgage-related securities into the world. They didn't foist predatory loans on unsuspecting retirees or place bogus AAA ratings on financial toxic waste or design CDOs so that they would fail. The Raj, arguably, had nothing much to do with the financial crisis. Even Judge Holwell admitted as much during sentencing. The Raj was only trying to make money, big money, by mining insider information. There's no evidence that his avaricious and unethical behavior caused the Great Recession.

Judge Holwell's questionnaire for the Raj jury pool shows that he was worried that the broader financial crisis would infect his trial:

> This case does not have anything to do with the recession or who is to blame for the financial problems we face. . . . [D]oes the fact that the case involves the financial industry, Wall Street executives, hedge funds, mutual funds and the like, make it difficult for anyone to render a fair verdict? (Packer 2011)

Yet in the end, it was impossible for the judge to exorcise the financial crisis demons from the trial, according to *New Yorker* writer George Packer.

> In spite of the Judge's caveat, the catastrophic events of 2008 haunted the proceedings. All the wiretaps had been made that year, and so the jurors heard tapes of a hedge-fund manager running his business as one investment bank after another fell. . . . The wiretaps, which breached the normally soundproof wall of hedge funds, told a breathtaking tale of selfish, short-term thinking. (Packer 2011)

Without a doubt, the Raj's story indeed is a "breathtaking tale of selfish short-term thinking." But compared to what? The Raj looks like a choir boy next to those who created, sold, and distributed every lousy form of mortgage-related security known to the human race. While the Raj was illegally plying his sources for information, cutthroat hedge funds were actively trying to take down bank after bank. Now that's a dazzling display of short-term thinking.

And guess what? They're still at it.

• • •

When I suggested to my agent, lawyer, and good friend Bill Lee that we should question whether Raj Rajaratnam's form of corruption really was criminal, he thought I was nuts. "Of course, it's a crime," he said. "Nobody can seriously argue that insider trading is good for us."

They do, however. There's a boatload of very serious economists, lawyers, and other academics who present arguments that would totally exonerate the crime of insider trading. In fact, many claim that this so-called crime is a *benefit* to the economy. That should be welcome news for those who wish entry into the million-an-hour club.

Even if trades such as Raj's don't benefit society, some argue, at least insider trading shouldn't be criminalized. There are no victims, just as in marijuana cases. Who knows why some anonymous souls wanted to sell shares just as the Raj was buying them? That's their business. Nobody put a gun to their heads to sell Goldman Sachs shares. Yes, the Raj profited, but no one was robbed—and no one should serve time because of a little buying and selling in a victimless crime.

Yet some economists go much further, to argue that insider trading actually is *good* for us. These apologists, to be sure, have a high hurdle to clear. They will need to justify why it's okay for the Raj to haul in $900,000 overnight because he gets an illegal tip from a board member that Warren Buffett is about to invest.

Here's one classic defense: When an insider has information that could affect the price of a stock, it means by definition that the stock is not correctly valued. The sooner the valuation is corrected, the better our society's resources will be allocated. Let's take an extreme example—Enron. Some people inside Enron and its accounting firms and other consulting groups knew the company was cooking the books and that the company's shares were greatly overvalued. This meant that the markets were allocating capital to a company that didn't warrant it.

Donald Boudreaux describes the kind of economic damage that could ensue. He uses a fictitious company, Acme, Inc., as an example, but he, no doubt, is talking about Enron and WorldCom.

> Investors will buy Acme shares at prices that conceal the company's imminent doom. Creditors will extend financing to Acme on terms that do not compensate those creditors for the true risks that they are unknowingly undertaking. Perhaps some of Acme's employees will turn down good job offers at other firms in order to remain at what they are misled to believe is a financially solid Acme Inc.
>
> Eventually, of course, those misled investors, creditors and workers will suffer financial losses. But the economy as a whole loses, too. Capital that would otherwise have been invested in firms more productive than Acme Inc. never gets to those firms. So compared with what would have happened had people not been misled by Acme's deceitfully high share price, those better-run firms don't enhance their efficiencies as much. They don't expand their operations as much. They don't create as many good jobs. Consumers don't enjoy the increased outputs, improved product qualities and lower prices that would otherwise have resulted.
>
> In short, overall economic efficiency is reduced.
>
> It's in the public interest, therefore, that prices adjust as quickly and as completely as possible to underlying economic realities—that prices adjust to convey to market participants as clearly as possible the true state of those realities. (Boudreaux 2009)

How do we ensure that prices adjust quickly? That's easy: let insiders trade on their information. If knowledgeable Enron employees had traded heavily on their awareness of cooked books, the price of Enron's shares would have dropped quickly before doing any more harm to unsuspecting employees, investors, and creditors. As the late Milton Friedman put it in 2003,

You want more insider dealing, not less. You want to give people most likely to have knowledge about deficiencies of the company an incentive to make the public aware of that. (Fisher 2009)

To Friedman, free markets always are miraculous. In this instance, by trying to make a buck off their confidential information, insiders become de facto whistleblowers ferreting out corruption! He's right, at least in that perhaps there should be an exception if your hands are otherwise clean and you're only selling shares in the company you work for because you think your colleagues are corrupt and you're hoping to jump ship and blow the whistle soon.

Yet isn't the Raj's kind of insider trading not quite as noble? The Raj didn't ferret out corruption. He *was* the corruption. Apologists argue, however, that even if he didn't sniff out wrongdoing, his profitable maneuvers at least had the effect of rapidly bringing a company's stock closer to its true value.

There's more. Some claim that the Raj's corrupt stock sales actually *benefited* those he ripped off! You see, the Raj created excess demand for the shares of Goldman Sachs, which means that as he bought those shares, the price would begin to rise. Why? Because in theory, more demand for a given supply—no matter how slight, no matter how late in the day—equals a higher price. You don't even have to show that it happened in real life, because economic theory says it must be true.

So when the Raj started snapping up tens of thousands of shares of Goldman at $125, he would probably have to pay a bit more for at least some of the 175,000 shares he rapidly purchased. This means investors who were selling their Goldman shares on that day and at that moment when the price was inching up actually got a bit *more* than they would have received if the Raj wasn't buying at all. The Raj's insider mass purchase, therefore, actually put a few extra bucks into the pockets of these needy sellers—who were about to sell anyway. According to this expert reasoning, the sellers, as well as the FBI, should be *grateful* to the Raj for his public service. Thanks to him, the markets found their true price a bit faster, sellers got a better price on the way there, and, well, the world is just a better place for it.

Not convinced? You're not alone. One can easily imagine alternative scenarios. Without the Raj stoking the markets at 3:58 p.m.—two minutes before the closing bell—those who wanted to sell their Goldman Sachs stocks might not have had any buyers at all at a price they were willing to accept. As a result, they might have been stuck with their shares overnight. And then by the morning, their stocks would have jumped $8 a share, based on the exciting Buffett news.

Even if you grant the dubious argument that these investors weren't really harmed by the Raj's criminal enterprise, one big question remains: Was the Raj's insider move "worth" nearly a million dollars? Isn't there supposed to be a connection between how much you earn and what value you create for the economy?

Only in finance could someone dare to argue that the Raj contributed a million dollars' worth of labor (though I'm sure suckering Gupta into the Raj's insider-trading network took some serious time and effort). But where was the sweat, the innovation, the insight, that "earned" him $900,000 overnight? If the Raj really had moved the price closer to its true value, as economists' shapely supply-and-demand curves predict, he didn't move it by much.

So, what *did* he do? Actually, economists have a term for it: The Raj took advantage of *asymmetrical information*. That is, he placed a sure bet, based on information he had that others didn't. Unless Goldman Sachs was hit by a drone missile overnight, its price would go up after the Buffett announcement. Insider information simply transferred money from unknowing investors into the Raj's pocket for no redeeming economic contribution. That's the very definition of a rip-off, not of economic value.

It's worth noting that the only people in a position to place such easy bets, legal or not, are the very wealthy or those connected to them. Only the important and powerful get access to this "asymmetrical information" *and* have the money to capitalize on it. (A lowly accountant with a look at Enron's books would not be able to pull it off.) So legalizing insider trading would give a green light to a maneuver that would make the rich even richer. Although that might be good for those who enter the million-an-hour club, is it good for our economy and society?

Some economists believe that inequality benefits the economy as a whole by creating a super-rich class of investors who can afford to take risks and innovate. Yet unfairness also has a high economic cost.

If the average investor knows that insiders will always get the good investments before they do, why should they invest at all? If the entire stock market system is rigged against you, why bother? That's precisely what most worries Judge Holwell. Don't let it worry you, though, unless you don't know any insiders.

· · ·

Insider trading, at least, is based on accurate information. The rumormongering that Jim Cramer touts is based on lies. Yet he claims that spreading rumors is a vital part of a hedge-fund manager's job. If you aren't willing to manipulate markets by planting false information, you're a loser.

"Pump and dump"—pumping up stocks with optimistic rumors so that you can later dump them at a profit, or the reverse—has been with us ever since company shares were first traded on the Dutch bourses in the seventeenth century. It's just a part of everyday hedge-fund alpha hustling, says Cramer. No big deal.

Yet pump and dump looks a bit more sinister in the midst of a major meltdown. In the wake of Lehman Brothers' collapse in 2008, several government agencies banded together to investigate the spread of malicious rumors that may have contributed to the demise of that esteemed company. On September 19, 2008, just four days after Lehman declared bankruptcy, the SEC's Division of Enforcement issued a statement assuring investors that it was going after any profit-seeking rumormongers:

> Hedge fund managers, broker-dealers, and institutional investors with significant trading activity in financial issuers or positions in credit default swaps will be required, under oath, to disclose those positions to the Commission and provide certain other information. . . .
>
> Linda Chatman Thomsen, Director of the SEC's Division of Enforcement, added, "Abusive short selling, market manipulation and *false rumor mongering* for profit by any entity cuts to the heart of investor confidence in our markets. Such behavior will not be tolerated. We will root it out, expose it, and subject the guilty parties to the full force of the law."
>
> The Commission's actions follow recent reports of trading irregularities and allegations of *false rumor mongering*, abusive short selling and possible manipulation of financial stocks. [Italics added.] ("SEC Expands" 2008)

The SEC, so far, has come up with bupkes. Well, not quite. As of this writing, its sole "rumormongering" catch has been Paul Berliner, a proprietary trader at the Schottenfeld Group, who profited by spreading a false rumor about a company he was shorting. He had sent thirty-one instant messages to colleagues to kick it off. As the rumor spread through Wall Street, the company's shares were knocked down by 17 percent. Berliner had to give back his profits—a total of $26,129, plus a $130,000 fine, and he was barred for life from any association with a broker-dealer. Not all that scary. And that's about it for high-profile prosecutions and convictions related to rumormongering or, for that matter, the real causes of the 2008 crash.

Yet for a time, governments here and abroad were also chasing down malicious rumormongers. Back in 2008, in the heat of the financial crisis, the SEC and the British Financial Services Authority (FSA) so feared rumormongering hedge funds that they enacted a ban on all short sales of financial institution stocks—thus robbing hedge funds of their most powerful tool. The ban, enacted on September 19, only a few days after the demise of Lehman Brothers and the rescue of AIG, was designed precisely to prevent hedge funds from betting against banks to bring them down. The agencies had effectively canceled rumormongers' pay day. Here's how SEC chairman Christopher Cox put it:

> The Commission is committed to using every weapon in its arsenal to combat market manipulation that threatens investors and capital markets. The emergency order temporarily banning short selling of financial stocks will restore equilibrium to markets. This action, which would not be necessary in a well-functioning market, is temporary in nature and part of the comprehensive set of steps being taken by the Federal Reserve, the Treasury, and the Congress. ("SEC Halts" 2008)

And temporary it was. In a few months, after markets stabilized (thanks to the enormous influx of federal cash and asset guarantees), the ban on short selling was rescinded. By then, the entire financial system was backstopped by taxpayers, so hedge funds heaved a sigh of relief and went back to their reckless pursuit of short-term profits.

In September 2011, however, rumormongering continued. This time the big European bank Société Générale (SG) was in a serious fight with rumormongers. The bank was overexposed to weak sovereign bonds in countries such as Italy, Spain, and Greece and owned too many failing banks in Greece, the whisperers said.

Was this true? Does it matter? The rumors, true or false, create their own reality—just as Cramer promised they would. The "noise" may spur nervous depositors to withdraw their money and may keep other banks from loaning money to SG. Hedge funds may flee SG, taking their bags of money with them. Then other investors join the exodus, and you get a modern bank run. So far, SG has survived.

Meanwhile, watch out for packs of hedge funds running around like hungry wolves. If they all short a particular bank, hoping for a quick, profitable kill, the share price may drop, just as the rumormongers had predicted. Then the short-betting hedge funds will walk away with the cash. If they get really vicious, hedge funds may cheat in yet another way, by selling shares that they haven't even borrowed—"naked shorts." (This contributed to Lehman's demise, where some 32 million shares of Lehman stock, that had been shorted during the company's slide to oblivion, couldn't be delivered.)

In August 2011, fearing a collapse of SG, authorities in France, Belgium, Italy, and Spain followed the path earlier taken by the UK and the United States, enacting a temporary (in this case, a fifteen-day) ban on short sales. The European Securities and Market Authority announced that

> European competent authorities will take a firm stance against any behaviour that breaches these requirements and ESMA will support national authorities to act swiftly against any such behaviour which is clearly punishable. While short-selling can be a valid trading strategy, when used in combination with spreading *false market rumors* this is clearly abusive. [Italics added.] (ESMA 2011)

Why were so many hedge funds short-selling SG? One view is that they were simply betting on what they thought was true: Société Générale, they thought, is a weak bank whose price still doesn't reflect its low value. So the ban could be viewed as just another example of government authorities protecting a risky too-big-to-fail institution.

The other view? Jim Cramer's. Rumormongering is critical to hedge-fund success, and if you don't do it, "maybe you shouldn't be in this business." You can't afford to pass up a hot asymmetrical Soros-like play. If the banks crash, you win big, and if they don't, you don't lose that much. If you share this view, then European authorities are trying to stop hedge funds from doing what comes naturally: making speculative asymmetrical attacks based on lies.

IS RUMORMONGERING GOOD
FOR THE ECONOMY?

That depends. According to economic theory, if the rumors are false, then hedge funds are defacing our sacred supply-and-demand curves. They are *not* moving prices closer to their "true" value. In fact, false rumors would further distort the price, leading to all of the dire consequences of resource misallocation. The rumormongers are creating inefficiencies, not a better allocation of our scarce resources. Bad, bad, bad.

Yet what if the rumors are even partly true—say, in the case of SG? Then the curves are again doing their duty by crossing at a lower price point. In this case, the hedge funds that spread these rumors *do* serve the greater good by warning the world of the bank's poor health. Unfortunately, these infallible supply-and-demand curves can't tell us whether the rumors are true or false.

The European Securities and Market Authority's statement that short-selling, "in combination with spreading false market rumors," is "clearly abusive" raises genuine concerns about free speech (ESMA 2011). Should you be prosecuted because you are spinning tales? What if you really believe the false rumors you spread? What if you never tell the truth about the hands you play in the financial casino? Isn't that just the way you're supposed to play the game? And besides, why should you be blamed if some bozo reporter prints or broadcasts your fictitious stories without really doing his or her homework? You can see why prosecutors are not eager to go after these crimes.

The European authorities, however, have no patience for such hand-wringing as they try to stave off another economic crash. They don't give a hoot about abstract efficiency or the fine points of free speech. Their goal is to enhance *stability*, and they are sure that the hedge funds aim to profit from increased instability.

It's a battle of financial wills that resembles the battle between Soros and the Bank of England. Today, the entire economic stability of Europe is at stake. If hedge funds succeed in "disrupting what needs disrupting," then we may see our whole economy disrupted as well.

So compared to the potentially catastrophic effects of rumor-mongering in Europe, don't the Raj's crimes seem trivial?

Yet there's a much bigger point that U.S. Attorney Bharara wants to make. He's not just going after the Raj because of an isolated case of insider trading. Rather, Bharara worries that the entire hedge-fund barrel may be rotten:

> Given the scope of the allegations to date, we are not talking simply about the occasional corrupt individual. We are talking about something verging on a corrupt business model. (Lattman 2011)

• • •

No sooner had I completed this chapter than the following headline appeared in the *New York Times*: "Judge Says Hedge Funds May Have Used Inside Information" (Duhigg and Lattman 2011).

In this case, the insider information came from confidential bankruptcy proceedings involving Washington Mutual, the now-defunct savings bank that had morphed into one of the largest predatory mortgage companies in the country. Apparently, "lawyers from Fried, Frank, Harris, Shriver & Jacobson, which was involved in the bankruptcy negotiations, told its clients, the hedge funds, about the secret agreement. As a result, those hedge-fund investors were able to buy bonds on the cheap, and then wait for their value to rise when the agreement came to light" (Duhigg and Lattman 2011).

Sound familiar?

The four hedge funds that may have profited from the tip-off include our old friend Appaloosa, as well as Aurelius Capital

Management, Centerbridge Partners, and Owl Creek Asset Management.

"All have denied any wrongdoing."

Or how about this one from the *Wall Street Journal*:

> Securities regulators have sent subpoenas to hedge funds, specialized trading shops and other firms as they probe possible insider trading before the U.S. government's long-term credit rating was cut last month, people familiar with the matter said.
>
> Securities and Exchange Commission officials demanded more information about specific trades made shortly before Standard & Poor's Corp. downgraded the U.S. to double-A-plus from triple-A on Aug. 5, these people said. SEC officials are zeroing in on firms that bet the stock market would tumble.
>
> Those trades could have reaped huge profits when the Dow Jones Industrial Average sank 5.5% on Aug. 8. (Eaglesham 2011)

To top it off, in the 2012 Rajat Gupta insider trading trial, the defense team is arguing that because the Raj had so many insider shills, how could you possibly pin the leaks on just one person? To which Judge Jed Rakoff responded, "The most disturbing part of this case is what it says about business ethics. It's not just one bad apple, but a whole bushel full" (Ahmed and Lattman 2012). Corrupt business model? Maybe that's closer to the truth than we dare to believe.

• • •

Let us all learn from the Raj's sad example. His network united various international financial elites, many of whom just happened to have dark skins and to be of Asian descent. They met while attending elite universities and business schools in

England and the United States. Yet had the Raj and his associates been part of the (white) American old boy network, they
might have parlayed valuable insider information without fear
of reprisal.

Here's how the old boy network plays the game.

Think back to July 2008. Bear Sterns had already collapsed,
home prices were falling fast, and the stock market had the jit-
ters. With foreclosures hitting record levels, hedge-fund sharks
turned their attention to Fannie and Freddie, which were sure to
experience enormous financial difficulties. Hank Paulson, the former head of Goldman Sachs and then serving as Bush's Treasury
secretary, had a mess on his hands. He needed to find a way to
stabilize Fannie and Freddie and keep the predators at bay. He
decided on a two-part public strategy. First, he asked Congress for
authority to buy equity in the firms, which usually signals a move
toward nationalization. He also set about to audit their books,
in order to assure investors that all was well. Yet he told both
Congress and the press that he had no intention of taking over the
ailing firms. "If you have a Bazooka, and people know you have
it, you're not likely to take it out," he said, according to *Bloomberg
News* (Teitelbaum 2011).

Paulson's public pronouncements heartened investors. For if
Paulson nationalized Fannie and Freddie, shareholder value would
plummet to nothing. Yet if Paulson bolstered the firms and kept
them in private hands, share prices would recover, which is precisely what happened after Paulson spoke publicly in mid-July.

Just a few days later, however, Paulson took a quiet little sojourn
up to New York City to have lunch with some of the boys—his old
comrades at Goldman Sachs who now ran hedge funds. "Around
the conference room table were a dozen or so hedge fund managers and other Wall Street executives—at least five of them alumni
of Goldman Sachs," reported *Bloomberg News*. There, Paulson
made it crystal clear that the government would soon seize Fannie
and Freddie. And just in case his former employees at Goldman
Sachs were too dimwitted to figure out what that meant, he
explained "that under this scenario, the common stock of the

two government-sponsored enterprises . . . would be effectively wiped out. So too would be the various classes of preferred stock" (Teitelbaum 2011).

Hmm. You tell the public all is well, and the stock goes up. But you tell your hedge-fund cronies that you're about to wipe out the stock! Think you could make money with that information?

Well, someone did. No one knows for sure who was at the meeting and whether they used the secret Paulson information to short the firms. Yet on the day of the meeting, short-selling of Fannie and Freddie stock reached record highs and then went even higher during the next few days. A little more than a month later, Paulson took out his bazooka and fired away, nationalizing both Fannie and Freddie, which crashed the stock and made millions upon millions for the short sellers.

All of it was legal, or mostly so. You can't nail Paulson, because he didn't make any investments based on his information, and it's hard to prove that he lied to Congress. You can't really nail those who used the information for fun and profit, because you don't know who was there, and it's not clear that using the information violates any law.

So step back and compare the Paulson and Raj Mafiosi. If you're the Raj and you're plying corporate boardrooms for hot tips, you can land in jail, if you're caught. But if you get the info from your friends who are appointed to top economic positions in government, well, you're both in the clear and in the money, even if *Bloomberg News* writes a stinging exposé of it all. You want to cheat? Then, as always, it pays to have friends in high places and to look like you can play the part.

―――――――――――― DO'S AND DON'TS ――――――――――

- **Do** conduct all insider trading near noisy traffic.

- **Don't** be afraid to explain how insider trading is actually good for the economy.

- **Do** get your insider tips from high government officials who can't be prosecuted.

- **Don't** hope that your FBI tape will win a Grammy.

- **Don't** bob for apples in the hedge-fund barrel.

- **Do** remember that a corrupt business model is better than no business model at all.

STEP 9

Bet on the Race *after*
You Know Who Wins

On the first day of autumn 2011, I'm driving to leafy Chatham, New Jersey, to get my first live look at a trading room. Located in a bright new office townhouse complex, it's exactly like what you see in the movies, only smaller. Eight casually dressed traders speak in hushed tones to one another and to clients on the phone, each monitoring multiple screens. One desk holds five screens, including two Bloomberg terminals and another streaming Twitter.

Yet beneath this modest, ordinary trading room, powerful forces lurk in dark pools. At this very moment, the traders are struggling to protect their clients from invisible sharks that can gobble up foes at the speed of light. They are doing battle with strange predators who shun the sunshine and others whose mysterious movements will entrap you without your ever realizing it. If this is a movie set, it's for the *Twilight Zone*, not for *Wall Street*.

My guide into this netherworld is Joe Saluzzi, the cofounder of Themis Trading, LLC. Joe and his partner, Sal Arnuk, run this small firm, which navigates the shoals of electronic trading for its thirty-five or so institutional clients. They seem as if they're doing alright, but they don't make a million dollars an hour. They don't trade any of their own money. Instead, their focus is helping their clients trade stocks, while protecting them from the predators that now stalk electronic markets.

Joe, a slim, athletic Brooklyn native, fills the room with his energy and friendliness. A born storyteller, he makes me feel right at home in this foreign world as he bubbles with ideas and insights. In terms of vivaciousness, he rather resembles another Brooklynite—the late union leader Tony Mazzocchi, whose life I chronicled in my first book, *The Man Who Hated Work and Loved Labor*. Like Tony, Joe obviously loves what he's doing. In fact, he's on a mission, an urgent one that gets him talking faster and faster as he warms to his subject. This man is on a crusade to expose the dangers of high-frequency trading and the perils of a fragmented electronic financial market. (Sal, who is the talented writer of this pair, is busy dealing with clients, but you can tell from Joe's comments that the two of them form a tight team.)

Joe starts by giving me a crash course on how our modern financial markets work. Until a decade ago, a few stock exchanges had a three-hundred-year-old market monopoly on trading. Then it all broke apart. "The market" turned into an arena for rapid electronic trading, and new competitors flocked to the scene. There are now thirteen electronic exchanges in the United States on which you can buy the same financial instruments. "They are the same shoe store," Joe says. "There are thirteen shoe stores selling exactly the same item."

Yet buying and selling on these exchanges without getting fleeced is a lot harder than going to your local shoe store for a pair of Keds. "That's where it gets really tricky," says Joe. "Because sometimes there are the invisible shoe stores called dark pools, which are basically exchanges that are not lit up."

Dark pool? Is that a shoe store on Diagon Alley?

Each of the thirteen exchanges is a lit venue, something I can see on my machine. I can see their quotes. And then there are dark pools that are inside these quotes. So they sell shoes, but you also don't know what shoes they are selling because no one sees them. But you can still buy them if you want.

Naturally, this all makes perfect sense to Joe, who's been navigating these dark pools for years. Yet I'm still wondering how you buy shoes in an unlit shoe store, and how quotes can harbor dark pools. Joe tries to help me out:

You go in there, and you're just guessing. You're hoping there is something in there. Other traders will hide in the dark. They will say, "Okay, I'm willing to sell something at $12.16 when the [lit] quote was offered at $12.19."

What I gather is that Joe is looking to buy some shoes that are being offered on his "lit" screen at $12.19 (must be a pair of flip-flops). So Joe hunts around in the dark pools for someone who might sell him the shoes at a lower price:

Then I come along to see if anyone is hiding in the dark, and I buy it at $12.16. Boom, we've got a match. Nice trade. Theoretically, that's how it's supposed to work. It's called a crossing market. You can cross stocks without the noise of the [lit] market. That's really a valuable thing.

So Joe saves some money for his client by hooking up directly with a seller who was hiding in the dark pool. The lit shoe price on his screen was $12.19, but Joe got it in the dark for $12.16, for a savings of three cents per share, which adds up if you are buying a lot of shoes.

All in all, Joe says that beyond the thirteen "lit" shoe stores, we can shop in forty to sixty dark pools that also sell the same shoes. The downside of pool shopping, though, is that we don't know which shoes and what sizes until we wade in.

On the upside, however, at least with all of those lit shoe stores and dark pools, we have many venues for buying and selling shoes. All of that competition should ensure that we'll get good prices and low transaction costs wherever we go. Yes?

No, says Joe. Because lurking in all of these markets, whether sunny or shady, are high-frequency traders (HFTs)—mostly hedge funds and investment banks. With their super-computers (and super-programmers, mathematicians, and computer scientists), these guys can complete trades in nanoseconds. They trade so often during the day that they now account for up to 50 to 80 percent of all of the volume we see on the stock exchanges. This is a very big deal: HFTs are estimated to rake in from $8 billion to $20 billion in profit per year. Now, *this* is the business you want to get into.

The problem, says Joe, is that many HFTs—though not all— are predators. They lurk in the dark pools waiting to ambush you. So as Joe wades into a dark pool to buy or sell a certain stock, he has to protect himself from predator HFTs.

You have to find the [stocks] before someone realizes that you're looking to buy them. If they realize that you're doing it, they're going to buy them ahead of you and sell them back to you later [for a higher price]. That's a predatory hit.

When Joe wants to place a large order for a client, he often has to scour all thirteen markets and many dark pools to find enough reasonably priced stocks to buy. He has no choice but to venture into dark pools from time to time. If he's not very, very careful, though, a high-frequency trading computer owned by a hedge fund or a large investment bank will sniff him out and front-run his trade, squeezing money out of Joe's clients.

To understand how this works, let's follow Joe deeper into his Twilight Zone.

Joe wants us to understand that the stock quote we see on our computers is not reality. It's a picture of reality that is slightly delayed. When high-frequency traders look at their screens, they see something different. In fact, they see the future. It's as if they occupied a parallel universe that runs on an accelerated clock. We're not talking about minutes here. Not even seconds. Joe tells me,

> They can see in microseconds, which is a millionth of a second. They can see in nanoseconds, which is a billionth of a second. They are approaching the speed of light. So they can see inside the quote. It's getting really crazy.

And it gets even crazier. HFTs buy data feeds from the electronic exchanges that contain a trove of information about who is doing what on the exchanges. Joe explains that "every nugget, every little key stroke that I enter is being tracked by some exchange and is in the feed." That includes "What time did you enter your order? How long was the order in? Did you cancel the order? What time was the order canceled? Did you reenter the order? What price did you adjust it to?"

HFTs use that information to develop models for figuring out exactly how orders are flowing. "That's how they make their predatory assessments," says Joe.

It all happens at a warp speed the rest of us can't even see. We end up with two realities:

> There's one quote that the public sees . . . and then there's the orchestrated, reengineered quote that you [the HFTs] can derive yourself, if you buy all those data feeds and bring them into processing power.

To ensure that they can move at close to the speed of light, HFTs "co-locate" their machines right next to one or more of the electronic exchanges. That's extremely expensive, but it cuts down on the distance their data have to travel and therefore reduces the time. The aim: to predict the quotes before they are posted. An HFT, says Joe, "can build a quote faster than what the public sees. *You can see the future.*" And if you, the HFT, are seeing the future, he adds, "You can pretty much make money guaranteed every time."

I scratch my head. It sounds like Joe is saying that in their alternate high-speed universe, HFTs can see the end of a horse race before it's over in our universe. They even have time to place their bets on the winner before the winner is declared. That's how these hedge funds and banks can win up to $20 billion a year?

It's all perfectly legal, too, even though it has the stench of the insider-trading behavior that sent poor Raj Rajaratnam to the hoosegow. Joe agrees.

They're seeing the future. How is that different from those research analysts that were giving Galleon tips on insider information? Oh, he [the Raj] was getting a tip a few days beforehand. If I'm telling you a price two nanoseconds before anyone else, isn't that the same?

The one significant difference, as Joe points out, is that the information HFTs are collecting isn't coming from a corporate insider. Anyone could get access to it—at least in theory. This is the "key to their argument," says Joe.

You can do it. I can do it. Since it's available to everybody, there's nothing wrong here. Well, technically . . . But you need millions. You would need an army of programmers, and they've got to be the best, too. There's so much competition among [HFTs], you can't just be some hack HFT and enter the market to play that game. You won't be able to play with the big boys who are co-locating—hundreds of thousands of dollars a month' worth—putting in the best computers, constantly changing them.

What does all of this fancy action mean for you and me—or anyone who has a regular stodgy old 401(k) or mutual fund? It means that when we or our pension fund does a trade, a little bit of our money—maybe just pennies—is siphoned off by the HFTs. The vigorish is so small that no one pays much attention, but those pennies add up.

In their white paper "Toxic Equity Trading Order Flow on Wall Street," Joe and Sal sum it up:

> High frequency trading strategies have become a stealth tax on retail and institutional investors. While stock prices will probably go where they would have gone anyway, toxic trading takes money from real investors and gives it to the high frequency trader who has the best computer. The exchanges, ECNs [electronic communications networks] and high frequency traders are slowly bleeding investors, causing their transaction costs to rise, and the investors don't even know it.

As Joe was walking me through all of this, I again felt like a rube—like a hopelessly naive outsider who falls for the media hype about the genius of quantitative analysts, the "quants." Before talking with Joe, I had read and believed depictions of how these wondrous hedge-fund quants made big money for their firms by expertly digging into historical market patterns, while trying to predict future trends over months or years. It seemed like my grad school statistics classes on steroids—using mathematical probabilities to make accurate guesses about the economy down the road. Sure, there are guys out there like Cramer and Soros, who don't so much predict what markets will do as force them to do it. But these quants really do make quality, informed predictions, right? That seemed like a potentially worthwhile contribution that could increase the stability of markets and the economy as a whole.

Joe punctured my bubble, though. The quants couldn't care less about what the rest of us call the future—the world as it might become down the road. The future event horizon for quants is a few nanoseconds from now. Months or years down the road? You've got to be kidding.

So, the riches aren't going to the ultra-brilliant mathematical forecasters. No, they're going to those who can jump in and out of markets in nanoseconds, fleecing slower buyers and sellers, again and again. At least George Soros was out in the open when he did battle against the Bank of England. HFTs slither through the grass.

Here's the other shocker for the naive and trusting: It's not about the quality of the companies you're investing in, either. Or about allocating capital efficiently to help corporations grow. That stuff is for chumps. It's hardly even about buying and selling. It's about extracting pennies from millions of trades, while cruising undetected beneath the surface and doing it all on autopilot—automated on your high-speed computers. That way, you never have a losing day, ever.

. . .

Is there any justification for this type of fleecing? Of course there is, as with every other big money move. It's all about making markets more efficient and cheaper to run and use. The claim is that electronic markets are a major improvement over what preceded them. So let's see how far we've really come.

Back in those ancient times (the 1990s), before all of the markets went electronic, a bunch of specialists in green coats took buy and sell orders on particular stocks. If you wanted to sell a hundred shares of IBM, the guy in the coat who specialized in IBM would make the trade. In fact, he *had* to make the trade. That was his function in the old marketplace. He would give you the bid offer (such as $12 for the shoes) and the ask offer ($12⅛). It was all done in fractions back in the old days, where an eighth was the finest gradation. That eighth of a dollar spread was the market-maker's fee for always being there to buy or sell your shares.

With the advent of electronic markets, the green coat guys got squeezed out of the trading room, and the spreads between buy and ask turned to decimals, which in turn reduced the spread. This, of course, was perceived as an enormous boon to investors large and small. You can now go on E-Trade and make a trade for a minuscule cost, compared to the old days, when your broker had to call your order in to market makers on the floor of the New York Stock Exchange. HFTs further drive down these costs by buying and selling shares by the billion each day. Economists will tell you that this dramatic reduction in transaction costs is a damn good thing. It makes financial markets, and therefore the entire economy, more efficient.

High-frequency traders also bring enormous liquidity to markets. It is estimated that they are responsible for up to 80 percent of all volume on our exchanges. As you may recall from our earlier discussions, liquidity is next to godliness. In a liquid market, you can always find what you want to buy when you want to buy it and at a reasonable price—like having 24/7 low-cost shoe stores. Furthermore, when you buy or sell, your actions won't affect the market price. Deeply liquid markets attract investors from all over the world. It's one reason why the United States is the world's leading financial power.

Here's one more important justification for HFTs: all of their buying and selling every day smooths out the market, reducing day-to-day price volatility. That makes for a less terrifying roller-coaster ride for all of us.

So, by narrowing price spreads, increasing liquidity, and reducing volatility, HFTs must be well worth the billions they "earn." Right? Then what's the problem, Joe?

This is where Joe sees red. He starts with the great benefit HFTs supposedly provide by reducing the cost of each trade. Yes, Joe says, the cost that meets your eye is dramatically lower, but not low enough to offset the true cost of what HFTs do, which is hidden. (Clearly, we're back to the Twilight Zone, where two realities exist side by side.)

> The way I measure it, [HFTs] are actually increasing my transaction costs. I don't look at just the explicit. I look at the implicit. So what value is it when they trade 8 billion shares a day, when there really only should be two or three billion shares a day? What value to society is that? What value is drilling a hole in a mountain in Pennsylvania so that you can lay a cable to get to Chicago from New York a millisecond faster? What value is that?

Joe believes strongly that the prices he sees on his multiple screens and terminals during the day are not the real ones. He believes that the HFTs *are using their computing power to run prices up or down to levels that are far from what they should be.* So although the cost per transaction has dropped, Joe sees that the real cost of buying and selling has gone up, because most of the time you're not paying the right price for what you're buying—you're not paying what it's really worth.

If you have too many speculators creating a price of a security, do you feel comfortable that all of those who could care less about a security have set the price correctly? I don't think so. That's where my main problem is. I don't think these guys are setting the price right. They don't care what the company does. They just care about [fleecing] that one buyer who came in to invest for his mutual fund.

Do you think the price you're paying for that security is the actual price that it should be priced at? Or are HFTs artificially moving it up? . . . Volumes are being distorted. Prices are being distorted until events happen [in the real world] and then prices revert to where they should be. Bubbles burst.

You don't see any of these costs when you execute your trades, either.

Joe describes how high-frequency, high-speed traders push investors up and down when buying or selling stocks. Take the practice known as "pinging." HFTs can make and cancel thousands of trades per second just to see how high or low a regular investor will go to make a trade. Some HFTs make and cancel millions of trades per day.

Joe explains how this game works. "Imagine," says Joe, "that you're about to buy a stock at the price you see listed on your screen. Then suddenly, the deal disappears on you." Joe snaps his fingers. "It's hard to believe the [HF] seller saw you coming. But he did."

What is the HF seller up to here? "They really don't want to sell the stock to you," says Joe. "They just want to find out what you want to do and go out and buy the stock ahead of you. So, let's say the stock is a twenty-cent bid, offered at twenty-two cents." (By this, he means cents on a dollar—as in a \$10.20 bid price and a \$10.22 offer price.) "You want to buy two thousand shares at twenty-two cents—and two thousand are offered to you at that price. But eighteen hundred are canceled, and all you're able to buy is two hundred shares at twenty-two."

"Where did the rest of the stock go?" asks Joe. Well, they saw you coming and bought the stock ahead of you. So, next thing you know, "someone buys at twenty-three, twenty-four, twenty-five. It's a twenty-five-cent bid offered at twenty-six."

If you weren't paying attention, you'd just go along with the deal, says Joe. "You would just say, 'Okey-dokey.'"

Joe would like us to understand that the real cost to investors and our economy of these crazy rising and falling share prices is much greater than what we're saving on transaction costs. The billions of extra shares bought and sold by HFTs actually move prices *away* from their true value.

As any economist would confirm, that's not okey-dokey. In fact, Joe is making a powerful critique of HFTs and the fragmented electronic markets that make them possible. For if HFTs move prices away from their true worth, then they are doing what economists say is extremely harmful for any modern economy. Prices are supposed to reflect real value. When they do so accurately, then our resources are more efficiently allocated throughout the economy. When they don't, you get a serious misallocation of society's scarce resources, which reduces our overall well-being. If Joe is correct, and HFTs are screwing up prices all over our financial markets, then we have an inefficient and misshapen economy.

Not only is capital being misallocated among firms because their price signals are off, but capital is also erroneously flowing into the financial sector as a whole in terms of profits, bonuses, and wages based on HFTs' stealth fees. If all of the price signals were close to their real values, the extra capital flowing to finance would have been better spent in other sectors of the economy. You can easily see how this, in turn, could translate rapidly into more top college graduates flocking into the hedge-fund world, instead of into relatively lower-paying fields such as medicine. No wonder we've got too many hedge-fund managers and not enough obstetricians.

What about liquidity, though? Aren't HFTs helping the markets deepen through all of their incessant buying and selling?

It's hard to deny that hedge funds bring tens of billions of dollars into the market. If they really account for 80 percent of the trading, then all of that liquidity just has to be good for us. No?

Joe doesn't buy it. He goes back to the guys in the green jackets who made markets in specific stocks. They had to be there to buy and sell. Even if markets crashed, they *still* had to be on the job to buy and sell. Those were the rules.

Yet now HFTs have wiped the little green-coated men off the planet, and HFTs are under no obligation to make markets. In fact, at the end of every day, they close out their positions, so that they have no overnight exposures. One HFT even bragged that holding a stock for the long term meant *two seconds*! As Joe puts it,

> The guys running around in the green coats on the New York Stock Exchange . . . would say, "I will buy 5,000 at this price and sell 5,000 shares at that price." That's a quote. It means "I know there's a bid at this price and offer at that price. That's the price of the security." But today, it's an order-driven market. It's my bid placing it and it's somebody else's offering. And either one of us can disappear at any moment.

Yet surely with HFTs trading billions of shares, there will always be somebody there to buy your shares. The HFTs won't all disappear at once, will they?

Welcome to May 6, 2010.

. . .

On that tumultuous day, the Greek government passed an austerity measure, while protesters mobbed the streets of Athens. At the time, markets hadn't yet become familiar with this routine. The possibility of an ongoing populist revolt unnerved people, so everyone started selling. By noon, the euro took a dive against the Japanese yen and the U.S. dollar. That led to more selling. By 2 p.m., the markets were down 300 points.

Waddell and Reed, a Midwestern mutual fund, wanted to protect its portfolio from further declines caused by the European turmoil. So at 2:30 p.m., it activated a widely used automated algorithm to sell more than $4 billion worth of futures contracts to hedge Waddell and Reed's long positions in stocks—meaning the mutual fund was protecting itself from further losses. Normally, such a trade would be spread out during the course of the day, but supposedly the program dumped them all in about a half hour. (This fact is contested. All we know for sure is that Waddell and Reed sold a lot of futures.)

For reasons no one could fathom at the time, this firm's large, but not unusual, sell orders ignited a series of rapid-fire automated moves by HFT firms. At first, the HFTs jumped into the markets to profit from the turmoil. But then, when their programs detected so much selling and other irregular patterns, the HFTs withdrew their money entirely, dumping their positions and sucking all of the liquidity out of the futures market.

One economist who investigated the crash likened the sell-off to a game of hot potato, as one HFT tried to dump its positions onto another. When the hot potato game came to a screeching halt, many HFTs began slowing down or even shutting down their operations entirely. Because this futures market was linked to other markets, liquidity quickly dried up in equity markets as well. Within minutes, the entire stock market dropped 700 points. Then, a few minutes later, the market jumped back up 700 points as automatic buying programs kicked in.

Had this "flash crash" struck at the end of the day before the buy programs kicked back in, a financial panic could have spread around the globe.

The SEC was obliged to investigate this near disaster. Its lengthy report attempts to explain the cascading events. Although the report has many critics, everyone more or less agrees that high-frequency trading was the transmission belt that turned a rapid sell order of futures contracts into a near catastrophic meltdown.

Joe Saluzzi was at his desk when the crash hit.

It was crazy. Phones started lighting up. People couldn't get their orders in. Systems were overloading. No one got anything done. It was the violence of the move that scared the crap out of everyone. We had no idea what was going on. Maybe it was a nuclear bomb. Who knows? There has to be a major event going on right now. Who declared war on whom? What the heck? No one's ever seen anything like that. Then all of a sudden it just stopped. It started coming back, and it came back real fast.

Joe and Sal think they have a pretty good idea what happened: the HFTs took their money and ran. They don't buy the theory that one mutual fund was at the root of the collapse. "It was an easy scapegoat for the SEC," Joe offers.

The more likely occurrence was a feedback loop. An HFT bought a [large futures] contract [from the mutual fund] and all of a sudden realized that there was another contract for sale and then decided to sell [the one it had just purchased] to somebody else, who then realized that there was another for sale, and he sold it and there was the boom, boom, boom, boom, hot potato. And before you knew it, things were getting a little crazy.

Why didn't the HFTs want to hold the hot potato?

They didn't want to hold a position. No [HFT] wants to hold a position. They each have a certain risk level. Normally, they can manage that risk in a manner of minutes or seconds. All of a sudden, their risk level got too high. They said, "Oops, I'm not going to hold that. Things are getting hairy."

Why did the HFTs run for the hills? To understand Joe's answer, we need to remember that HFTs rely on their high-speed data feeds from the electronic stock exchanges to make their millions of trades. If those data feeds appear corrupted in any way, the entire HFT firm risks total failure—especially if the company is leveraged to the hilt. (By *corrupted*, Joe means that the HFTs saw different values for the same stock on different exchanges. They didn't know which one was correct. Or that they saw unusual delays.) They could lose it all in a hurry.

Their data was off. All of a sudden, they're getting lags in data. If they see that one feed from the New York Stock Exchange is slower than another feed from NASDAQ, now they have a potential error on their hands, because they don't know which one is right. And what they'll normally do when they have a data corruption is to just pull out [Joe wipes his hands clean]. "Get me the heck out of there." Flatten out and wait and see what happens.

Joe is the first to tell you that he has no concrete proof for this scenario. Yet many others corroborate his story about what happened on May 6—and about how HFTs operate in general. These firms hold shares for only seconds, and they win day after day. The *New York Times*'s Julie Creswell reported,

The founder of Tradebot, in Kansas City, Mo., told students in 2008 that his firm typically held stocks for 11 seconds. Tradebot, one of the biggest high-frequency traders around, had not had a losing day in four years, he said. (Creswell 2010)

After the May 6 "flash crash," the *New York Times* interviewed Manoj Narang, an MIT graduate who runs Tradeworx, a firm that looks a lot like Joe and Sal's and is located only a few miles away in Red Bank, New Jersey. Like Joe's company, Tradeworx has a few people and lots of screens. Yet Narang is on the other side of the deals. His programs operate automatically, buying and selling stocks and indexes he may never have heard of. Literally, he has no idea what his machines are buying and selling. It's not clear, either, if they're running predator programs that lurk in the dark pools.

He certainly did make a killing in 2008, however, when the stock markets were nearing collapse. As he told the *Times*, "It was like shooting fish in the barrel in 2008. Any dummy who tried to do a high-frequency strategy back then could make money" ("Speedy New Traders" 2010). Sure sounds like a shark waiting in a dark pool for a kill.

So, what did Tradeworx do on May 6? It pulled the plug. Why?

> Mr. Narang said Tradeworx could not tell whether something was wrong with the data feeds from the exchanges. More important, Mr. Narang worried that if some trades were canceled—as, indeed, many were—Tradeworx might be left holding stocks it did not want. ("Speedy New Traders" 2010)

Joe and Sal are fond of repeating a metaphor from Andrew Haldane, the erudite executive director for financial stability at the Bank of England. In a speech two months after the May 6 meltdown, Haldane took on the grand myth of HFT liquidity: HFTs, he said, could be credited with "adding liquidity during a monsoon and absorbing it during a drought" (Haldane 2011).

• • •

Have HFTs helped turn the stock market into a roller-coaster with a few wheels off the track?

In their paper "The Dark Side of Trading," professors Ilia D. Dichev, Kelly Huang, and Dexin Zhou provide academic backing for Joe and Sal's view of the market. Like our two antipredator crusaders from Chatham, New Jersey, these professors question the widely held theory that "higher investor participation and trading volume," much of it due to HFTs, "lead to better price discovery and therefore to prices that are closer to fundamental values" (Dichev et al. 2011, 1).

Instead, their research suggests that HFTs create enormous "noise" in the marketplace and cause prices to diverge from their true value. They posit that "the large presence of what is collectively known as noise . . . can lead prices away from fundamentals, whiplashing them in temporary swings and reversals" (2). The professors conclude that HFTs and the enormous liquidity they bring are also roiling the marketplace, injecting "an economically substantial layer of volatility above and beyond that based on fundamentals, especially at high levels of trading" (34).

Really, those are remarkable claims. First, Dichev, Huang, and Zhou undercut one of the most cherished economic justifications for all speculative activity—that prices are moved closer to, not further from, their true values. They demonstrate that prices are moved further from their true worth. Second, they show that the enormous extra liquidity brought to markets by HFTs and other speculative hedge-fund activities doesn't stabilize markets, as we are often told. Rather, it makes them more volatile. All of this is very bad news for the free-marketeer economists who are ideologically certain that the markets are growing ever more efficient and self-correcting. If these professors are correct, it means that financial resources are being misallocated, day in and day out, by swarms of HFTs and hedge funds. It also means that there will be hell to pay in terms of lost economic output, bubbles, and meltdowns.

Joe and Sal have another favorite metaphor to describe this entire process. In their white paper "What Ails Us about High Frequency Trading?" they wrote,

The market is like an ocean. To the extent that there are many different trading styles and participants trading against and interacting with each other, the market is healthy, like an ocean teeming with many species. But when one participant accounts for so much volume, something is out of balance, the same as an ocean where one of its more predatory species, such as a shark, becomes the dominant inhabitant. (Arnuk and Saluzzi n.d.)

Joe tells me that he's not against speculators in general:

Well, the markets used to be a nice variety of investors. There were value investors, growth investors, short-term speculators, day traders, all representing a relatively equal function in the market. That's a healthy market, so there's nothing wrong with speculators. They are actually providing a very good function, taking risk off the market at certain points.

Take farmers who grow crops. It's a good thing to have a speculator on the other side [to buy your crop at a fixed price before you bring it to market]. You'll feel comfortable that you'll make your profit [as a farmer]. Excessive speculation is the problem. [Having] no obligations [as a market maker] is the problem.

Joe adds insects to his list of predator metaphors:

The locusts will come into a farm, and they'll swarm it and eat everything they possibly can, and when they're done, they leave and go to another farm. That's kind of happened here. They're eating it all. They're now looking for new farms, and the new farms are different markets, different asset classes.

Yet Joe and Sal don't blame HFTs for doing what they do, any more than they blame sharks for being sharks. The underlying problem, they say, is the deterioration of the ecosystem. It's the way the exchanges are now organized. It's the *fragmentation*:

Why do you have 13 exchanges, multiple ECNs [electronic communications networks], and 40 dark pools, each trading the same security? What is going on there? Why do you need all of that?

High-frequency traders are a function of the fragmentation. They just took advantage of a corrupt system. They're not doing anything illegal. Is it immoral and unethical? Yes, in my opinion. How the system became corrupt is a whole other story. It was years and years in the making.

And how are HFTs taking advantage of the system?

They're demanding things from the exchanges. They're saying, "I want this information faster. I want this in my data feed. And if you don't give it to me, I'll walk down the block to a different exchange." So, do they have a quasi-partnership with the exchanges? Yes. Are the exchanges, ECNs, and dark pools making a ton of money off this? Yes. Is this how the market is set up? Yes. So [the exchanges] are relying on the HFTs to supply that liquidity, which they are making money off of as well.

Joe and Sal believe that more flash crashes are in our future—lots of them. They don't believe the SEC or Congress has the knowledge or the guts to take on this billion-dollar industry, whose lobbyists are running all over Capitol Hill. So far, says Joe, the SEC has tried only superficial fixes:

They put in circuit breakers. If the stock moves more than 10 percent, they're going to stop it for five minutes. They put in a short-sales rule. They put in a rule to get rid of guys who don't have risk checks. More Band-Aids. What they're not looking at—and this is the key—is the fragmentation.

And the next time there's a flash crash? "It's going to be more violent. It will go to 10 percent like that," says Joe, snapping his fingers yet again.

If it happens at the end of the day, that's when it might really be a problem. If overseas [markets] see that, then they're going to open and panic—and we all know that markets many times are panic driven—then you've got yourself a real issue. And it will happen again. And it will happen again after that. And then maybe someone will come along and say, "Hmm, this isn't quite working. We need a new approach." And then maybe things will change.

• • •

For those of us who don't regularly visit this financial Twilight Zone, it's hard to grasp the dangers posed by high-frequency trading. So here's another framework to consider.

It comes from Yale University sociologist Charles Perrow, whom I heard speak in 1985, shortly after the deadly explosion at the Union Carbide plant in Bhopal, India. All of us, at the time, were struggling to understand how this catastrophic event could have happened. The prevailing view was that it must have been caused by human error—a presumption that workers in developing nations didn't have the skills to handle complex technologies. In his talk, however—and in his book *Normal Accidents*—Perrow argued that the human error framework was not suitable for understanding accidents at modern complex facilities. Rather, the combination of *system complexity* and very *tight coupling* among the many complex systems creates unanticipated events. That is, stuff happens.

He writes that these events are "not only unexpected, but are *incomprehensible* for some critical period of time" (Perrow 1999, 9, italics in the original). To be sure, they are also incomprehensible to workers and managers, in both developing and developed nations.

Perrow's work focuses largely on chemical plants and nuclear reactors, where many complex systems function in close proximity to one another. Because these systems are designed to work together, most system crashes are contained and do not lead to catastrophic events—but not always. On a shockingly regular basis, system failure leads to fatalities. For example, the United Steelworkers Union, which represents employees at many chemical and nuclear plants, suffers on average one worker fatality per week. Every few years, these system failures both here and abroad are so large that they kill multiple employees and send toxins spewing into the surrounding communities. The catastrophe at the Union Carbide facility in Bhopal, where tens of thousands died or became seriously ill, was unusual only because of the numbers involved. The systemic failure was all too familiar. In catastrophic events with fatalities such as these, Perrow's theory usually proves true: complexity and tight coupling are almost always at play.

Here's an example of how the unexpected happened at a Texas oil refinery. A pressurized pipe containing a highly flammable substance ruptured and ignited. That was bad enough, but not impossible to contain. When the ignited pipe fractured, however, it also broke loose from some of its fastenings, so that it could pivot wildly back and forth. Basically, it turned into a giant blowtorch, cutting through nearby pipes in a different system that contained highly volatile substances, which in turn exploded. It's doubtful that anyone could have predicted this unusual interaction. Yet with two very volatile complex systems operating in close proximity, it was always possible that one could take down the other.

Although the electronic stock exchanges are unlikely to explode and kill nearby workers, the world of electronic trading is far more complex than a chemical factory. Not only do we have at least thirteen electronic market exchanges and forty-plus dark pools, but they are all connected to an unknown number of independent HFT firms whose automated systems account for billions of stock trades per day. Millions of other investors, traders, and fund managers from all over the world are also hooked into these exchanges. HFTs do their speed-of-light trading using proprietary algorithms that are considered trade secrets. To this murky mix, we add large mutual funds and online trading services (not HFTs) that use common algorithms to buy and sell securities automatically. All of this is happening within fractions of a second. As a result, it is highly likely that strange interactions might occur that could spin out of control, affecting nearby systems in a myriad of unknown ways.

Our complex financial markets have all of the markings of a "normal accident" just waiting to happen. No wonder Joe is already braced for the next flash crash. When it happens, it will be, as Perrow wrote, "incomprehensible for some critical period of time," just as it was during the May 6 flash crash.

Well, it's happening already in the stock market, but we can't see it because it's happening near the speed of light. Researchers Neil Johnson, Guannan Zhao, Eric Hunsader, Jing Meng, Amith Ravindar, Spencer Carran, and Brian Tivnan explored the nanosecond parallel universe occupied by high-speed computer trading. They were shocked to discover "18,520 ultrafast black swan events that we have uncovered in stock-price movements between 2006 and 2011" (Johnson et al. n.d., 1). Those "black swans" are flash crashes that in less of a second rectified themselves. The reason there are so many flash crashes is that most of the high-speed computer traders deploy similar algorithms, which then can reinforce one another. So, while humans are diverse in their trading strategies, machines are much more homogenous. These researchers warn that the high-speed crashes are like "micro-fractures" on the wings of airplanes. They are growing in number and could cause a fatal crash—one that we'll see and not soon forget.

Although there are many other ingredients in this toxic electronic stew, none is more potent than the high-frequency traders and their automated systems. They are supercharged actors who drive much of what happens in the market. Furthermore, their actions tighten the links among the market's complex systems, ensuring that uncontrolled events will indeed spread and do so in an instant. Then, in the midst of the catastrophic breakdown they helped cause, HFTs are designed to suddenly withdraw, taking their fabled liquidity with them just when it is most needed.

So, my dear would-be members of the million-an-hour club, be careful where you swim in this complex world of dark pools and flash crashes. Today's shark may be tomorrow's taste treat for a bigger shark.

What's wrong with that, you might wonder? Isn't the invisible hand of the market supposed to work all of this out? Or, if not, maybe Darwinian competition or Joseph Schumpeter's "creative destruction" will weed out the weaker players and corrupted structures so that only the strong and good HFTs and hedge funds will win the day. As our exploration sadly suggests, however, the very competition for "alpha" riches and quick, supercharged profits can also create catastrophic meltdowns throughout our tightly coupled and complex electronic markets.

Insider trading, rumormongering, and HFTs may do much more than create a very exclusive million-an-hour club. These fundamental hedge-fund strategies may be placing our entire economy at risk—you included.

(For total immersion into dark pools and such, see Joe Saluzzi and Sal Arnuk's new book, *Broken Markets: How High Frequency Trading and Predatory Practices on Wall Street Are Destroying Investor Confidence.*)

—— DO'S AND DON'TS ——

- **Do** buddy up when swimming in a dark pool.

- **Do** brag about bringing liquidity to markets even if you never hold a stock for more than a second.

- **Don't** brag about how much money you make by holding stocks for less than a second.

- **Don't** name your high-speed computer "Hal."

STEP 10

Milk Millions in Special Tax Breaks

Long before Stephen Schwarzman became a wealthy private-equity mogul, he was a Yale student—and a member of its most prestigious secret society, Skull and Bones. In its spooky windowless mausoleum sealed with a vaultlike door, Schwarzman congregated with the Yale student elite, including the progeny of presidents and potentates. Schwarzman was tapped for the secret society by an august group of upperclassmen that included George W. Bush.

If you're not a member, and you say the words "Skull and Bones" in the presence of Schwarzman (or any other member), he's supposed to walk out of the room. In the secret argot of Skull and Bones, all outsiders are "Rians"—short for "barbarians"—and you have no business uttering the sacred name of this elite society.

When a Skull and Bones member gets too full of himself, he gets "flushed": the other members gang up on him, put his head in the toilet bowl, and flush. During Schwarzman's tenure, a Yale class president was allegedly kicked down the stairs during an unsuccessful flushing foray and broke his arm. We don't know whether Schwarzman joined the flushing vigilantes or was flushed himself during his time at Yale. Yet we do know that lots of people would like to give him a good flushing now.

Schwarzman made his fortune as cofounder (with Peter Peterson) of the Blackstone Group, a private equity fund that buys undervalued companies, restructures them, and then sells them again—at a huge profit—as public companies (think Mitt Romney and Bain Capital). Over time, the fund evolved into an all-purpose firm that combined mergers and acquisitions, hedge-fund activities, real estate, and leveraged buy-outs.

In 2007, at the peak of the housing bubble and of Schwarzman's fame and fortune, he threw himself an over-the-top sixtieth birthday party. It was so big, he had to rent the Armory on Park Avenue to accommodate his admirers. He also rented Rod Stewart for a cool million to croon for his guests. The whole shebang reportedly cost $5 million, but for the billionaire Schwarzman it was chump change.

The sheer obnoxiousness of his excess put Schwarzman into the limelight, which he apparently enjoyed. Yet the light blazed even brighter a few months later, when Schwarzman turned his prosperous private equity firm into a publicly traded company. Blackstone's initial public offering (IPO) put about $4 billion into Schwarzman and his partners' pockets. (To his credit, a year later he made a well-publicized tax-deductible donation of $100 million to the New York Public Library.)

But pride goeth before a fall—or, at least, we hope it does. In pitching the IPO, Schwarzman bragged openly about a wonderful tax feature that really sweetened the deal: Blackstone paid only 15 percent in taxes on its profits, compared to 35 percent for a normal corporation.

Oops. In the process, Schwarzman inadvertently alerted Washington politicians and the public that the richest of the rich were profiting mightily from this enormous tax loophole that showered money on financial partnerships but not on regular corporations. Many of Schwarzman's fellow private-equity and hedge-fund managers probably wanted to give the guy a good flushing, right then and there, for drawing unwanted attention to their billion-dollar tax loophole.

When you get to be an elite financier, however, you don't feel that you should be subject to the same income tax rates as all of the little "Rians" who labor far below. You've earned the right to use the "carried interest" loophole that classifies almost all of your income as capital gains. Your well-compensated chauffeurs, pilots, and personal assistants might be paying at the 35 percent rate (the top tax bracket)—but why should you? If you have to pay at all, then 15 percent is about all Schwarzman can stomach.

• • •

As Rod Stewart gently rocked Schwarzman's birthday guests, Victor Fleischer, an unknown, untenured law professor at the University of Colorado, was bopping away on his keyboard, writing a wonky piece on the virtues of taxing private-equity and hedge-fund companies at something beyond 15 percent. His obscure paper, "Two and Twenty: Taxing Partnership Profits in Private Equity Funds" (later published in the *NYU Law Review*), turned him into the rock star of hedge-fund taxation. The paper just happened to catch the eye of congressional staffers who were desperately searching for revenue sources that could substitute for the Alternative Minimum Tax. (The AMT, which had begun to hit middle-income earners, was political poison.)

Fleischer's unassuming article crushed all of the justifications for Schwarzman's enormous loophole. Like the little boy who saw through the emperor's new clothes, Fleischer wasn't afraid to say so.

Having failed to secure an interview with Rod Stewart, I gave Professor Fleischer a try. Lo and behold, fame had not gone to his head. He was happy to talk with me by phone in October 2011 from his law school office at the University of Colorado, where he now has a tenured position.

It all started so innocently, he told me. Back in 2007, he posted a draft of his tax article on TaxProf, a website that caters to, what else, tax professors. "It's common practice to seek out comments on your draft before you finalize and submit it to a law journal," Fleischer said. He had no idea that staffers on the Senate Finance Committee patrol that website to keep up with what academia is saying about taxes. They spotted Fleischer's piece and asked him to come share his ideas at a closed-door session of the committee. Little did he realize it was the equivalent of playing before a full house at the Superdome. "If you want to draw attention to something in Washington, you make it a closed-door hearing," Fleischer said. "It brought incredible attention to what we were doing. It was off to the races from there."

Practically overnight, Fleischer became a hot commodity. He was all over TV, especially the financial shows, and he was interviewed in the *New York Times*. Not only did Fleischer give good, very clear, blunt answers, but his boyishly handsome face looked good on TV. All of a sudden, he became the lodestar for an enormous tax fight that still rages on today. Or, as the young, starstruck professor put it, "The most pleasant surprise was that I'm not writing for an audience of twelve."

Fleischer knows that he has Schwarzman to thank for his newfound fame. "Schwarzman has a knack for making himself look like an ass," said Fleischer. Case in point: As reported on BusinessInsider .com, Schwarzman used these ill-chosen words to describe the Obama administration's efforts in 2010 to raise taxes on private-equity firms and the wealthy: "It's a war. . . . It's like when Hitler invaded Poland in 1939." Was Schwarzman implying that if you wanted to take away his precious tax loophole, you were a Nazi?

"He's obviously a very smart investor, but he thinks that because he's really good at what he does, he must be good at making government policy as well," said Fleischer. The professor said that Schwarzman has an "arrogance" that shows in both his lifestyle and in his words.

Fleischer (whom Schwarzman would probably liken to Rommel) fired the opening volley in the campaign to close Schwarzman's beloved loophole. In his article, Fleischer zeroed in on the subject of outsize hedge-fund compensation:

Ironically, while the public and the media have focused on the "excessive" pay of public company CEOs, the evidence suggests that they are missing out on the real story. In 2004, almost nine times as many Wall Street managers earned over $100 million than did public company CEOs; many of these top earners on Wall Street are fund managers.

Then he added the kicker that ignited the debate:

And fund managers pay tax on much of that income at a fifteen percent rate, while the much-maligned public company CEOs pay tax at a thirty-five percent rate on most of their income.

What's more, the good professor argued, he could find no reasonable justification for giving fund managers such an enormous tax break.

Lawmakers created the carried-interest tax break in 1954 as a way to support small businesses built up on sweat equity and very little capital. Because there was no simple way to value the sweat equity until the firm produced profits, the business was exempted from paying taxes on that labor. If the business was sold down the road, then any increase in value would be taxed as capital gains, not as regular income.

Fleischer used a gazebo metaphor to explain. Say you build a gazebo in your backyard with your bare hands. It may have required a lot of labor, and it may be very valuable (at least, to gazebo lovers such as you), but you don't have to pay taxes on it until you sell your home. Even then, you pay only if your home appreciated in value—and the increase would be taxed at the capital gains rate, not as regular income.

Yet this doesn't exempt mom-and-pop partnerships from paying regular income taxes. What they pay depends on how they make their money. As Fleischer explained,

If the partnership is running a restaurant, and most of its income comes from the receipts for meals that the restaurant provides, that's going to be ordinary income, so it will be taxed at the ordinary rate, depending on the partners' income bracket. All of it is ordinary income until they sell the business. Then they might get a capital gain taxed at the lower rate.

The mom-and-pop partnership tax break took on an entirely new dimension when extremely wealthy and profitable investment firms and hedge funds started to hijack it. These managers obviously put an enormous amount of labor into their firms. In exchange, they receive two kinds of income. First, they get a 2 percent yearly management fee of all of the assets under management for their investors. And second, they get a very big incentive bonus of 20 percent of all of the profits they churn up. They often put some of their own money into the fund, but it usually amounts to only a small percentage. The idea behind the 20 percent incentive bonus is to align the managers' interests with the investors'. To get rich, the managers also have to make their investors rich (or, more typically, even richer than they are already).

Yet the two kinds of income are taxed at different rates. The 2 percent fee on assets under management is taxed as regular income, but the 20 percent incentive fee on investment income is treated more like the gazebo: if it comes from assets held one year or longer, it is taxed at the 15 percent capital gains rate.

Fleischer pointed out that this arrangement is pretty similar to what happens when financial company employees get incentive stock options (ISOs): that money is also treated as capital gains when sold, rather than as regular income. Yet there's one enormous difference. In their case, only the first $100,000 of ISO profit can be claimed as capital gains. No such limit applies to fund managers.

Here's how it plays out for someone making a million an hour from income derived from incentive bonuses or ISOs. If he worked at an investment bank and the $100,000 cap were applied, his tax bill would be $15,000 for the first $100,000 and another $315,000 in taxes on the remaining $900,000, taxed at the 35 percent rate. The total tax bill for this very prosperous banker would be $330,000 an hour.

If this same million-an-hour star ran a hedge fund or a private-equity fund, however, there would be no cap. Therefore, his tax rate on incentive fees could be 15 percent for a total of $150,000 an hour. For every hour worked at that rate, our mogul saves $130,000 in taxes, compared to the super-rich banker. No wonder Schwarzman and company did not take kindly to Professor Fleischer's paper. Fleischer noted:

> I received a lot of hate mail, dozens of them. People mailed me out of the blue. They called me a socialist. They compared me to Stalin. You can't blame them. If the loophole were closed, we'd be more than doubling their tax bill.

Yet Fleischer had serious admirers as well, including in Congress. Senator Carl Levin and others used Fleischer's information and arguments to fashion a bill that would greatly tighten this tax loophole. Versions of that bill passed the House several times, but the Senate bill hasn't seen the light of day. President Obama has also repeatedly called for closing this loophole—including as a way to help finance the job stimulus bill he proposed in September 2011. The loophole's fate remains unclear.

Nevertheless, because Congress rarely sides against Wall Street, expect the carried-interest loophole to still be there when you make your first billion.

• • •

Hedge-fund moguls aren't the only ones to benefit from this mother-of-all-tax-loopholes. There are other billionaire-producing funds, such as "venture capital" funds—"VCs," to those in the know.

If you saw the movie *The Social Network*, you might remember the scene where Facebook founder Mark Zuckerberg is introduced to Peter Thiel, a venture capitalist. Thiel then bestows on Facebook a $500,000 "angel investment," putting the start-up on the road to glory.

That's a classic VC success story: VCs are all dying to find the next Facebook.

Venture capitalists have to be brilliant at distinguishing between good and bad start-up companies, as well as at helping the start-ups they've picked develop into something viable. As Professor Fleischer put it, "They are filling an information gap between the market for financing, which doesn't know anything about these entrepreneurial start-up companies, and the entrepreneur, who has all the information. The VCs are better at discovering the information and picking the winners."

They have a lot of picking to do, because everyone seems to have an idea for a new company. As then Harvard president Larry Summers says to the Winklevoss twins in *The Social Network*, "Everyone at Harvard is inventing something. Harvard undergraduates believe that inventing a job is better than finding a job. So I suggest again that the two of you come up with a new project."

Another kind of fund, the private equity fund, has a similar role but with an evil twist: Fleischer said that private-equity funds are "good at finding companies that are undervalued by the stock market for whatever reasons." They take the companies private and then make "operational changes," said Fleischer, "which is French for firing people." The dirty deed safely done, they take the company public again. "With private equity it's a combination of financial engineering, like loading it up with debt, and this information discovery. . . . That's basically the same thing that Warren Buffett does."

Yet the line between hedge funds and private equity funds and venture capital can blur. Traditionally, Fleischer said, hedge funds focus on "looking for mispricing in the market: a commodity that's undervalued, a stock that's undervalued, or whatever it may be, a currency that's undervalued and they're making a bet on that."

Certain hedge funds, however, and certain divisions within hedge funds act very much like private equity or VC funds. Take the "activist" hedge funds that James Altucher describes in *SuperCash: The New Hedge Fund Capitalism*:

Activist hedge funds try to find undervalued companies, build positions in those companies and then declare war.

Whatever it takes, the activists will attempt to unlock value. As one activist hedge fund manager, Bob Chapman, told me, "It takes a certain type of personality to be an activist. You can't hold back from the battle." (Altucher 2006, 22)

Activist hedge funds, as do private equity firms, seek out undervalued companies and buy large positions in them. Yet rather than taking them private in order to exert full control over their operations, activist hedge funds beat the hell out of management until it agrees to make changes that supposedly bring higher value to the shareholders. Altucher quotes several amusing/cringe-inducing letters that hedge funds sent to the companies they were browbeating. Here's just a taste of one:

Sadly, your ineptitude is not limited to your failure to communicate with bond and unit holders. A review of your record reveals years of value destruction and strategic blunders which have led us to dub you one of the most dangerous and incompetent executives in America. . . . I have known you personally for many years and thus what I am about to say may seem harsh, but is said with some authority. It is time for you to step down from your role as CEO and director so that you can do what you do best: retreat to your waterfront mansion in the Hamptons where you can play tennis and hobnob with your fellow socialites. The matter of repairing the mess you have created should be left to professional management, those who have an economic stake in the outcome. (39–41)

How would you like to get a letter like that from your largest investor?

Jim Cramer's hedge fund played an "activist" role with the regional savings and loan banks it had a major stake in. Other hedge funds tried to beat down the value of Cramer's holdings in order to force him into a fire sale. Cramer turned to the banks and implored them to do something—anything—to increase the value of their stocks. And, most urgently, could they please buy back their own shares to push up the price? Here's Cramer:

> Dutifully, I called the chief financial officer of BayView, the repulsive San Francisco S&L that had fallen some 60 percent during the last few months—I couldn't believe he was in that early given how poor his performance was—and told him what a disgrace his stock was. The fall from $30 to $12.50 since we had bought it, especially the decline in the last few weeks from $19 to barely a teenager, was criminal, just criminal. He had to find buyers of his stock or accept that we were going to have to puke it up all over him in the open market [meaning that Cramer would dump his shares], something that would take it down to the mid-single digits and presumably into the arms of some large bank that would swallow them up. (Cramer 2002, 222–223)

Why are these VC-fund and hedge-fund bullies taking such a strong interest (to put it mildly) in the companies they've invested in? Because they really are invested: to qualify for that all-important 15 percent capital gains loophole, they've got to hold onto that stock for a year, and it has to show gains. So let the harassment begin!

In contrast, hedge funds that make high-frequency trades or trade in nanoseconds to extract small differences in prices do *not* qualify for the loophole on the profits that result. I'm sure many a tax lawyer has stayed up into the wee hours, trying to magically transform short-term gains into long-term gains, but I know of no one who has succeeded.

So, do these VC and private-equity funds play a more useful role in society than hedge funds that specialize in short-term trades? Maybe, said Professor Fleischer:

> VCs do produce real social utility by identifying a great entrepreneur and then providing that entrepreneur the resources he or she needs to build a new technology. There's much more social value from that activity than there is from

a hedge fund that knows a mutual fund is going to buy a stock and buys it a millisecond before them so they can take half the spread away. There's no real social value there.

Wait, does this mean there are good justifications for the carried-interest loophole?

• • •

First, a brief detour into the history of the income tax.

Federal income tax rates and tax loopholes have always been a battleground for class tensions. Until the late 1800s, the federal treasury was mostly filled through regressive excise taxes and tariffs. The rich barely noticed.

Although a temporary income tax had been imposed during the Civil War, it took the emerging populist movement in the 1880s to put the question of an income tax back on the national agenda. The populists made a compelling case that such a tax was needed to rectify the crippling disparities of wealth created by the new class of industrial robber barons sitting astride their colossal empires of coal, steel, railroads, meat, sugar, tobacco, and utilities. In 1894, the Democrats, pushed by populist sentiment, enacted a 2 percent income tax on individuals and corporations that earned more than $4,000 a year. Because the average income that year was only $440, this was clearly a direct hit on the rich. Yet the decidedly conservative, pro-business Supreme Court declared the legislation unconstitutional in 1895. (In *Pollack v. Farmers' Loan & Trust*, the Court ruled that under the Constitution, such a "direct tax" had to be apportioned to the states based on population—which would not have been practical for a federal income tax.) Finally, the question of the constitutionality of a federal income tax was put to rest by the Sixteenth Amendment, passed in 1913.

From then on, the super-rich had to pay more than the rest of us, as a percentage of income, in order to pay for the government functions that enabled and protected the accumulation of great fortunes. The rates have seesawed, however, depending on the social and economic environment. From 1913 to 1915, those earning more than $500,000 a year were subject to a 7 percent federal income tax. Yet during the height of World War I in 1918, millionaires paid a substantial 77 percent of their incomes above $500,000 into the federal treasury. Then, during the laissez-faire, pro-business 1920s, the rate fell to 24 percent.

The 1929 stock market crash and the ensuing Great Depression changed American attitudes toward the super-rich. During the New Deal, tax policy reflected a growing national (and global) perception that excessive wealth was the cause of the economic misery. The Great Depression and all of the union organizing that accompanied it created a national consensus that the economic crash was caused by runaway finance and the vast concentrations of wealth that had accumulated during the Roaring Twenties. With nearly one out of three Americans without work, it seemed obvious that high taxes on the rich were needed to help pay for New Deal jobs programs. Roosevelt turned against his own class and pressed Congress to ratchet up top tax rates, step by step. By 1940, people with annual incomes greater than $5 million paid 81 cents in federal taxes on every dollar above that threshold.

The onslaught of another world war further jacked up the rates paid by the well-to-do. By 1944, the top federal tax bracket dropped to $200,000, and the rate on every dollar earned over that amount faced a nearly confiscatory tax rate of 94 percent.

Yet something unexpected happened after World War II. Although America was in a decidedly conservative mood, especially during the Eisenhower years (1952–1960), tax rates on the super-rich remained sky high. The top tax bracket stood at $400,000 per year from 1948 all the way through 1963, and the top marginal tax rate hovered between 91 and 92 percent on incomes higher than that amount.

How could that be? How could this high tax rate survive in such a conservative era? What were we thinking?

We were thinking more like a "we." We were worried about the Cold War. In order to protect democracy from another round of totalitarian threats, we saw the need to build up our infrastructure, our military, and, most important, our people. The result: a new interstate highway system, an arms race, a vastly expanded educational system, and a dramatic rise of the middle class.

The Great Depression also still haunted us. The generation who had experienced the 1930s learned that prosperity was ever fragile. They also believed that to protect our economy and keep people at work, we needed to contain the financial sector and avoid vast disparities of wealth. Scholars today debate whether these shared ideas were based on an accurate understanding of what caused the Great Depression. At the time, though, the common wisdom called for continued high tax rates on the super-rich.

Although this may come as a shock to our million-an-hour aspirants, the nation then showed a striking ambivalence toward money making. The "Greatest Generation," who had just fought both the Depression and the Fascists, believed that public service was a high calling—something that many of their kids also believed during the 1960s. Millionaires, to be sure, were also greatly respected, but public officials, both civilian and military, ranked even higher in the social pecking order. This may sound corny to us today, but back then, making the world a better place for its people actually meant at least as much or more than making money for its own sake.

Yet as memories of economic hardship and world war receded, the tax bite on the rich receded as well. In response to the deep but relatively short recession that had begun in the late 1950s, JFK applied Keynesian tax cuts in an effort to stimulate the economy. Even after those tax cuts, though, the marginal rates hovered between 70 and 77 percent all the way from 1964 to 1980. In fact, the top income tax bracket dropped to $200,000 a year and stayed there during the presidencies of LBJ, Nixon, Ford, and Carter. (To be sure, the tax code became riddled with arcane loopholes for the rich, but the effective tax rate after all deductions remained high.)

Then came the ideological revolution of the mid- to late 1970s that we discussed previously. Many economists blamed regulation and high taxes for our bout of stagflation and argued that prosperity would return only if we reduced both.

There was more to this argument than economics. It also reflected a pro-elite worldview made famous by Ayn Rand and made respectable by economist Milton Friedman. In the Randian universe, the achievers, the successful, and the rich were simply superior beings. We should applaud them for creating wealth. Rand disdained the envious who wanted to shackle the wealthy through state power, especially the collectivist unionists who sought to siphon away hard-earned riches through strikes.

Milton Friedman argued that the pursuit of profit would, by definition, lead to a more prosperous society. In fact, he argued, putting social morality ahead of profit making was both foolish and destructive. Greed in the marketplace is good, he believed, because it results in the best possible allocation of resources. This is still the ultimate justification for hedge-fund profiteering.

Enter the Reagan era of tax cuts. In 1982, the top federal tax rate dropped from 70 percent to 50 percent. In 1987, it fell to 38.7 percent. Then in 1992, it reached a fifty-year low of 31 percent. The Clinton administration bumped it back up to 39.5 percent, where it stood until 2000. Then along came George W. Bush, who inherited a budget surplus (imagine that!). Backed by Alan Greenspan (an Ayn Rand acolyte), G. W. reduced the top tax burden to 35 percent, where it stands today. As a result we have one of the most unequal income distributions on earth. (The CIA's *World Factbook* lists the United States as the 42nd most unequal country, compared to the United Kingdom, 91st; Canada, 103rd; Germany, 124th; and Sweden—the most egalitarian—136th.)

• • •

The Private Equity Council has spent more than $6.5 million to counter the frightening impact of Professor Fleischer's paper and to block any efforts to take away the beloved 15 percent tax (Lerer 2007). In fact, the council's money now supports a whole genre of apologists who could be called the Carried Interest Defense Industry. Researchers and commentators can't wait to justify why it's good for the economy to let billionaires pay a lower tax rate than the rest of us.

Douglas Holtz-Eakin, the president of the American Action Forum, along with Cameron Smith and Winston Stoody, came up with a startling defense of the tax loophole, which they presented in a paper published in June 2010:

> Perhaps most damaging, the higher taxes on carried interest will re-allocate managerial talent, as the entrepreneurially-inclined are deterred by these higher taxes and seek their outlets elsewhere in the economy. (Holtz-Eakin et al. 2010)

Now that's a through-the-looking-glass theory. The argument they are making to *support* the loophole is the one most people use to *oppose* it! They are claiming that if hedge-fund managers and others like them have to pay regular tax rates, they might flee their multibillion-dollar financial funds and have to run companies or start new ones for only millions or even hundreds of thousands of dollars instead.

Behind this argument lurks a good deal of circular logic blurred into billionaire worship. Because hedge-fund managers make billions, they must produce billions in value for our economy, and they produce all of this value because of their brilliant entrepreneurship. Since they are so successful and valuable, we don't want to do anything that could possibly hold them back, because, by definition, the stuff they do makes so much money, creates so much value, and therefore is so good for the economy. Hands off the blessed wealth creators!

Let's suspend reality, though, and grant their premise. Let's assume that we don't want to lose a single precious hedge-fund manager by raising his taxes to the level the rest of us must pay. Do we actually have any evidence that these guys will run for the hills if they have to pay 35 percent? Professor Fleischer thinks not:

> The argument that people will stop becoming private equity managers or venture capitalists if you raise the tax rate seems absurd to me. Just about everyone who graduates with an MBA wants to become a venture capitalist or go into private

equity. There's no shortage of financial recruits, like there is, let's say, of obstetricians. It's just seems crazy to me to think that we would have an undersupply of private equity fund managers—that they need a tax subsidy in order to survive.

Fleischer is talking to you. Would you walk away from your million-an-hour career because your take-home pay was reduced from $850,000 an hour (with the carried-interest loophole) to only $650,000 an hour (if the loophole were removed)? Hmm, maybe not.

Yet the Carried Interest Defense Industry has other, more cynical arguments in its arsenal. For instance, if we pass a law closing the loophole, those crafty fund managers will just find ways to evade the new measure. Fleischer says this argument actually once kept him up at night:

> It's the idea that there may be some workarounds—that there may be some devices that people can come up with to get the same tax result using a slightly different economic structure. But while I'm still concerned about it, the proposed legislation does a pretty good job of closing all the loopholes within the loophole and at least shutting down the obvious workarounds.

Or, if we close the loophole, fund managers will just pass on the extra cost to their investors. That, in turn, will reduce investment in venture capital, private equity or certain hedge funds. "It's just not true," says Fleischer:

> Because the tax is imposed on managers and because these funds exist in a competitive marketplace, the managers can't just shift the incidence of the tax over to investors. If they could increase their fees, they already would have done so. They are already charging the most that the market will bear. They can't just unilaterally raise fees or the investors will just go to another fund. It's a very competitive marketplace.

Another argument thrown at legislators is that closing the loophole isn't worth the effort: the U.S. Treasury might gain only $1.8 billion a year or less, a mere trifle in the scale of things. Yet Leo Hindery Jr., who earned hundreds of millions as head of the Yes Network and ATT Broadband, estimates the yearly revenue gain to be more like $10 billion.

Even the lowball estimate of $1.8 billion used by the Obama administration would be enough to hire more than fifty-one thousand entry-level teachers. More teachers or more millions for hedge-fund managers? Your choice.

Why such a discrepancy in numbers? According to an article by Hindery in the *Huffington Post*, the explanation is dark:

> [M]uch of the difference between my calculations and the revenue estimates used by the White House, some in Congress and, especially, the self-serving Private Equity Growth Capital Council is that their revenue estimates "take into account taxpayers' likely behavioral responses in attempting to avoid higher taxes under proposed legislation, as well as the likely success of the proposed legislation at preventing avoidance and collecting those revenues."
>
> This methodology—that tax avoiders will just find other ways to avoid taxes—has, without any persuasive supporting evidence, been used repeatedly over the years to put off fair-minded Members of Congress from closing tax loopholes. Having been around this space myself for 23 years, I'm not aware of any possible "avoidance schemes" which these managers might possibly take to avoid paying these particular taxes—and of course the difference between $1.8 billion and $10 billion per year implies an absurd and unrealistic amount of tax avoidance. (Hindery 2011)

Essentially, the argument is that hedge-fund managers will hire the best lawyers, who will help them avoid taxes no matter what we do. Or they'll just hide their profits offshore and cheat.

Maybe so, but it's a very curious argument. Isn't it the same as saying that we should eliminate all taxes on billionaires, because they have the means to avoid them? And why should we ever try to make tax evaders pay their fair share? It seems like a pathetically weak argument.

Then, of course, there's the ultimate zinger: that raising taxes—*any* taxes—destroys jobs. Even some liberal politicians are barfing up this one. On Politico.com, you can find a letter by Democrats Jared Polis and Mike Quigley urging the president to please keep the loophole in place. Increasing taxes for hedge-fund managers and the like, they wrote, would "not only damage our already fragile economy, but it would also cripple the spirit of innovation and entrepreneurship that makes our country so strong" (Smith 2011).

When I first read that letter, I thought it was a spoof—a way to make fun of these liberals. After all, how could anyone still argue that financial funds that so proudly brought us toxic CDOs and the like "embody the spirit of innovation and entrepreneurship that makes our country so strong?" But no, these guys are serious.

More amazing still, Polis is viewed as an exceptional liberal. If you check his labor record, it's almost perfect (as measured by the AFL-CIO). As Paul Waldman points out in the *American Prospect*, Polis is even a member of the Congressional Progressive Caucus. Wrote Waldman,

Elected in 2008, he's a member of the Progressive Caucus and known as a left-winger. He wants to end federal marijuana prohibition. He represents Boulder. He's gay. He's also really rich—on the order of a couple hundred million dollars in net worth (dot-com money)—but as Robert Frank described him in 2007, "Rather than using government as a tool to cut taxes and boost his personal fortune, he's using his personal fortune as a tool to change government. The changes he seeks are aimed at lifting up the underclass, rather than providing further support for the overclass. Or at least that's the way he puts it on the campaign trail." (Waldman n.d.)

How can this radical guy support such an egregious loophole? It would be enlightening to hear him explain to the underclass why the richest people on the planet need this tax break, so I requested an interview. This was going to be great. Maybe the Leopold-Polis interview would rank right up there with Frost-Nixon!

A dream deferred. I got this note instead: "As you may have seen, Jared and his partner just welcomed their new baby into their home, so we will not be able to accommodate your request at this time." Oh, well, let's hope the little darling distracts the congressman from continued loophole lobbying.

And we'll be watching. As fate would have it, Professor Victor Fleischer lives in Jared's congressional district. The professor had a few choice words after I read him Jared's letter in defense of the carried-interest loophole:

> That's a crock of [crap]. The entrepreneurial spirit comes from the founders who start the companies that the venture capitalists and private equity managers invest in. The founders are the ones who are providing the innovation. They're the ones who are relying on the creative spirit to do great things. The VCs are providing financing and providing advice, and some are very good at it. But the idea that VCs are going to disappear or that they're so fragile that they can't survive if they have to pay 35 percent tax—that's crazy.

Since Polis isn't here to defend himself, we will: If taxes go up on these fund guys, won't they just move their business overseas, causing us to lose thousands upon thousands of jobs, not to mention all of the jobs we get from servicing these billionaires? Fleischer, in fact, told me that some of these guys actually had suggested to him that they might just move their companies to India if we took their loophole away. Fleischer doesn't buy it, though.

> But you know what? People aren't going to move their businesses offshore. If you're a venture capitalist in Silicon Valley, you've got to stay close to where the companies are. If you're a private equity manager in New York, you probably like living in New York.

Unfortunately for the Fleischer position, the current legislation to eliminate the loophole is quite broad, giving opponents such as Polis more reasons to oppose it. Not only does it include the billionaire hedge funds, private equity firms, and VCs, but it encompasses all manner of partnerships, large and small. This allows lobby groups such as the Private Equity Growth Capital Council to quietly airbrush hedge funds out of the debate. The council makes it seem that virtually every red-blooded American owns a stake in this loophole: "Changing the tax treatment of carried interest will have widespread ramifications, adversely affecting start-up ventures, small businesses, interests in real estate and natural resources, and other enterprises," they warn us (Private Equity Growth Capital Council 2007).

Yet billionaires and those who want to get there should take comfort from the way this debate is framed. Most people on both sides are assuming that the entire process of hedge-fund profiteering is economically worthwhile. It's only a matter of how much tax they should pay.

What if their activities aren't worthwhile, though? What if hedge-fund profits are largely the product of cheating, perilous high-speed trading, and spurious bets such as the Greatest Trade Ever? What if the entire industry is a drain on our economy and society? If that's the case, then we may need to do much more than simply close a ridiculous loophole.

Stay tuned, hedge funds: the attack on your carried-interest loophole may be the least of your worries.

———— Do's and Don'ts ————

- **Don't** accept being taxed at the same rate as those who aren't job creators like you.

- **Do** remind people that the real innovators in Silicon Valley are the hedge funds, not the techies.

- **Don't** worry about losing your tax loopholes. You can always count on millionaire lawmakers to bail you out.

STEP 11

Claim That Limits on Speculation Will Kill Jobs

You want a million an hour? Then you'd better watch out for those who are dying to tax your good fortune away even before you get it. How dare they?

The do-gooders dare to believe that the financial sector is collecting hidden and unauthorized taxes from the rest of us. Unfortunately, they may have a case, and it's catching on.

When hedge-fund managers (such as George Soros) conduct speculative raids on a nation's currency (as Soros did on England and later on Sweden), the money they waltz away with actually comes from taxpayers, via their central banks. In the Soros deal, the Bank of England lost funds, and the British people either received less from their government or had to pay more in taxes to make up for it. Although that process was opaque and prolonged, the final ledger was clear: money went from the British and Swedish people to Soros and other financial speculators. Is this compulsory payment to speculators really a hidden tax?

When hedge funds use insider information or rumormongering to extract money from markets, isn't this a hidden tax on the buying and selling of financial instruments?

When high-speed traders suck up small sums from virtually every trade made by the rest of us, aren't they pocketing a hidden sales tax on our mutual funds, pension funds, and 401(k)s?

Or how about our too-big-to-fail hedge funds and banks that gorged themselves on trillions in bailouts and federally subsidized loans? Wasn't that transfer from the public purse to financial elites a hidden wealth tax on the rest of us?

Then there's that handful of "winners" who extracted billions through the creation and peddling of toxic assets and rigged securities that were designed to fail. Unfortunately, that money had to come from somewhere—namely, from "losers" such as those five Wisconsin school districts. Unless they win their court case, isn't it likely that either Wisconsin schoolkids will get fewer services or their parents will see tax increases, as a result of what the hedge funds did?

Add it up: bailouts, dubious high-speed trading fees, illegal insider-trading scams, rumormongering, securities designed to fail, and speculative raids on currencies—that's a lot of taxation without representation. Meanwhile, state and local governments are cutting services and raising overt taxes to make up for the losses and to provide services for the eight million workers who lost their jobs due to the financial crash.

So, first we pay hidden taxes to financial elites and then we pay overt taxes to clean up the financial mess?

Of course, hedge-fund managers aren't the only ones who extracted money from this toxic process at our expense. There were the predatory mortgage lenders, the investment banks that gobbled up the crap mortgages and then packaged, repackaged, and repackaged them again into CDOs of all shapes and stripes. There were the ratings agencies whose rapidly rising profits depended on blessing these CDO monstrosities with AAA ratings. There were the proprietary traders and hedge funds and brokers who peddled the crap. Many, many financiers grew rich from hawking securities that had no real value. Now we're paying for all of their ill-gotten gains.

It doesn't bode well for the million-an-hour club when we examine the contours of our economy. During the last generation, the financial sector mushroomed in size and garnered a larger and larger share of all corporate profits. Is that because of the "value" it produced for the economy or because of the hidden taxes it extracted?

All in all, the million-an-hour club might want to bolt the door and draw the shades tight. Outside, the public sees a bloated financial sector that extracts humongous hidden taxes from the rest of us. In the rigged casino that is high finance, those hidden taxes are the house's money—and the public wants it back.

That's why the do-gooders are scheming away right now to put an end to these hidden taxes. As they see it, the drunken gamblers who wrecked the place should pay for the damages done. More important, the casinos should be shut down entirely to save us from the next greed-inspired crash.

So, take cover as those do-gooders line up their big gun that's pointed squarely at the million-an-hour club. It can be summed up in three words: financial transaction tax.

• • •

During the 1970s, James Tobin, the late Yale economist and Nobel laureate, observed the new world of fast-moving money and saw an enormous problem. He feared that the power of money racing around the globe would rob nations of the power to tackle their citizens' most pressing problems. "Private financial markets have become internationalized much more rapidly and completely than other economic and political institutions," he said. "That is why we are in trouble" (Tobin 1978, 155).

Tobin's problem has now become a global one, with the aid of very large speculators. In fact, James Tobin practically predicted the currency raids that Soros and others visited on Britain and Sweden years later.

The problem started when President Richard Nixon took the United States off the gold standard and ended the Bretton Woods agreements, which had guided world finance for a quarter century. At that time, it was a sensible move: the rapidly developing world economy had outgrown the Bretton Woods framework. (Short version: in the late 1960s, for a variety of reasons, it was a lot more profitable for foreigners to trade dollars for gold than to exchange them for pounds or pesos, so the United States started to run low on gold. As a result, we jettisoned the gold standard.)

Instead of measuring currencies using the gold benchmark, we would now value currencies relative to one another: free-floating rates. Governments would no longer decide how many yen equaled one dollar. It was all up to the foreign exchange markets. Most economists thought that was fine, including Tobin.

Tobin could see, however, that speculators were going to have a field day. Under the old system, governments prevented currency speculation by controlling the amount of capital that could be moved in and out of the country. Under the new system, that would be next to impossible. So the field was again open, as it was during the Great Depression, for speculators to bet on currencies.

Most economists didn't take Tobin's worries very seriously. They figured that speculation on different currencies would more or less balance out. In the process, currencies would move more quickly to their real value—a value based on the fundamental strength of each economy that would include productivity, inflation rates, budget deficits, and the like.

Yet Tobin feared that speculators would periodically set off wild destabilizing gyrations in exchange rates—and that fear of such gyrations would give the money markets political clout. A country might feel compelled to enact austerity policies to please the markets, even if those policies were detrimental to its own citizens—or it might shun social and economic policies that could displease the markets. For example, a government might back away from passing measures to boost job creation if it feared that currency speculators would react too violently, weakening the economy further. Tobin predicted that we would soon live in a world where currency and bond markets took on human qualities, "liking" and "disliking" this policy or that. According to Bob Woodward's account in *The Agenda*, President Bill Clinton realized this early in his first term, saying, "You mean to tell me that the success of my program and my reelection hinges on the Federal Reserve and a bunch of fucking bond traders?" (Woodward 1994, 73).

Tobin puzzled about how to curb the speculators without hindering global trade and prosperity. The problem was complex, but his solution simple: "Throw some sand in the well-greased wheels" of finance, he wrote (Tobin 1978, 158).

Of course, the defenders of unfettered markets were scandalized. After all, most economists pray to the gods of efficiency. They praise floating exchange rates for efficiently reducing the overt cost of transactions and for allowing money to move at lightning speeds to wherever it's needed. That way, money is deployed productively, not siphoned off or wasted in financial administration. Tobin was happy to grant those positive attributes to free-floating rates, and he had no quarrel with financial speculation as such. He just didn't think that financial efficiency was the end-all and be-all of human wisdom.

In fact, Tobin seemed to view "financial efficiency" as an oxymoron. In a conventional economist's perfect world, financial speculators drive prices toward their true value—their true equilibrium price. For instance, a speculator might guess (and then speculate on) the real value of a goods-producing company and on what that value will be in the future. Yet Tobin questioned whether this kind of forecasting could really apply to estimating the long-term real price of a currency. How could a speculator formulate an accurate prediction? Instead, Tobin thought, speculators would push currency values all over the place, hoping for a quick kill, while wreaking havoc on national economies left and right—a financial bull in a china shop.

So Tobin proposed slowing down that bull through a tax, which is the sand in the wheels. Because most economists and policy makers wanted nothing to do with it, they were only too happy to refer to it as the Tobin Tax. Yet now, more than a decade after his death, the idea is gaining adherents, both here and abroad. Along the way, the name changed to a *financial transaction tax*. Some even call it a *financial speculation tax* or *Robin Hood Tax*. Tobin's aim was to rein in speculators by taking away their short-term profits and therefore their motivation to destabilize currencies to make a quick killing. The tax would not only yield income for the commonwealth, but also would allow national governments to regain some control over their economic policies.

Tobin was no socialist. He always retained a deep and abiding respect for the markets. Yet his ultimate aim was to make life better for the citizens of the world, not just for banks and hedge funds. We can be sure that if James Tobin were alive and well today, he'd want to dump a bargeload of sand into the speculative wheels to prevent the next crash.

• • •

Unfortunately for the million-an-hour club, economist Dean Baker *is* alive and well and more than willing to heave all of that sand into the wheels of finance. As codirector of the Center for Economic and Policy Research in Washington, Baker is a forceful American proponent of financial speculation taxes. I interviewed him by telephone (October 2011) about how such a tax might work.

Baker got into economics because, as he puts it, "It occurred to me that a lot of things didn't look very good in the world, and it seemed to me that you needed to know economics to do anything about it." So he went to economics graduate school in the early 1980s and graduated with a PhD from the University of Michigan. In 1992, after a few years of teaching at Bucknell, Baker came to Washington, D.C., to do battle with the economic policy establishment. With a combination of confidence, competence, and hard work, Baker has become a powerful advocate for progressive economic policies and a formidable foe of the financial industry.

Baker became interested in financial transaction taxes long before he arrived in D.C. "Back in the 1980s, I was thinking that there were a lot of wasted resources in the financial sector," he recalls. "And then I stumbled onto Tobin. Even before that, I'd noticed that Keynes talks about it in passing in *General Theory*, which I read as an undergraduate."

Baker believes we should look at the rapidly growing financial sector the same way cold-blooded capitalists would look at most other industries. They don't like bloat and waste, and they're happy to slice an industry down to size to increase its efficiency.

Finance's true productive value is steering resources from savers to those who want to borrow and invest. In principle, you'd like to have that done as efficiently as possible, which means we should treat it the way capitalists would treat any other industry: employ as few people in the industry as possible, and pay them as little as possible. Capitalists don't want to pay their autoworkers a lot, and they don't want to pay people who play with money a lot. We want that same efficiency in financial markets. We want as few resources as possible tied up in the sector itself—in the flipping back and forth of assets and the other very short-term moves speculators make.

A hard-nosed capitalist would notice finance's wasteful habits, practices that have nothing to do with moving savings into productive investment.

You have a lot of rent seeking. People can become very good at out-guessing the market. For example, they might realize oil is about to go up before it actually does and place their bets. Some of that could be because of insider trading, or maybe they're lucky or smart—they study it and get it right. But getting in there [to trade] an hour ahead of someone else, that's something of very little value, particularly if you're doing it through insider trading or through some program that allows you to take advantage of trading patterns and gets you in there a quarter of a second ahead of anyone else. There's no benefit to the economy at all from that. People who get rich by figuring out a way to know that oil prices are going to go up or down an hour before someone else are adding absolutely zero value to society. They basically skimmed off profits that someone else produced.

Okay, Dean, so what do we do about it?

Baker advocates placing a very small tax, not only on currency transactions as Tobin suggested, but on *all* financial industry transactions—stocks, bonds, and all manner of derivatives, including credit default swaps, which are a form of financial insurance. In short, he wants to tax just about everything a billionaire hedge-fund manager does!

Baker suggests that we may have a workable model for this tax, because the European Union is likely to impose one soon. Although Baker says he'd prefer a higher tax, he thinks the proposed European rate is "probably more realistic. They're proposing a tax rate of one-tenth of 1 percent of stock trades—so it would be five one-hundredths of a percent on the stock buyer and another five one-hundredths of a percent on the stock seller." The Europeans will also probably impose a tax of one-hundredth of 1 percent on various options, futures, credit default swaps, and other derivative instruments.

Baker notes that he and Bob Pollin (an economist at the University of Massachusetts, Amherst), "calculated that even with a 50 percent decline in trading volume due to the tax, it would raise on the order of $150 billion a year in the United States. That's real money."

Very real, indeed. And most of it will come out of your million-an-hour pockets!

For Baker, the financial speculation tax is a thing of beauty, precisely because it does no harm at all to the truly valuable work of financial markets—moving savings into productive investments. Yet the tax does punish unproductive speculation.

A financial transaction tax has almost no impact on what we want the markets to do, which is allocate money to people who have innovative ideas for producing, say, better cars or better software or computers, or whatever the product might be. On those activities, the financial transaction tax will have almost no impact. The whole point is to make this tax very small. So for someone who has a productive plan for good investment and needs to raise capital, it's almost inconceivable that this very small difference in transaction costs could have any effect at all on their plans.

However, it would have a big impact on those people who are looking for short-term profits, which by definition must be small. Obviously, you'd love to double your money in a day, but if you're looking to get in at one o'clock and out at two o'clock, you'd be happy to make a half of a percent gain—that's fantastic. If you do that twice a day, you can get incredibly rich. That's the sort of trading that this tax would have the biggest impact on.

Baker and his colleagues at the Center for Economic and Policy Research stay on top of the debate over a financial transaction tax, often acting as a rapid response team when other economists trash the idea. For example, Kenneth Rogoff, the noted Harvard economist and coauthor of *This Time Is Different* (a bestselling account of eight hundred years of financial crises), wrote a scathing op-ed against proposals for a European financial transaction tax. Rogoff argued that such taxes are dangerous because they reduce liquidity, make trading harder, and obscure the real value of stocks and bonds. Furthermore, Rogoff wrote, "While raising so much revenue with so low a tax rate sounds grand, the declining volume of trades would shrink the tax base precipitously. As a result, the ultimate revenue gains are likely to prove disappointing" (Rogoff 2011).

Yet Rogoff's most stinging critique is that the tax will slow the economy, hitting the little guy hardest. As Rogoff puts it,

Over the long run, the tax burden would shift. Higher transaction taxes increase the cost of capital, ultimately lowering investment. With a lower capital stock, output would trend downward, reducing government revenues and substantially offsetting the direct gain from the tax. In the long run, wages would fall, and ordinary workers would end up bearing a significant share of the costs. (Rogoff 2011)

This reasoning makes Dean Baker chuckle. "When people make arguments like that, I jump on them. It's encouraging to me. There aren't a lot of economists who are better than Rogoff, and if this is what he's got to say, then I figure we've got a pretty good case." Baker rebutted Rogoff's argument in a blog post that was translated into German and Italian—and probably other languages as well.

The heart of this debate brings us back to our talk with Joe Saluzzi. What is the real cost of trading stocks? Without question, these costs have dropped dramatically during the last twenty years as a result of electronic trading. Rogoff is claiming that if we tax this process, those efficiencies will be lost. That will make it more expensive for corporations to raise capital, which in turn will mean slower growth, fewer jobs, and lower incomes.

Baker agrees that technology and deregulation have dramatically lowered the cost of trading during the last three decades. Yet even after a small transaction tax, he argues, "Trading costs would still be lower than they were in the eighties and much lower than they were in the fifties and sixties," when they could be up to 1 percent of the price of the stock. Besides, Baker can find no evidence that those higher transaction costs slowed growth. In fact, economic growth was much greater then than now.

Baker concedes that the tax would indeed reduce trading volume by as much as 50 percent, but so what? Much of the explosion of trading comes from high-frequency traders who add little or no value to our economy. As for Rogoff's liquidity fears, Baker points out that we had no liquidity problems fifteen or twenty years ago when transaction costs were much higher than they would be even if we did impose a new tax.

Baker sees absolutely no evidence—either in economic literature or in the real world—for Rogoff's claim that a small transaction tax will drag down the economy. In fact, he notes, England has had a financial transaction tax on stock trading for centuries—and it's five times as large as the one Europe is proposing. Yet there are no signs that it is harming the British economy. As Baker tells me,

> They've had their tax in place since 1696. They have one of the largest stock markets in the world, and they get between 0.2 to 0.3 percent of GDP just from taxing stocks. That would be the same as $30 to $40 billion a year in the U.S. And that's just from taxing stocks, not derivatives. And they've been able to collect this tax quite effectively. Their Inland Revenue Service—their equivalent of our IRS—says it's their least costly tax to administer.

Doesn't Rogoff have a point about liquidity, though? If the tax reduces the volume of trading by 50 percent, won't that make it harder for people to make trades when they want or need to make them?

Not according to Baker. He patiently walks me through the argument:

> Clearly [the tax] does reduce liquidity, almost by definition. If you have less trading, you have less liquidity. But what does that mean? [Even with this reduced liquidity], if I want to sell shares of GE stock, I'll be able to do it instantaneously, since the volume will still be millions a day. I'm not going to have to wait more than a minute, maybe a second, and there will be someone on the other end to pick that up.

What about lightly traded stocks, such as those of a small start-up company?

> There are some stocks—over-the-counter-stocks—that aren't that big. To trade those right now, even without a tax,

you might have to wait several days. But the transaction costs for those stocks are much higher already. So here's a nice feature of the tax: While the tax might double the costs of trading on GE stocks, it's a much smaller percentage increase when I buy or sell my shares of this new computer or software start-up. That's because those transaction costs without the tax might already be 2 or 3 percent on those harder-to-trade stocks. So the increase in transaction costs from the proposed tax is relatively small for that [kind of trade].

So, who *will* feel the pinch from this tax?

It's going to hit the whole class of people who are making their money by trying to jump in ahead of you and me when we're trying to make our trades, who try to skim some profit that should be going to us. We don't need that person to hold the stock for a second so that they could get some of the movement in price.

Yet won't the real costs get tossed back to the ordinary investor, who is just trying to make the best of his or her 401(k)? We may think we're taxing the super-rich, the argument goes, but are we really hitting the little guy?

Baker has no patience for this argument:

They have to get their logic straight. What you expect to happen—and there's a fair bit of research on this—is that people will reduce their trading in response to an increase in costs. . . . So let's say the mutual fund I have in my 401(k) currently turns over 20 percent in the course of a year. And now we throw this tax in, and it doubles trading costs. So instead of my 401(k) turning over 20 percent in a year, it'll turn over 10 percent in a year. If I'm paying twice as much per trade but am only trading half as much, then I'm not paying one extra penny for my trades in total. And what do

I care about the number of trades I do? I care about what I get on my investment and, on average, more trading doesn't actually get me more money.

The last argument, thrown at Baker again and again—including by me—is that financial markets will simply run to notorious tax havens such as the Grand Cayman Islands.

Baker returns to the English example: the tax has been in place there for more than three hundred years, and England's stock market is doing just fine. "You might see some shift to tax havens," he conceded. "But it really depends on how much you step up the effort to combat it. In Europe, the proposed tax would be based on residence. So to evade it, you'd have to set up a shell company to do your trading." That wouldn't be impossible to do, says Baker. But it's not exactly easy, either.

Besides, says Baker, it's not as if we couldn't do anything about markets fleeing to the Grand Caymans or elsewhere. "You know, if they were running guns to Al Qaeda, we'd figure out ways to stop them. We're not that defenseless before the Cayman Islands. It's one of the bogeymen that they hold up."

Enough said. My advice to you million-an-hour seekers: Beware of financial transaction taxes—and of Dean Baker.

• • •

My bracing discussion with Baker about a financial transaction tax made me rethink my visit with Joe Saluzzi (who says he's not sure whether he favors a transaction tax).

Remember that Joe and his partner, Sal, earn their fees by protecting their clients from high-frequency traders—predators who lurk in dark pools, waiting to jump ahead of each trade in a matter of nanoseconds.

Joe and Sal told me that 70 to 80 percent of stock market trading today is "noise"—high-frequency trades that last no longer than a few seconds. Plus, there is more noise that comes from "pinging"—testing the market for certain prices and then disappearing before the trades are consummated. They've also warned that such liquidity is phony—it won't be there when we really need it.

What's more, they're sure that because of this high-frequency trading rip-off, the real transaction costs we're paying right now are much higher than what they seem to be. Your real cost is not just what E*Trade charges you. Your real cost also includes the extra hidden tax you pay when high-frequency traders jump ahead of you. Because of them, the price you end up paying when you buy is higher than it should be, and it's lower than it should be when you sell. As Joe told us, the fee you pay E*Trade for the transaction is only the "tip of the iceberg." The rest of the iceberg is also your real cost, but it's submerged, harder to see, and often overlooked—much to the pleasure of the high-frequency traders.

What the financial transaction tax really does is replace the hidden tax (which is now extracted by hedge funds and banks) with an out-in-the-open tax that goes to the commonwealth. It may even *reduce* the true transaction costs. Rather, the tax will help eliminate most of the hidden part of the iceberg. Pension funds, mutual funds, and the average trader might not see a rise in the actual cost of trading—only a change in who is collecting the tax.

The "financial speculation tax" is both aptly named and carefully targeted, much to the chagrin of the million-an-hour club. It goes after useless speculation. It reclaims for the nation the money that is being siphoned from markets. It makes it much harder for the sharks to make enormous profits from high-frequency trading. It will move about $150 billion a year from the pockets of financial elites and put enormous downward pressure on their inflated incomes. Who knows, it might even motivate business school grads (and any avid young business readers of this book) to forsake Wall Street for more productive careers in rebuilding the real American economy or, God forbid, for careers in public service.

If this tax is such a no-brainer, though, why don't we have one in the United States? Timothy Geithner, our Treasury secretary at the time of this writing, does not like the idea, so I called his office to ask him why. Unfortunately, he was unable to make time for me. Yet his office did give me a statement on October 11, 2011, that I'm permitted to attribute to a "Treasury Department official."

A financial transaction tax (FTT) is not an idea we are planning to support in the U.S.

FTTs are hard to implement globally, are generally borne by retail investors, are prone to regulatory arbitrage, depress asset prices and trading volumes, and increase capital costs.

The Obama Administration's Financial Crisis Responsibility Fee applies at the institutional level, levied as a tax on certain liabilities of large financial firms in order to discourage excessive leverage. This is fully consistent with the principles agreed to by the G-20 Leaders.

In our view, a tax on liabilities is a better way to generate funding while addressing excessive leverage.

The response, as we can see, mirrors Rogoff's argument that Baker decimated previously, but the Treasury folks are also trying to turn our attention to a proposed fee on "certain liabilities" of very large banks. Does this move us in the right direction?

Not really, says Baker. He thinks the bank tax is a fine idea but largely a "diversion" from the much more significant financial transaction tax. The bank tax, he explains, would apply only to the relatively small number of banks with assets of $50 billion or more. He estimates that the tax would raise $8 or $9 billion a year. What's more, the Geithner plan wouldn't touch the major hedge funds whose socially destructive practices we've been discussing in this book. It lets them off scot-free—as if they had nothing to do with the economic crisis, our increasingly skewed income distribution, or the siphoning away of our productive wealth into money games. Fortunately for hedge funds, Geithner doesn't seem troubled by any of this.

What about President Obama? Supposedly, the president once liked the speculation tax idea. According to Ron Suskind in

Confidence Men, he told his economic team, "We're going to do this!" (Suskind 2011, 389). But Larry Summers, then Obama's top economic adviser, was of the same mind as Geithner and killed the idea.

If Obama truly wanted a financial transaction tax, he could have compelled Summers and Geithner to move on it. In fact, if he really wanted one, maybe he wouldn't even be dealing with top economic advisers who come from Wall Street and who venerate hedge-fund billionaires.

Is there any hope for a financial speculation tax in the United States? Dean Baker thinks so.

> The movement for this is hugely growing. Occupy Wall Street has been fantastic for it. People like Nicholas Kristof [*New York Times* columnist], who is a little left of center, have come out for it. Steve Perlstein at the *Washington Post*, a decent guy who also is probably a little left of center, a former business reporter, now a columnist who's been at the *Post* 30 years—he came out for it. You've got a lot of very centrist people suddenly talking about it. Other business reporters are writing things like, "Yeah, that makes sense. Why wouldn't we do this?"

Why not? Because very wealthy, powerfully connected financial elites would lose by it. And they will do all they can to make sure it doesn't see the light of day, unless forced to do so by a very large and very vocal popular movement.

P.S. Watch out for the National Nurses United, a union of 150,000 nurses from all over the United States who are fighting for a Robin Hood Tax. Wherever there's a protest about high finance, you'll find nurses, dressed like Robin no less, pressing for the tax. Who would have thought that kindly, caring nurses could stand in the way of you making it into the million an hour club? (See NationalNursesUnited.org.)

Do's and Don'ts

- **Do** remind lawmakers that any tax on your trades is a death tax on jobs.

- **Do** remind lawmakers that any tax on your trades will destroy market confidence and cause a financial crash.

- **Do** remind lawmakers that their campaign funds will evaporate if they so much as whisper the words "Robin Hood."

STEP 12

Distract the Dissenters

Well, one more step and you'll be knocking at heaven's door. Take care, though, this last one is a doozy. As you enter the high-income stratosphere, you'll find that the envious and the outraged are nipping at your heels. Sure, we all know that you just want to keep winning the game and get your just rewards. You didn't write the rules or make the laws. You may bend them a bit, but basically, you're just going after the financial riches that are waiting for those who are ruthless and smart enough to snatch them.

Yet that's not good enough. The natives are growing restless. If you're not careful, they'll be blaming you for the Wall Street crash, the high unemployment, the draconian cuts in state and local services, the outrageous bailouts, and the mounting deficits. Before you can say "Ponzi," you'll be playing tennis with Bernie.

Let's face it: you'll never make it into the million-an-hour club without skating out to the ethical edge—and beyond. Sure, a few of you may try to play it squeaky clean, at least for a while. Sooner or later, though, you're going to cut a corner or two. It's part of what the New York DA calls the "corrupt business model." It's built into what Professor Lynn Stout says is your "criminogenic" culture.

Even if, by some miracle, you stay within the letter of the law, some of what you do is certain to look shady and slimy to an aroused public. There's no way to be a boy scout and make a million an hour.

So we need to prepare you for the political onslaught. You'll need to learn how to crush your opponents before they can do you harm. You'll need to rig the political process. You'll need to redirect public anger away from you. In short, you've got to do everything and anything you can to intimidate those who are foolish enough to mess with you. Forget about fair play—you've got to stomp your critics into the ground, overtly and covertly. Here's some advice that you'd best not ignore.

1. If Someone Writes Your Name and the Word "Crime" in the Same Article, Sue Them!

You cannot let anyone associate you with law breaking. It doesn't matter if you're innocent or guilty as sin. Use your money and put some high-powered lawyers on retainer to send nasty, threatening letters to anyone who dares to malign you, even two-bit bloggers who have a two-bit following. Why? Because in today's world of social media, stuff happens in a hurry. Yesterday's two-bit blogger could become tomorrow's giant slayer. If the blogger strikes a raw nerve, it could reverberate around the world. Next thing you know, you've got the FBI interviewing your secretary. Not good.

So you need to come down hard and fast. You should flash your financial sword at anyone who dares to cross you. In fact, you should follow the lead of one of the richest hedge-fund players in the world who went after a hapless blogger no one had ever heard of: yours truly.

Let me serve as an object lesson on how to intimidate your critics. I can tell you, it gets your attention when one of the big boys fires a shot across your bow. You see, I'd written a pointed piece for the *Huffington Post* about a hedge-fund guru who'd cut what I considered to be an odiferous financial deal with a too-big-to-fail investment bank. While others were writing melodious odes to this fellow for brilliantly predicting the housing market collapse and then betting against it, I wondered out loud how the guy had gotten away with this "near-criminal conspiracy" to defraud investors. To date, the bank has paid hundreds of millions of dollars in SEC penalties for misleading its investors, while our hedge-fund guru (He-who-must-not-be-named) has walked off with more money than God and no penalties whatsoever. The entire episode, I argued, revealed the rot deep within our financial system, and we needed reforms to protect us from this kind of financial malignancy.

Yet He-who-must-not-be-named was a bit sensitive about having his name associated with (1) a slimy deal, and (2) the words *criminal conspiracy*. And for good reason. The SEC and congressional committees had already demonstrated that he was deeply involved in rigging failed mortgage-related securities so that he could bet big against them. In principle, he violated no securities law, because the bogus security was issued by the investment bank. Yet in the eyes of the public—and of this blogger—that was a mere technicality. Surely, it should be against the law to rig a security to fail and then pocket the money. Imagine the uproar in virtually any other industry if new products failed almost immediately by design. There would be hell to pay, if, for example, a firm designed a spanking new car to crash so that the car manufacturer could collect the insurance. So you can understand why this hedge-fund titan was on the lookout for any hint of impropriety attached to his name.

One week after I had written the piece, I received this note from a *Huffington Post* editor:

We have received a complaint regarding the blog post below:
In the post, you accuse [X] of criminal behavior. Because accusations of criminal conduct without a factual basis (an

indictment, complaint, or conviction) are libel per se, could you please back up these accusations further with facts or remove them within 24 hours?

Please let me know if you have any questions.

Well, at least I had one avid reader.

Notice how in this e-mail my "near-criminal conspiracy" turned into a charge of "criminal behavior" (which, I think, is like transforming "nearly having sex" into the real deal). It seemed that this billionaire's legal minions had applied some serious heat to *Huffington Post*. Even though I was reasonably certain that accusing someone of a "near-criminal conspiracy" was not libelous, I had no interest in hiring a panel of high-priced lawyers to defend myself against a touchy billionaire. The blog already had run its course and hit tens of thousands of readers and websites. I convinced myself that my point had been made, and I pulled the piece.

Yet in truth, I was shaken. I just couldn't believe that a multibillionaire was coming after me. Was it possible that one small voice posed a threat to such a mighty financier?

A few days after skulking away from this fight, I got another jolt. My sage agent, Bill Lee, received an e-mail from someone who claimed he was representing a book publisher: Could we send him a copy of my latest book proposal (which was for this book)? Yet when Bill asked for the name of the publisher, the inquirer refused to provide it, saying it was just a small one. Bill said he'd never before encountered this odd behavior, and neither had any of his agent friends.

Did this phantom publisher have anything to do with the *Huffington Post* kerfuffle a few days earlier? Was I paranoid to wonder whether that alleged publisher had been sent by my thin-skinned billionaire and that I was being investigated up and down? It didn't take long to imagine myself in a grade-B movie where my computer was hacked, my garbage inspected, and my family held for ransom.

Look, I'm not all that brave. I love my wife and kids and will do anything to protect them, which includes shutting my big mouth. For the first time since becoming a writer, I felt threatened.

And that is precisely what I was meant to feel. Whoever was checking me out intended to send me a warning: "Be careful what you write. We are powerful. Go too far, and we'll use our bottomless bank accounts to tie you up in legal knots and make your life miserable. You don't know who you're messing with. You're out on a limb, all alone."

Bravo to our million-an-hour aggressor. He got the result he wanted, and he didn't even have to go to court. He got me to withdraw the piece, and now I am careful not to associate He-who-cannot-be-named with "near criminal behavior" or "nearly having sex."

2. Divert the National Conversation from Wall Street to Government Debt

Just as you can silence little bloggers, you can silence Washington. All it takes is cash, lobbying, and an epidemic of financial amnesia. (More details in Number 6, further on.) Your goal is clear: to prevent a federal witch hunt that focuses on Wall Street's high crimes and misdemeanors. Come on, let's be honest. No one has been prosecuted for taking down the economy. Sure, for a while after the crash it seemed as if the Wall Street villains would at least be dragged before Congress to confess their sins—how they gambled away our wealth and rigged mortgage-backed securities to fail. After all, the public wanted to know why we bailed out the bastards and why the too-big-to-fail banks are now even bigger. President Obama even hurt their feelings by calling them "fat cats."

If federal investigations got out of control, it could lead to criminal indictments, which at the very least would be bad for the wallet. No one wants to invest in a hedge fund that's under indictment, even if it's vindicated.

Well, a few hearings took place, but Watergate they were not. Then a miracle happened.

Financial amnesia set in as Congress debated health care, instead of Wall Street. Pretty soon, everyone seemed to forget that Wall Street was to blame for our collapsed economy. Instead, with the help of many financial lobbyists and campaign contributions, the conversation turned to debt. (The word on the Street is that in the 2010 and 2012 elections, most of the big hedge-fund money poured to the Republicans. Even a weak Dodd-Frank bill was too much to bear, and Wall Street's feelings were still smarting from Obama's "fat cat" jibe.)

This was a remarkable feat. At first, it seemed certain that Washington would understand that the Wall Street crash was the fundamental cause of the deficits. After all, it was directly responsible for the humongous loss in tax revenues and a rise in costs to aid the millions of unemployed. Of course, the Bush tax cuts for the wealthy, combined with two unfunded wars, further eroded the tax base.

Yet after Wall Street financed a finance-friendly Congress, Republicans, along with many Democrats, focused on cutting back government. In fact, big bad government, not Wall Street, was increasingly viewed as the cause of the economic collapse and the reason why the recovery was so tepid. Sensing the mood, Obama froze federal wages and offered a grand compromise to cut long-term deficits by "reforming" so-called entitlements.

By the summer of 2011, you could see the miracle unfold. The deficit hawks in both parties preened about, in order to outdo one another in cutting the social safety net and screwing the poor. America, we were told, was teetering on the edge of insolvency. Even our pristine debt rating was slashed by one of the ratings agencies.

How amazing is that? The same whorish ratings agencies that for hefty sums gave bogus AAA ratings to every toxic mortgage security that ever winked at them now had the nerve to downgrade U.S. debt securities—and to be credible? How is that possible? Why would anyone ever again believe them? Didn't anyone notice that these Wall Street shills were once again doing Wall Street's dirty work?

Yet the media sucked it up and amplified the message, and Congress genuflected before the ratings agencies, while collecting gobs of campaign donations from Wall Street. Pathetic, but very effective.

Very Serious People then wanted to show how they were mature enough to cut Medicaid, Medicare, Social Security, and other public services. You had to have *cojones grandes* as you called for the layoffs of firemen and teachers, even as the unemployment rate reached the highest sustained levels since the Great Depression. And you had to have a severe case of financial amnesia never to mention that the crash of the financial casinos, the ensuing layoffs, and the collapse of the economy caused the debt "crisis" in the first place.

So learn from this, my friends. See how Wall Street got precisely what it wanted. By the end of the summer of 2011, we were all Greeks, living on the dole, drinking too much retsina. The political establishment was demanding that we tighten our belts to pay off the debts caused by the million-an-hour club. It doesn't get any better than that.

What a relief. You can gamble, keep your winnings, and then when you lose, have the American public pay off all of your losses. Sweet Jesus!

It was working perfectly until those pesky kids turned up at Zuccotti Park, just two blocks from Wall Street.

3. UN-OCCUPY WALL STREET

Mother of God, where the hell did they come from? And how do you get rid of them, once and for all?

Talk about your living nightmare. A bunch of scraggly kids turn up in New York, set up camp, rail against Wall Street—and the media jump all over it! Next thing you know, there are so many reporters on the scene that they end up interviewing one another. It's a big story that soon spawns similar encampments all over the country. The game is on.

More amazing still is that none of the usual suspects had anything to do with the uprising. It didn't come from the labor movement (although the pitched battles in Wisconsin may have set the stage). It didn't come from the myriad of progressive think tanks or liberal-issue organizations or even MoveOn.org. It didn't come from the aging sixties radicals, either. Instead, it grew out of a loosely knit group of young anarchists and slightly older creative artists who were fed up. It was a movement miracle.

Did astute progressive analysts (such as me) see it all coming? No. As a matter of fact, two years before the Zuccotti Park revolt, I expressed my disappointment about the lack of protest against Wall Street in a piece on *Huffington Post* called "Obama's No FDR, We're No Mass Movement." I lamented,

> We can moan all we want about Obama's shortcomings, the mistakes his Administration has made and his inability to take on Wall Street. But we haven't exactly applied a lot of heat. A million people on the mall demanding "Jobs Now" along with serious Wall Street reforms might help. A million people showing up repeatedly might actually get the job done. Why have we forgotten how to build a mass movement just as the Tea Party shows that it can be done?
>
> The free market on Wall Street is dead and has been for a long time. It's been replaced by a billionaire bailout society that will provide decades of chronic unemployment and ongoing bailouts for the super-rich.
>
> It's a damn shame Obama can't deal with it. It's a bigger shame that we won't force him to. (Leopold 2010)

Then the Occupy Wall Street kids came out of nowhere and applied the force. In a matter of weeks, the entire spotlight shifted back to Wall Street and to the mal-distribution of income.

The 99 percent/1 percent framework became the new common sense, something that progressives had failed to accomplish during the previous thirty years. It was like the million-an-hour club was being hauled out for a public stoning. Oh, no!

The possibilities were explosive. Although a couple thousand folks participated in Zuccotti Park, another million or so in the New York area were extremely sympathetic. If that larger group joined the fray, then Wall Street might be confronted with a major mass movement. Yet these million middle-class progressives were not about to sleep in the park. They seemed to be waiting for more traditional approaches, such as marches, demonstrations, and organization building. It didn't happen. The traditional progressive movement, from labor on down, was unable to seize the moment and build a mass movement, although a few large protests did take place. Occupy Wall Street was on its own. As long as it was there, however, the question of accountability for the crash hung over the heads of the super-rich.

Next came the hard part: how to make them go away.

Clearly, cooptation was not going to work. These young people were not about to clean up and go door knocking for the Democrats. They were way outside of the established system and had no reason to get back in. Many were recent graduates who couldn't find work. Many were saddled with crushing student loans. The Wall Street crash made their future bleak. Yet there was meaning to be found in the encampments as they set about creating their own political community. Their "General Assemblies," their mic checks, their hand signals, and their work committees were both exhausting and exhilarating. It was brilliant street theater, with Wall Street starring as the villain, each and every day. And it was working because

1. They hit the right target—Wall Street,
2. They used the right framework—the 99 percent, and
3. They came up with creative visual tactics—the encampments.

Nope, they weren't going away on their own.

Brute force wouldn't work, either. The more the police pepper-sprayed and arrested folks, the more press Occupy Wall Street received. This was not Chicago 1968, when the police could smash the heads of antiwar protesters on the nightly news and still count on more than half of the country to support the head smashers. This time, the country was not divided: just about everyone now hates Wall Street.

So, how do you get them to go away?

First, let nature take its course. It's harder to sleep out in winter. A certain amount of attrition was bound to set in, especially if you assist nature by prohibiting space heaters and such, due to fire considerations, of course. More important, though, you needed to quietly convince mayors all over the country to reclaim the parks and remove the encampments—there's public health and the like to consider, isn't there? Raid the suckers in the middle of the night and force them out!

Of course, we don't as yet have concrete proof that billionaire financiers persuaded the billionaire New York mayor to do their dirty work. It probably wasn't necessary. No mayor likes permanent demonstrations targeting his or her city's leading industry, especially a mayor who made his billions by supplying most of the information terminals for Wall Street.

Whatever happened behind the scenes, it worked. By the winter of 2011, Occupy Wall Street went into hibernation. As of this writing, we don't know whether it will ever reappear with anything close to the impact it had in the fall of 2011. It's also too soon to know whether the 99 percent framework sticks or fades or if Wall Street remains the public target. Yet one thing is certain: as the Occupy Wall Street hiatus set in during the winter of 2011–2012, the national conversation shifted back to debt and deficits, much to the relief of the million-an-hour club.

4. ENCOURAGE PROGRESSIVE SILOS

There are tens of thousands of progressive nongovernmental organizations all over the country, staffed by many who are hostile to the million-an-hour club. Will they rise up to challenge Wall Street?

Not yet, and maybe never. On the surface, that's very puzzling. Why is there a Tea Party but no anti–Wall Street equivalent coming from these progressives? I had a chance to pose that question to hundreds of activists around the country.

After more than two years of asking, here's my theory: An entire generation of progressives became imprisoned in their issue silos and didn't know how to break out. Most progressive organizations had turned into (perfectly worthy) interest groups—each with its own issues—environment, women, people of color, gay/lesbian, labor, peace, food, health care, and so on. Very few cared about macroeconomic issues—that was someone else's silo. In fact, it seemed that most had grudgingly accepted the permanence of neoliberalism and financial domination. That's just the way it was.

The economic collapse in 2008 should have been a silo-busting event. After all, progressives of all stripes had for years and years been warning about the perils of cutthroat capitalism. Well, the throats were slashed and the bleeding profuse. The long-awaited collapse had arrived, splat, right before our very eyes. Yet most progressives remained within their silos. (Apparently, tackling economic crashes also was someone else's silo.)

Of course, many progressive individuals and organizations did join together to support Barack Obama's 2008 election. In fact, it was remarkable how many pinned their hopes on this knight in shining armor, who they hoped would be the next FDR. (We seemed to forget about the vast roiling movements that had been agitating for much of Roosevelt's agenda for years before he was elected.) After Obama's election, each silo went to Washington to press its own particular cause, almost as if the crash hadn't happened, and as if the economy would soon repair itself. And as if Obama, whose election was partly sponsored by Wall Street, was now going to challenge its prerogatives. People hoped for the best but didn't act to make it happen. There certainly was no hue and cry for a massive jobs program, combined with a drastic overhaul of Wall Street. The tens of thousands of progressive organizations all over the country did not drop what they were doing to build a mass movement for change. Instead, they continued to deliver carefully crafted work products aimed at enacting specific policy changes in Washington and, of course, aimed at keeping their foundation money flowing.

What the country got after 2008 was precisely what you would expect in the absence of a mass movement. The stimulus bill was too small and too weak; the Dodd-Frank bank reforms were weaker still; and a full-throttled attack on the sky-high unemployment rate was absent. Instead, we got a health-care plan designed to placate private insurance companies and the pharmaceutical industry—no single payer, no public option.

Meanwhile, the Tea Party filled the void and directed public outrage toward big government and our paltry national health care. After the Republicans won a landslide during the 2010 midterm elections, the Democrats and the silos people hunkered into a defensive crouch, hoping to escape the worst of the brutal global push for austerity that, in the United States, was abetted by the Tea Party.

Forget about labor's most important bill, the Employee Free Choice Act, which didn't even come up for a vote in the Democratic-controlled Senate. Forget about global warming bills. The reflexive actions were all defensive: Public-sector unions were fighting for their lives in Wisconsin, Michigan, Ohio, and New Jersey. Planned Parenthood saw its budget slashed and its finances investigated. State and local governments laid off workers, cut their benefits, and pared public services. The already inadequate new health-care law faced court challenges. Both parties backed deficit-reduction bills targeting Medicaid, Medicare, and even Social Security. (The Wisconsin struggle, however, showed enormous solidarity and creativity that some argue inspired Occupy Wall Street.)

So much for the silo strategy.

Yet there was one simple framework that had resonance with nearly every American: *Make Wall Street pay for the damage it caused.* The silos people didn't use it, though. Heck, I'm living proof that it works. Using that framework, I even was invited on conservative talk shows to discuss the perils of Wall Street, and no one would argue against it.

As the retreat accelerated, the silo gang flocked to the only mobilization strategy it understood: electing Democrats. They might be disappointed with Obama, but hey, he was far better than the alternative, wasn't he? You know the arguments.

Meanwhile, the progressive publications and the talk shows came up with their own analysis for the eerie pre-Occupy silence. There was a general moaning and groaning about growing apathy and about how average Americans were helpless in the face of overwork, technology overload, and the general economic onslaught. The idea of "broken" Americans was bandied about. The media were demobilizing us, and right-wing money controlled the agenda. Yet no one had any idea what to do about all of this, except the same old thing—toil away in our issue silos. By the summer of 2011, every "serious" commentator was bloviating about how much we all had to sacrifice to reduce the national debt and deficit. No one bothered to point out that the debt crisis was caused directly by the Wall Street crash. That would've been "immature"—a failure to face up to the world as it is. So both parties and the president played capture-the-deficit-flag: Who would be the first to slash the safety net? After all, "responsible" leaders had to show courage to be cruel to the poor when necessary. If we didn't face up to the hard sacrifices, we'd become the next Greece.

This is where it really gets dicey for the million-an-hour club. If the progressives stay within their silos, then our billionaires can quietly go about their business as if nothing much has happened. Yet if the silos become more porous, then a real *movement* might form. If that happens, financial elites will face a new kind of challenge.

(As a matter of fact, if you have big bucks, you might want to make considerable tax-free donations to the silo of your choice, just as many hedge-fund moguls are doing right now. The silo folks are unlikely to join a mass movement that bites the hands that feed them.)

What kind of mass movement are we talking about, though? Will it blossom like the Arab Spring? Will it smash the silos open and operate outside the confines of our two political parties?

If it does, we'll be taking a page from our own agrarian populist movement of the 1880s, which was a genuine uprising against the biggest New York banks. Small farmers from all over the country, starved for credit and deeply indebted, struggled to break free from Wall Street's domination of the financial system. The Bank of North Dakota, our nation's only state bank, grew out of this rebellion, and still serves as an example of what an alternative to "too big to fail" banks might look like. So watch out for populism—it's as American as a pitchfork.

5. FOMENT FINANCIAL AMNESIA

Perhaps the biggest protective shield for financial elites is the public's fleeting and selective memory. With careful PR and lobbying, we might forget that it was Wall Street's reckless leveraging and financial engineering that froze the economy and killed eight million jobs in a matter of months. We might not recall that the vast majority of the workers who saw their jobs evaporate were *not* in the financial sector. Rather, most came from the goods-and-services sectors, which had been starved for credit and then were squeezed even harder by the recessionary drop in demand. Companies such as GM had problems before the crash, but it was the financial implosion, not issues with production, products, or labor, that drove GM over the edge.

In short, financial amnesia can make Americans forget that Wall Street took the economy down—not their bosses at work, not their corporations, and not capitalists in general. It was the captains of finance who had gambled away America's prosperity. You really don't want people to question the worth of financial speculation—even if they don't know the ins and outs of synthetic CDOs.

Do hedge-fund moguls really have to worry, though? Isn't the populist moment already passing as the economy mends, ever so slowly?

We all expected that a reasonably steady economic comeback was likely. Perhaps the ultradynamic forces of the global economy, combined with the stimulus and the bailouts, could stop the hemorrhaging and bring down the unemployment rate. After all, China, India, and Brazil were still booming. Early on, economists, both in and out of government, predicted that the jobless rate would come down to 8 percent by 2009 and would fall to 6 percent by 2012. They were wrong. The financial crash was bigger than advertised. Unemployment only started to decline oh so slowly in late 2011 and early 2012. As of this writing, it's stalled again. At our current glacial rate of job creation, we'll be stuck with miserably high unemployment for another decade or more. And if Europe crashes? Then all bets are off.

Meanwhile, the financial industry is perking up, thanks to taxpayer bailouts and guarantees. Yes, there are many layoffs in the financial sector, and profits are not rolling in quite the way they used to. But basically, Wall Street is back with little remorse.

The big Wall Street banks and hedge funds are getting cocky again and striving to regain control of the national debate. With the help of financial lobbyists, they've battled to shift the conversation from Wall Street's recklessness and the job crisis to overregulation, tax cuts, and deficit-obsessed austerity. By 2010, much of the country seemed ready to embrace their antigovernment, anti-union frame. Attacks on public-sector union wages and benefits ensued, along with calls to slash Medicaid, Medicare, and Social Security. And why not? No one else had a credible alternative.

Wall Street managed to evade serious financial reforms and happily collected the next round of bonuses. And hedge funds? A few billionaires are getting nabbed for insider trading or Ponzi schemes. For everyone else, the party has resumed. The business media are still offering a free ride, marveling at the wondrous geniuses as before. Yet do the awed reporters and commentators even know how these stars of high finance earn all of that money as the economy sputters along?

So, will we forget or remember? Will attacks on Wall Street grow or decline? Will a new movement form or fade? The answers will determine whether the million-an-hour club prospers or explodes.

Don't hang your head or fret, though. You don't get on the road to a million an hour without the enormous willpower to succeed. Yes, the American people may pose obstacles, and those pesky Occupy Wall Street kids may kick up a fuss again. But making money however you can, as fast as you can, is in the American DNA. Grab it, savor it, and lord it over everyone. Cheat, lie, rig bets, front-run trades—do whatever it takes. Don't worry about justice or fairness or all the little "Rians" laboring far below. Money and more money must be your one and only goal. Only then can you enter the cherished million-an-hour club.

Will the club still be there, however, by the time you are ready to enter? That depends on the rest of us. If we forget, if we retreat into our silos, and if we continue to view uprisings like Occupy Wall Street as spectator sports, then financial elites will tighten their grip on the economy and on our democracy. Life will go on, but our wealth will be transferred, bit by bit, to financial elites.

If, however, we can organize a movement built for the long haul, one that clearly focuses on financial elites and the ways they harm our economy and society, then we may find, as Dr. Martin Luther King Jr. put it, that "the arc of the moral universe is long but it bends toward justice."

Conclusion

For those of you on the path to great riches, I leave you here. If this step-by-step guide hasn't discouraged you, nothing will. Good luck. (You'll need it.)

Yet as I write these words, I am also thinking of friends and neighbors who work hard at banks, investment companies, and even hedge funds. Although none are financial moguls, most are quite well off and deeply immersed in Wall Street's culture. They believe that their high incomes are justified and that super-rich financiers are well worth what they earn. They surely are upset by the protesters who are vilifying them. I won't be very popular in town when this book comes out (unless they follow my steps and make it really big!).

Of course, our description of Wall Street isn't about good or bad people. It's about the structures that allow our nation's wealth to be siphoned off by just a handful of people. It's about what happens to wealth when we fail to regulate finance. It's about what happens to our income distribution when we allow the nation's wealth to accumulate in the financial sector. It's about the ungodly belief structure that says that wealth is always the best sign of true worth.

Many talented college graduates are drawn into the wild chase for the vast riches that our system allows people in the financial industry to acquire. If we change this system, more bright people will go into other professions that contribute much more to the common good.

Without systemic reforms our obscene income distribution will grow even uglier. Poorly regulated financial casinos will again run wild, imperiling us all at some point in the future. The middle-class dream just might fade from memory, a relic from an odd and fortunate moment in American history.

This turbulent future is almost perfect for those in the million-an-hour club: the more chaos, the more financial possibilities for the shrewd, the brave, and the brilliant. Yet if we fail to rein in the financial industry, we'll probably be reading more stories like the one in the *New York Times* on October 24, 2011, about "surging poverty" in the suburbs. New research shows that in at least nine major metropolitan areas, more than half of the poor now live in the suburbs (Tavernise 2011).

Who could have imagined that we'd see food banks in suburbs, once the living embodiment of America's post–World War II aspirations?

In fact, the old-fashioned suburban ideal is now reserved for those who can afford to live in gated communities. That's about the only way to wall yourself off from the general urban, suburban, and rural blight. That may be the price we pay for allowing the formation of the million-an-hour club. That may be the America we are leaving to our kids.

For the last thirty years, we've run an experiment to find out whether cutting taxes on the rich and deregulating finance would create a bigger, stronger economy for us all. The experiment failed spectacularly.

Yet, financial elites are brilliant at evading all responsibility (and at convincing themselves they were not responsible). They've been quite successful at blaming the government for what happened—or denouncing regulations or scapegoating unions or poor people who couldn't afford their mortgages. Making a million an *hour* means never having to say you're sorry.

So how does it feel when you're in the 1 percent, and suddenly everyone's vilifying you? It doesn't feel good. My Wall Street neighbors dote on their children and contribute to charities. They also enjoy all of the creature comforts they can afford and feel that they are contributing mightily to our nation's success. Many whom I know well are loving, caring people, but they are also highly competitive and feel that they've played by the rules and won. They took risks and believe that their rewards are justified. Yet now, for the first time since the 1960s, their success is being challenged. The rules they have lived by are under fire.

The anti–Wall Street framework may be with us for a long time, and it may never sit right for those who identify with financial elites. It draws a sharp line that splits us apart. Yet that splitting did not start with Occupy Wall Street. It started with the financial billionaires who are grabbing a million dollars an *hour*. It started with banks and hedge funds that set up synthetic CDOs that were designed to fail. It started with morally bankrupt ratings agencies that sold AAA ratings to the highest bidder. It started with mortgage companies that pushed high-risk, high-interest mortgages on unsuspecting clients. It started with the insider traders, the rumormongers, the high-frequency predators, and all of the others who violate the spirit and the letter of the few financial rules that remain. If any of that bothers you, welcome to the 99 percent.

If not, enjoy your quest for a million an hour, and pray you don't get caught.

ACKNOWLEDGMENTS

Writing social commentary, at least for me, combines solitude with community as the effort builds from staring at an empty screen to collaboration with researchers, editors, and other colleagues. What binds us together is a deep passion to take on the injustices that permeate our society. I'm forever grateful to Laura McClure and David Dembo for their excellent editing, research, creativity, and rock-solid commitment to creating a more just and sustainable world. Whatever I write, they make it better—much better. It's an honor to work with them. Another crucial team member is my agent and friend, Bill Lee, who skillfully nurtured this project from idea to reality. And special thanks to our newest collaborator, Eric Nelson, our Wiley editor whose guidance, insight, and humor added enormous value to the effort. Many thanks also to the exceptional production and marketing teams at Wiley who so professionally moved this book into the real world. Also, special thanks to my good friend Ted "Ding" Robinson, who, as a keen student of Wall Street scamming, provided expert guidance from the investor point of view.

I also am deeply indebted to my partners at the Labor Institute—Sally Silvers, Rodrigo Toscano, and Jim Young—for their ongoing support. They make it possible for me to write, and I can't thank them enough for that precious opportunity.

Most important, all of this springs from my family, whose love inspires everything I do. My wife, Dr. Sharon Szymanski, the real economist in our family, provides never-ending support, guidance, inspiration, and powerful ideas for these projects. Our children, Chester and Lilah, give us all the motivation we need to work for a more just society. I also thank my sister Evelyn for her love and for showing us what good reporting and writing are all about.

Finally, I sincerely thank all the generous and gracious trade union members and their leaders who have invited me into their conferences and meetings to conduct workshops and exchange ideas. Hopefully, this book will contribute in some small way to improving the lives of the 99 percent.

References

Step 1: Reach for the Stars—and Beyond

"2011 Preqin Global Investor Report: Hedge Funds." http://www.preqin.com/docs/reports/Preqin_Global_Investor_Report_Hedge_Funds.pdf.

Asness, Cliff. 2004. "An Alternative Future, Part II: An Exploration of the Role of Hedge Funds." *Journal of Portfolio Management* 31 (1): 8–23.

Bricker, Jesse, Arthur B. Kennickell, Kevin B. Moore, and John Sabelhaus. 2012. "Changes in U.S. Family Finances from 2007 to 2010: Evidence from the Survey of Consumer Finances." *Federal Reserve Bulletin* 98 (2): 1–5. http://federalreserve.gov/pubs/bulletin/2012/PDF/scf12.pdf.

Evans, Heidi. 2009. "Brain Surgeons Thomas Milhorat, Paolo Bolognese Suspended for Abandoning Anesthetized Patient in OR." *New York Daily News*, May 5. http://articles.nydailynews.com/2009–05–06/local/17923759_1_surgeons-thomas-milhorat-patient.

"A Family Affair: Intergenerational Social Mobility across OECD Countries." 2010. *Economic Policy Reforms: Goring for Growth*. Part II, chap. 5. Paris: OECD Publications. http://www.oecd.org/dataoecd/2/7/45002641.pdf.

Norton, Michael I., and Dan Ariely. January 2011. "Building a Better America—One Wealth Quintile at a Time." *Perspectives on Psychological Science* 6 (1): 9–12. doi:10.1177/1745691610393524.

Step 2: Take, Don't Make

Ahmed, Azam. 2011. "Paulson Tells His Investors: 'We Made a Mistake.'" *New York Times*, October 12.

Chen, Joseph, Samuel Hanson, Harrison Hong, and Jeremy C. Stein. February 2008. "Do Hedge Funds Profit from Mutual-Fund Distress?" Working Paper 13786. National Bureau of Economic Research. http://www.nber.org/papers/w13786.pdf.

Larkin, Nicholas. 2012. "Gold Bulls Expand as Billionaire Paulson Says Buy." Bloomberg. February 17. http://www.bloomberg.com/news/2012–02–17/gold-traders-get-more-bullish-as-billionaire-paulson-says-buy-commodities.html.

Mallaby, Sebastian. 2007. "Hands Off Hedge Funds," *Foreign Affairs* 86 (1): 91–101.

McCullough, Keith, and Rich Blake. 2010. *Diary of a Hedge Fund Manager: From the Top, to the Bottom, and Back Again*. Hoboken, NJ: Wiley.

Riordon, William L. 1905. *Plunkitt of Tammany Hall*. Reprint: Lawrence, KS: Digireads.com Publishing.

Strachman, Daniel A. 2008. *The Long and Short of Hedge Funds: A Complete Guide to Hedge Fund Evaluation and Investing*. Hoboken, NJ: Wiley.

Taub, Stephen. 2011. "The Rich List." *Absolute Return Alpha*, April 1. http://www.absolutereturn-alpha.com/Article/2796749/Search/The-Rich-List.html?Keywords=rich+list.

Wilson, Richard C. 2010. "Appaloosa Management Nets $6.5 Billion Profits in 2009." Hedge Fund Blogger (blog). http://richard-wilson.blogspot.com/2010/01/appaloosa-management-profits-2009.html.

Zuckerman, Gregory. 2009. "Fund Boss Made $7 Billion in the Panic." *Wall Street Journal*, December 23. http://online.wsj.com/article/SB126135805328299533.html.

Step 3: Rip Off Entire Countries Because That's Where the Money Is

Madrick, Jeff. 2011. *Age of Greed: The Triumph of Finance and the Decline of America, 1970 to the Present*. New York: Knopf.

Mallaby, Sebastian. 2007. "Hands Off Hedge Funds." *Foreign Affairs* 86 (1): 91–101.

———. 2010. *More Money Than God: Hedge Funds and the Making of the New Elite*. New York: Penguin.

Peter Hanns Reill and Balázs A. Szelényi, eds. 2011. *Cores, Peripheries, and Globalization: Essays in Honor of Ivan T. Berend*. New York: Central European Press.

Reinhart, Carmen, and Kenneth Rogoff. 2008. "Banking Crises: An Equal Opportunity Menace." National Bureau of Economic Research, Working Paper No. 14587. http://www.nber.org/papers/w14587.

Step 4: Use Other People's Money

Johnston, David Cay. 2009. "Is Our Tax System Helping Us Create Wealth?" *Tax Notes*, December 21.

———. 2010. "Tax Rates for Top 400 Earners Fell as Income Soars, IRS Data Show." *Tax Notes*, February 18.

"President Jackson's Veto Message Regarding the Bank of the United States; July 10, 1832." *The Avalon Project: Documents in Law, History, and Diplomacy*, Lillian Goldman Library, Yale Law School. http://avalon.law.yale.edu/19th_century/ajveto01.asp.

Roubini, Nouriel. 2007. "Credit Derivatives, Hedge Funds and Leverage Ratios of 50: The Credit House of Cards." *EconoMonitor*, January 20. http://www.economonitor.com/nouriel/2007/01/20/credit-derivatives-hedge-funds-and-leverage-ratios-of-50-the-credit-house-of-cards/.

Step 5: Create Something You Can Pretend Is Low Risk and High Return

Drobny, Steven. 2011. *The Invisible Hands: Top Hedge Fund Traders on Bubbles, Crashes, and Real Money.* Hoboken, NJ: Wiley.

Leopold, Les. 2009. *The Looting of America: How Wall Street's Game of Fantasy Finance Destroyed Our Jobs, Pensions and Prosperity and What We Can Do about It.* White River Junction, VT: Chelsea Green. First chapter available online at http://www.alternet.org/economy/140208/the_looting_of_america:_how_wall_street_fleeced_millions_from_wisconsin_schools.

Prins, Nomi. 2009. *It Takes a Pillage: Behind the Bailouts, Bonuses and Backroom Deals from Washington to Wall Street.* Hoboken, NJ: Wiley.

United States Senate Permanent Subcommittee on Investigations, Committee on Homeland Security and Governmental Affairs, Carl Levin, Chairman, Tom Coburn, Ranking Minority Member. April 13, 2011. *Wall Street and the Financial Crisis: Anatomy of a Financial Collapse.* Majority and Minority Staff Report, Washington. http://www.ft.com/cms/fc7d55c8-661a-11e0-9d40-00144feab49a.pdf.

Zuckerman, Gregory. 2009. *The Greatest Trade Ever: The Behind-the-Scenes Story of How John Paulson Defined Wall Street and Made Financial History.* New York: Crown Business.

Step 6: Rig Your Bets

"Blankfein Says He's Just Doing 'God's Work.'" 2009. DealBook, *New York Times*, November 9. http://dealbook.nytimes.com/2009/11/09/goldman-chief-says-he-is-just-doing-gods-work/.

Eisinger, Jesse, and Jake Bernstein. 2010. "The Magnetar Trade: How One Hedge Fund Helped Keep the Bubble Going." *Propublica.org*, April 9. http://www.propublica.org/article/the-magnetar-trade-how-one-hedge-fund-helped-keep-the-housing-bubble-going/single.

Smith, Yves. 2010. *ECONned: How Unenlightened Self-Interest Undermined Democracy and Corrupted Capitalism.* New York: Palgrave Macmillan.

Taibbi, Matt. 2010. "The Great American Bubble Machine." *Rolling Stone*, April 5. http://www.rollingstone.com/politics/news/the-great-american-bubble-machine-20100405.

United States Senate Permanent Subcommittee on Investigations, Committee on Homeland Security and Governmental Affairs, Carl Levin, Chairman, Tom Coburn, Ranking Minority Member. April 13, 2011. *Wall Street and the Financial Crisis: Anatomy of a Financial Collapse.* Majority and Minority Staff

Report, Washington. http://www.ft.com/cms/fc7d55c8-661a-11e0-9d40-00144 feab49a.pdf.

Zuckerman, Gregory. 2009. *The Greatest Trade Ever: The Behind-the-Scenes Story of How John Paulson Defied Wall Street and Made Financial History*. New York: Crown Business.

Step 7: Don't Say Anything Remotely Truthful

Bagley, Judd. 2007. "Jim Cramer on Market Manipulation: In His Own Words." http://antisocialmedia.net/antisocial-multimedia/jim-cramer-on-market-manipulation-in-his-own-words.

Cramer, James J. 2002. *Confessions of a Street Addict*. New York: Simon and Schuster.

"Jim Cramer and Aaron Task." December 22, 2006. Video clip. Accessed October 5, 2008. YouTube. http://www.youtube.com/watch?v=EaNuRsNA0OU.

Johnson, Bruce. 2010. *Hedge Fund Fraud Casebook*. Hoboken, NJ: Wiley.

Lack, Simon. 2012. *The Hedge Fund Mirage: The Illusion of Big Money and Why It's Too Good to Be True*. Hoboken, NJ: Wiley.

Mallaby, Sebastian. 2007 "Hands Off Hedge Funds." *Foreign Affairs* 86 (1): 91–101.

Marshall, Richard D. 2009. "Rumor-Mongering in the Crosshairs: Crackdown Raises Legal and Policy Issues." *New York Law Journal*, February 9. http://www.ropes gray.com/files/Publication/45ae8b87-1840-4c6e-9ad8-02d770a05439/Presentation/PublicationAttachment/b85b165c-daf5-4b93-a89f-036d7b4b0590/Ropes Gray_Article_MarshallNYLJRumorMongering.pdf.

Stout, Lynn. 2010. "How Hedge Funds Create Criminals." *Harvard Business Review*, December 13. http://blogs.hbr.org/cs/2010/12/how_hedge_funds_create_crimina .html.

Step 8: Have the Right People Whispering in Your Ear

Ahmed, Azam, and Peter Lattman. 2012. "P. & G. Takes Center Stage at Gupta Trial." DealBook, *New York Times*, May 29. http://dealbook.nytimes.com/2012/05/29/p-g-takes-center-stage-at-gupta-trial/.

Appelbaum, Binyamin. 2012. "Family Net Worth Drops to Level of Early '90s, Fed Says." *New York Times*, June 11. http://www.nytimes.com/2012/06/12/business/economy/family-net-worth-drops-to-level-of-early-90s-fed-says.html.

Boudreaux, Donald. 2009. "Learning to Love Insider Trading." *Wall Street Journal*, October 24. http://online.wsj.com/article/SB10001424052748704224004 574489324091790350.html.

Duhigg, Charles, and Peter Lattman. 2011. "Judge Says Hedge Funds May Have Used Inside Information." DealBook. *New York Times*, September 14. http://dealbook.nytimes.com/2011/09/14/judge-says-hedge-funds-may-have-used-inside-information/.

Eaglesham, Jean. "U.S. Probes Rate Cutting Trades." 2011. *Wall Street Journal*, September 20. http://online.wsj.com/article/SB1000142405311190410670457658 1133063805062.html.

ESMA. 2011. "ESMA Promotes Harmonised Regulatory Action on Short-Selling in the EU." Public Statement, August 11. http://www.esma.europa.eu/system/files/ESMA_2011_266_Public_statement_on_short_selling.pdf.

Fisher, Jonathan. 2009. "Stock Market Investing: Is Insider Trading Such a Bad Thing?" *Telegraph* (UK), June 10. http://www.telegraph.co.uk/finance/personalfinance/investing/5492729/Stock-market-investing-Is-insider-trading-such-a-bad-thing.html.

Lattman, Peter. 2011. "Guilty Plea Expected in Hedge Fund Case." DealBook, *New York Times*, May 27. http://dealbook.nytimes.com/2011/05/27/guilty-plea-expected-in-hedge-fund-case/.

Lattman, Peter, and Andrew Ross Sorkin. 2011. "Figure in Insider Case Sought to Quit Goldman." DealBook, *New York Times*, March 13. http://dealbook.nytimes.com/2011/03/13/associate-in-insider-case-sought-to-quit-goldman/.

Packer, George. 2011. "A Dirty Business." *New Yorker*, June 27. http://www.newyorker.com/reporting/2011/06/27/110627fa_fact_packer?currentPage=all.

"SEC Expands Sweeping Investigation of Market Manipulation." 2008. Securities and Exchange Commission Press Release. September 19. http://www.sec.gov/news/press/2008/2008-214.htm.

"SEC Halts Short Selling of Financial Stocks to Protect Investors and Markets." 2008. Securities and Exchange Commission Press Release. September 19. http://www.sec.gov/news/press/2008/2008-211.htm.

Teitelbaum, Richard. 2011. "How Paulson Gave Hedge Funds Advance Word of Fannie Mae Rescue." *Bloomberg*, November 29. http://www.bloomberg.com/news/2011-11-29/how-henry-paulson-gave-hedge-funds-advance-word-of-2008-fannie-mae-rescue.html.

United States v. Raj Rajaratnam. October 13, 2011. S2 09-CR-1184 (RJH). United States District Court, Southern District of New York. Transcript.

Step 9: Bet on the Race *after* You Know Who Wins

Arnuk, Sal L., and Joseph Saluzzi. 2012. *Broken Markets: How High Frequency Trading and Predatory Practices on Wall Street are Destroying Investor Confidence.* Upper Saddle River, NJ: FT Press, BrokenMarkets.com.

———. n.d. "What Ails Us about High Frequency Trading?" A Themis Trading LLC Mini White Paper. http://www.themistrading.com/article_files/0000/0508/What_Ails_Us_About_High_Frequency_Trading_--_Final_2_10-5-09.pdf.

Creswell, Julie. 2010. "Speedy New Traders Make Waves Far from Wall St." *New York Times*, May 16. http://www.nytimes.com/2010/05/17/business/17trade.html?dbk.

Dichev, Ilia D., Kelly Huang, and Dexin Zhou. 2011. "The Dark Side of Trading." Working Paper. April 3. http://www.accountancy.smu.edu.sg/research/seminar/pdf/IliaDICHEV_paper.pdf.

Haldane, Andrew G. 2011. "The Race to Zero." Speech given at the International Economic Association Sixteenth World Congress, Beijing, China, July 8. http://www.bankofengland.co.uk/publications/Documents/speeches/2011/speech509.pdf.

Johnson, Neil, Guannan Zhao, Eric Hunsader, Jing Meng, Amith Ravindar, Spencer Carran, and Brian Tivnan. 2012. "Financial Black Swans Driven by Ultrafast Machine Ecology." Unpublished manuscript, February 7. http://arxiv .org/ftp/arxiv/papers/1202/1202.1448.pdf.

Perrow, Charles. 1999. *Normal Accidents: Living with High-Risk Technologies*. Princeton, NJ: Princeton University Press.

Step 10: Milk Millions in Special Tax Breaks

Altucher, James. 2006. *SuperCash: The New Hedge Fund Capitalism*. Hoboken, NJ: Wiley.

Comstock, Courtney. 2010. "Steve Schwarzman on Tax Increases: 'It's Like When Hitler Invaded Poland.'" *Business Insider*, August 16. http://articles.business insider.com/2010-08-16/wall_street/30045366_1_tax-hikes-taxes-on-private-equity-poland.

Cramer, James J. 2002. *Confessions of a Street Addict*. New York: Simon & Schuster.

Fleischer, Victor. 2008. "Two and Twenty: Taxing Partnership Profits in Private Equity Funds." *New York University Law Review* 83 (1): 1–59.

Hindery Jr., Leo. 2011. "Carried Interest: A Very Big Wolf in Sheep's Clothing." *Huffington Post*, September 20. http://www.huffingtonpost.com/leo-hindery-jr/ carried-interest-a-very-b_b_971542.html?ir=Yahoo.

Holtz-Eakin, Douglas, Cameron Smith, and Winston Stoody. 2010. "The Tax Treatment of Carried Interest." American Action Forum. http://americanac tionforum.org/files/TaxTreatmentCarriedInterest.pdf.

Lerer, Lisa. 2007. "Professor's Proposal Angers Wall Street." *Politico.com*, October 30. http://www.politico.com/news/stories/1007/6594.html.

Private Equity Growth Capital Council. 2007. "Private Equity and the Treatment of Carried Interest: An Overview." May 4. http://www.pegcc .org/issues/comment-letters/private-equity-and-the-treatment-of-carried-interest-an-overview/.

Smith, Ben. 2011. "Carried Interest Break Gets Democratic Backers." *Politico .com*, July 18. http://www.politico.com/pdf/PPM192_obama_carried_interest_ letter_final.pdf.

Waldman, Paul. "Liberals for Hedge-Fund Manager Rights." *American Prospect*. http://prospect.org/article/liberals-hedge-fund-manager-rights. Accessed July 6, 2012.

Step 11: Claim That Limits on Speculation Will Kill Jobs

Rogoff, Kenneth. 2011. "The Wrong Tax for Europe." Project Syndicate, October 3. http://www.project-syndicate.org/commentary/the-wrong-tax-for-europe.

Suskind, Ron. 2011. *Confidence Men: Wall Street, Washington, and the Education of a President*. New York: HarperCollins.

Tobin, James. 1978. "A Proposal for Internatoinal Monetary Reform." Cowles Foundation Paper, reprinted from *Eastern Economic Journal* 4 (3–4), July/ October. http://cowles.econ.yale.edu/P/cp/p04b/p0495.pdf.

Woodward, Bob. 1994. *The Agenda: Inside the Clinton White House*. New York: Simon and Schuster.

Step 12: Distract the Dissenters

Leopold, Les. 2010. "Obama Is No FDR, We're No Mass Movement." *Huffington Post*, February 10. http://www.huffingtonpost.com/les-leopold/obama-is-no-fdr-were-no-m_b_457452.html.

Conclusion

Tavernise, Sabrina. 2011. "Outside Cleveland, Snapshots of Poverty's Surge in the Suburbs." *New York Times*, October 24. http://www.nytimes.com/2011/10/25/us/suburban-poverty-surge-challenges-communities.html?_r=2.

INDEX

NOTE: Page numbers in *italics* refer to illustrations.

Abacus 2007-ACI (Goldman Sachs), 105–111
ACA Management, 108–110
"activist" hedge funds, 21, 190–192
Advantage Plus, 31–32
African Americans. *See* minorities
Agenda, The (Woodward), 208
AIG, 44–45, 92, 103, 110, 139–140
"alpha" return rate, 19
Alternative Minimum Tax (AMT), 185
Altucher, James, 190–191
American Action Forum, 197
American Prospect, 200–202
Appaloosa Management LP, 25–30, 154–155
Apple Inc., 25, 27, 123, 125–127
arbitrage, 42–43
Ariely, Dan, 22
Arnuk, Sal
   Broken Markets: How High Frequency Trading and Predatory Practices on Wall Street Are Destroying Investor Confidence, 181
   on high-frequency trading and "flash crashes," 172, 177
   "Toxic Equity Trading Order Flow on Wall Street," 165
   "What Ails Us about High Frequency Trading?", 175–176

asymmetrical information, 50, 148–149
athletes, income of, 8–9, 18
Aurelius Capital Management, 154–155
authors, income of, 10

Baker, Dean, 209–216, 218–219
banking industry, income of, 11–12, 18.
   See also hedge funds; *individual names of banks*
Bank of America, 27–30
Bank of England, 49–57, 174, 204
BayView, 192
Bear Stearns, 87, 156
Berliner, Paul, 150
Bernanke, Ben, 73
Bernstein, Jake, 80, 98, 99
betting, by hedge funds, 30–32, 38–41
Bharara, Preet, 143, 154
Blackstone Group, 184
Blake, Rich, 42
Blankfein, Lloyd, 97, 141
Bloomberg News, 87, 156–157
Bretton Woods conference (1944), 57–59, 64–66, 67, 207. *See also* income distribution
British Financial Services Authority (FSA), 150–151
Brodsky, Reed M., 138

251

Broken Markets: How High Frequency Trading and Predatory Practices on Wall Street Are Destroying Investor Confidence (Saluzzi, Arnuk), 181

Buffett, Warren, 14, 142, 148–149

Bush, George W.
  Fannie Mae and Freddie Mac, 156–157
  housing bubble and, 90
  Skull and Bones membership of, 183
  tax cuts by, 69, 196
  Wall Street colleagues of, 28

BusinessInsider.com, 186

Carran, Spencer, 180

carried interest loophole
  arguments for and against, 196–202
  capital gains and, 184–185
  defined, 185–189
  See also taxes

Carter, Jimmy, 69, 195

cell phone market, Cramer on, 123–128

Centerbridge Partners, 155

Center for Economic and Policy Research, 209–216

CEO income
  highest-paid corporate CEOs, 10–12, 18
  worker pay gap, 5–6

Chen, Joseph, 39

Citigroup, 27–30, 83

Clinton, Bill, 196, 208

CNBC, 117, 125

Cohen, Steven A., 143

Cold War
  taxes and, 194–195
  wages and productivity, 65–66
  See also income distribution; productivity

"co-location," 163

Commodities Corporation, 51

communism. *See* Cold War

Community Readjustment Act, 89

Confessions of a Street Addict (Cramer), 114, 115, 128–131, 133–134

Confidence Men (Suskind), 219

Congressional Progressive Caucus, 200–202

corporate CEOs. *See* CEO income

correlation trade, 88

Countrywide, 37, 84

Cox, Christopher, 151

Cramer, Jim
  "activist" hedge funds and, 191–192
  biographical information, 115–118
  Confessions of a Street Addict, 114, 115, 128–131, 133–134
  Cramer and Company (Cramer-Berkowitz) hedge fund of, 117, 118–121
  Mad Money (CNBC), 114
  TheStreet.com, 114, 116, 121–128
  Task's interview of, 121–128

Cramer, Karen, 115, 119–121

credit default swaps (CDS), 44–46, 90–93, 110–111

Creswell, Julie, 173–174

"criminogenic" environment, 132, 222

crossing market, 161

currency pegs, 51, 56

"dark pools," 160–166

"Dark Side of Trading, The" (Dichev, Huang, Zhou), 174–175

debt
  free market and, 74
  government deficit argument, 225–227

"deepening the market," 40–41

deregulation
  housing bubble and, 89–90
  income distribution and, 63, 69, 70–72, 74–76
  by industry, 68
  innovation and, 35

derivatives market, 69

Diary of a Hedge Fund Manager
    (McCullough, Blake), 42

Dichev, Ilia D., 174–175

Dimon, Jamie, 98

directors/producers, income of, 7, 18

dissent, 221–236
    "financial amnesia," 234–236
    government deficit argument,
        225–227
    libel claims and, 222–225
    Occupy Wall Street, 219, 227–230
    progressive nongovernmental orga-
        nizations, 230–234

distribution of wealth. *See* income
    distribution

doctors, income of, 13

"Do Hedge Funds Profit from Mutual
    Fund Distress?" (Chen), 39

Dow Jones Industrial Average, 140

Druckenmiller, Stan, 50, 52

Duke University, 22

ECONned (Smith), 102

economic fairness, 1–3, 22–23

economic productivity. *See*
    productivity

Eisenhower, Dwight, 66, 194

Eisinger, Jesse, 80, 98, 99

electronic communications networks
    (ECNs), 176–178

England
    Bank of England and Soros, 49–57,
        204
    financial transaction tax of,
        214, 215

Enron, 145–146

entertainment industry, income of,
    6–10, 18

equity tranche
    defined, 85, 87–88
    Magnetar and, 100–101

European Court of Human Rights, 55

European Exchange Rate Mechanism
    (ERM), 49–57

European Securities and Market
    Authority, 152, 153

European Union
    Euro and Soros, 49–57, 204
    financial transaction tax and, 211,
        216

Fairfield Greenwich, 130–131

Fairfield Sentry, 20

Fannie Mae, 89, 156–157

FBI, 38, 142–143

Federal Reserve
    Great Recession of 2008 and, 28, 31,
        141–142
    income distribution and, 63, 73
    New York Federal Reserve and
        LCTM, 118
    productivity and innovation, 36

"feeder funds," 20

"financial amnesia," 234–236

financial risk, hedge funds and,
    43–46

financial sector, deregulation of,
    68. *See also* Glass-Steagall Act

financial sector *vs.* nonfinancial
    sector yearly compensation
    (2010 dollars), 72

Financial Services Authority (FSA)
    (Britain), 150–151

financial transaction tax, 204–220
    financial speculation and,
        204–209
    liquidity and, 216–219
    proposal for, 209–216

"flash crashes," 171–177, 180.
    See also high-frequency
    trading (HFT)

Fleischer, Victor, 185–189, 190,
    192–193, 196–198, 201–202

Ford, Gerald, 195

fragmentation, 174–178

Freddie Mac, 89, 156–157
free-market economic theory
    ERM and Soros, 53–54
    Friedman on, 68–69, 146–147, 196
    high-frequency trading and, 175
    income distribution and, 71
    insider trading and, 146–147
    taxes and, 196
    toxic assets and, 29
Fried, Frank, Harris, Shriver &
        Jacobson, 154
Friedman, Milton, 68–69, 146–147, 196
front-running, 38–41, 130–131
"funds of funds," 20

Galleon, 136
Gates, Bill, 14
Geithner, Timothy, 28, 142, 217–219
gender, income gap and, 10, 13–14
General Theory (Keynes), 210
Germany, currency of, 49, 52
Glass-Steagall Act
    dissolution of, 69
    inception of, 58
gold
    gold standard, 60, 67, 207
    Paulson and Company, 30–32
Goldman Sachs
    Abacus 2007-ACI, 105–111
    Cramer and, 115, 119
    Greatest Trade Ever and, 80, 83
    Gupta and, 140–142
    housing bubble and, 97–98, 105–111
    Paulson and, 156–157
    Rajaratnam and, 145–149
government deficit argument,
        225–227
Government National Mortgage
        Association (Ginnie Mae),
        101–102
Great Depression
    Bretton Woods conference (1944)
        and, 57–59, 64–66, 67, 207

taxes and, 194, 195
Greatest Trade Ever, The (Zuckerman),
        79–80
Greatest Trade Ever (GTE), 78–81
Great Recession of 2008
    credit default swaps, 44–46
    government deficit argument and,
        225–227
    hedge funds and, 27–30, 31
    insider trading and, 139–144,
        155–157
    See also housing bubble
Greece
    high-frequency trading and,
        171–174, 180
    PIIGS (Portugal, Ireland, Italy,
        Greece, Spain), 54–57
Greenspan, Alan, 73, 121, 196
Gupta, Rajat, 140–142, 148, 155

Haldane, Andrew, 174
Harvard Business Review, 132
Harvard Business School, 22
HedgeFundBlogger.com, 27
Hedge Fund Fraud Casebook (Johnson),
        129–130
Hedge Fund Mirage, The (Lack),
        130–131
hedge funds, 25–47
    "activist" hedge funds, 21, 190–192
    as betting, 30–32, 38–41
    Bretton Woods conference (1944)
        and, 57–59
    defined, 19–22
    deregulation and, 63, 68, 69, 70–72,
        74–76
    economic fairness and, 1–3, 22–23
    financial risk and, 43–46
    housing bubble role of, 88–90 (*See
        also* housing bubble)
    inception of, 59–61
    influence on national currencies,
        48–57

insider trading as business model of, 154–155 (*See also* insider trading)
leverage, 63, 72–74
liquidity and, 38–41
managers' income, 1–3, 16–19, 25–30, 117
managers' personality traits, 131–134
price efficiency and, 41–43
private equity funds, venture capital funds, and, 190–192
productivity and, 32–38, *63,* 63–72, *71, 72*
See also high-frequency trading (HFT); housing bubble
high-frequency trading (HFT), 159–182
cost of, 166–170
defined, 159–166
financial transaction tax and, 216–219
"flash crashes" from, 171–177, 180
fragmentation and, 174–178
risk of, 178–181
taxes and, 192
high-speed trading, 43
high-water mark, 117
Hindery, Leo, Jr., 199
Holtz-Eakin, Douglas, 197
Holwell, Richard, 136–139, 144
housing bubble, 78–96, 97–112
credit default swap (CDS) and, 90–93
equity tranche of, 85, 87–88
Goldman Sachs and, 97–98, 105–111
Greatest Trade Ever (GTE), 78–81
interest rates and, 85
Magnetar and, 98–105
mortgage-backed securities and, 85
predatory lending and, 84, 88–90
short selling and, 93–95
subprime bonds, 89, 102–103, 105, 107, 109–111

synthetic CDOs and, 81–83, 86–87
"How Hedge Funds Create Criminals" (Stout), 132
Huang, Kelly, 174–175
Huffington Post, 199, 223–224, 228
Hunsader, Eric, 180

incentive tax options (ISOs), 188
income distribution, 5–24, 62–77
celebrities' income, 6–10, 18
CEO and worker pay gap, 5–6
CEOs' income, 5–6, 10–12, 18
deregulation and, 63, 68, 69, 70 72, 74–76
doctors' income, 13
economic fairness and, 22–23
gender gap, 10, 13–14
hedge-fund managers' income, 1–3, 16–19
hedge funds, defined, 19–22
lawyers' income, 12–13, 18
leverage and, 63, 72–74
ongoing issues of, 237–239
productivity growth and wage gains, *63,* 63–72, *71, 72*
top one percent of U.S. population, *71*
U.S. income disparity, 14–16, 18
income tax. *See* taxes
individual responsibility, predatory lending and, 89
inflation, gold and, 30–32
innovation, productivity and, 34–38
insider trading, 136–158
arguments in favor of, 145–149
Great Recession of 2008 and, 139–144, 155–157
as hedge-fund business model, 154–155
Rajaratnam and, 136–139, 140–144, 145, 155–157
rumormongering and, 124–125, 149–154

insurable interest, 91–92
interest rates
    Abacus 2007-ACI (Goldman Sachs)
        and, 108
    housing bubble and, 85
    insurable interest, 91–92
    See also carried interest loophole
International Swaps & Derivatives
    Association (ISDA), 55–56

Jackson, Andrew, 75–76
jobs
    "financial amnesia" and, 234–236
    government deficit and, 226–227
    taxes and, 200–202
Johnson, Bruce, 129–130
Johnson, Lyndon B., 195
Johnson, Neil, 180
Johnson, Rob, 50
Jolie, Angelina, 10, 13
Jones, Paul, 51
JP Morgan Chase
    Greatest Trade Ever and, 80, 83
    hedge funds of, 21–22
    housing bubble and, 98, 99–100, 111

Kennedy, John F., 195
Keynes, John Maynard, 195, 210
King, Martin Luther, Jr., 236
Koch brothers, 14
Kovner, Bruce, 51
Krauss, Melvyn, 53
Kristof, Nicholas, 219

Lack, Simon, 130–131
lawyers, income of, 12–13, 18
Lee, Bill, 145, 224
Lehman Brothers, 139–140, 141,
    149–150
Leopold, Les
    libel claim against, 223–224
    The Looting of America, 79,
        81, 94, 102

*The Man Who Hated Work and Loved
    Labor,* 160
"Obama's No FDR, We're No Mass
    Movement," 228
leverage
    defined, 41
    income distribution and, 63,
        72–74
    Magnetar and, 103
Levin, Carl, 189
libel, claims of, 222–225
libertarianism, 68–69
liquidity
    financial transaction tax and,
        213–214, 216–219
    hedge funds and, 38–41
    high-frequency trading and,
        167–170, 174
"long" buying, 94–95, 108. *See also*
    housing bubble
Long-Term Capital management, 73,
    118–119
Looting of America, The (Leopold), 79,
    81, 94, 102

Mad Money (CNBC), 114
Madoff, Bernie, 19–20, 130–131, 137
Magnetar, 88, 98–105
Major, John, 50, 52. *See also* England
Mallaby, Sebastian
    on hedge fund income, 32–34, 36
    on hedge funds and risk, 43–44, 45
    on insider trading, 113–114
    on liquidity, 38, 40
    *More Money Than God: Hedge
        Funds and the Making of a New
        Elite,* 51, 52
*Man Who Hated Work and Loved Labor,
    The* (Leopold), 160
McCullough, Keith, 42
McKinsey and Company, 140
Meng, Jing, 180
mezzanine tranches, defined, 85

middle class, income of, 5–6, 14–16, 18. *See also* income distribution
Milhorat, Thomas, 13
minorities
  predatory lending to, 89
  wages of, 65
More Money Than God: Hedge Funds and the Making of a New Elite (Mallaby), 51, 52
Morgenthau, Henry, 57–59
mortgage-backed securities, 85. *See also* housing bubble
movie stars, income of, 10, 18
musicians/groups, income of, 8, 18

Naked Capitalism. See Smith, Yves
naked credit default swap (CDS), 93
"naked shorts," 152
Narang, Manoj, 173–174
Narvik (Norway), U.S. housing bubble and, 103–104
National Nurses United, 219
neoliberalism, 69
New Yorker, 144
New York Federal Reserve, 118
New York Stock Exchange, 38
New York Times, 154, 173–174, 186, 219, 238
Nixon, Richard, 60, 67, 195, 207
nonsupervisory weekly wages, productivity and (U.S., 2012 dollars), *63,* 65
Normal Accidents (Perrow), 178–179, 180
Norton, Michael, 22

Obama, Barack
  Great Recession of 2008 and, 225–226
  JP Morgan Chase and, 98
  "Obama's No FDR, We're No Mass Movement" (Leopold), 228
  on taxes, 186, 189, 199, 217–219

2008 election and, 231
2010 election and, 232
Wall Street colleagues of, 28
"Obama's No FDR, We're No Mass Movement" (Leopold), 228
Occupy Wall Street, 219, 227–230
oil, 31, 67, 68
OPEC, 67
Owl Creek Asset Management, 155

Packer, George, 144
PATCO, 69
Paulson, Henry, 28, 79–80, 156–157
Paulson, John
  Goldman-Sachs Abacus 2007-ACI and, 105–111
  income of, 16
  Paulson and Company, 25, 30–32, 106–111
pension funds, 20, 87–88
Peretz, Marty, 115, 122
"Perfect Hedge," 142–143
Perlstein, Steve, 219
Perrow, Charles, 178–179, 180
Peterson, Peter, 184
PIIGS (Portugal, Ireland, Italy, Greece, Spain), 54–57
"pinging," 168, 216–217
Pisani, Bob, 125
Plunkitt, George Washington, 29–30
"Poisons in Your Pensions" *(Bloomberg News),* 87
Polis, Jared, 200–202
Politico.com, 200
Pollack v. Farmers' Loan & Trust, 193
Pollin, Bob, 211
Ponzi schemes, 20
pound sterling, 49–57, 204
poverty, suburbia and, 238
predatory lending, housing bubble and, 84, 88–90
price efficiency, hedge funds and, 41–43
price fixing, Cramer on, 127–128

private equity funds, 183–185, 190.
    See also carried interest
    loophole
Private Equity Growth Capital
    Council, 196, 199, 202
productivity
    growth of, and wage gains, *63,*
    63–72, 71, 72 (*See also* income
    distribution)
    hedge funds and, 32–38
progressive nongovernmental
    organizations, 230–234
ProPublica, 98, 99
"pump and dump," 149

quantitative analysis, 165
Quigley, Mike, 200

Rajaratnam, Raj, 136–139, 140–144,
    145, 155–157
Rakoff, Jed, 155
Rand, Ayn, 196
rating agencies
    AAA-rated securities, 37, 54,
    82, 85–87, 95, 100, 103–104, 140,
    143, 205, 226
    government deficit and, 226–227
Ravindar, Amith, 180
Reagan, Ronald, 69, 196
Reinhart, Carmen, 59
Research in Motion (RIM),
    123–128
residential mortgage-backed
    securities (RMBS), 106
Rogoff, Kenneth, 59, 212–214
Rolling Stone, 97
Roosevelt, Franklin D., 194, 231
Roubini, Nouriel, 74
Rowling, J. K., 14
Royal Bank of Canada (RBC),
    81–83, 104
rumormongering, insider trading and,
    124–125, 149–154

SAC Capital Advisors, 126, 143
Saluzzi, Joe
    Broken Markets: How High Frequency
    Trading and Predatory Practices on
    Wall Street Are Destroying Investor
    Confidence, 181
    financial transaction tax and, 213,
    216
    on high-frequency trading and dark
    pools, 159–166
    on high-frequency trading and "flash
    crashes," 171–174, 177
    on high-frequency trading cost,
    166–170
    "Toxic Equity Trading Order Flow
    on Wall Street," 165
    "What Ails Us about High
    Frequency Trading?", 175–176
savings and loan industry, 69
Schottenfeld Group, 150
Second National Bank, 75–76
Securities and Exchange Commission
    (SEC)
    Citigroup and, 83
    Cramer, 124–125, 128
    Goldman Sachs, 80, 97–98, 105–106,
    109–111
    Great Recession of 2008, 149–151
    Paulson and Company, 31
short selling
    Great Recession of 2008 and,
    156–157
    housing bubble and, 93–95, 108 (*See*
    also housing bubble)
    insider trading and, 149–153
    "naked shorts," 152
Simoff, Michael, 53
Sixteenth Amendment, 193
Skull and Bones, 183–185
Smith, Cameron, 197
Smith, Yves, 98, 102–103, 111
social engineering, predatory lending
    and, 89

Social Network, The, 189, 190
Société Générale (SG), 151–153
Soros, George
Bank of England and, 49–57, 204
capital used by, 62 (*See also* income distribution)
Soros Fund Management, 51 (*See also* Soros, George)
Special Purpose Vehicles, 73
Spitzer, Eliot, 119
Squawk Box (CNBC), 117
stagflation, 67, 195
standard of living. *See* income distribution; productivity
Stifel Nichols, 83
Stoody, Winston, 197
Stout, Lynn, 132
Strachman, Daniel A., 26
TheStreet.com, 114, 116, 121–128
subprime bonds, 89, 102–103, 105, 107, 109–111
suburbia, poverty and, 238
Summers, Larry, 190, 219
SuperCash: The New Hedge Fund Capitalism (Altucher), 190–191
Suskind, Ron, 218–219
Sweden
economic fairness and, 22–23
Soros and, 51
synthetic collateralized debt obligations (CDOs), 35–38
Abacus 2007-ACI (Goldman Sachs) and, 105–111
CDO, defined, 86
CDO squared, 86
housing bubble, 81–83, 86–87, 100
income distribution and, 74
synthetic CDOs, defined, 93

Taibbi, Matt, 97
Tammany Hall, 29–30
TARP, 98
Task, Aaron, 121–128

Taub, Stephen, 31
taxes, 183–203
Alternative Minimum Tax (AMT), 185
carried interest loophole, arguments for and against, 196–202
carried interest loophole, defined, 185–189
financial transaction tax proposal, 204–220
George W. Bush and, 69
incentive tax options (ISOs), 188
income tax history, 193–196
post-World War II tax rates, 66
venture capital (VC) funds and, 189–193
of wealthy, 14
TaxProf, 185–186
Tepper, David, 25–30
Themis Trading, 160. *See also* Arnuk, Sal; Saluzzi, Joe
This Time Is Different (Rogoff), 212–214
Thomsen, Linda Chatman, 150
Tivnan, Brian, 180
Tobin, James, 206–209
"too big to fail," 76
toxic assets, Great Recession of 2008 and, 28–29. *See also* Great Recession of 2008; housing bubble
"Toxic Equity Trading Order Flow on Wall Street" (Saluzzi, Arnuk), 165
Tradebot, 173–174
Tradeworx, 173–174
trading. *See* high-frequency trading (HFT)
tranches
defined, 85
equity, 85, 87–88
mezzanine, 85
Tremont Group, 20

trust, in government, 67
Tudor Investment, 51
"Two and Twenty: Taxing Partnership
    Profits in Private Equity Funds"
    (Fleischer), 185

Union Carbide, 178–179
unions
    income distribution and, 66, 67–68,
        69
    taxes and, 194, 196, 219
    worker safety and, 179
United Steelworkers Union, 179
University of Chicago, 68–69
U.S. Senate
    Finance Committee, 186
    Permanent Committee on
        Investigations, 84, 97–98, 105
U.S. Treasury Department, 98
    Geithner, 142, 217–219
    Paulson, 156–157

"Vampire Squid," 97
venture capital, 21, 189–193
Vietnam War, financing of, 67
Volcker, Paul, 36

Waddell and Reed, 171
wages, nonsupervisory weekly. *See*
    productivity

Waldman, Paul, 200–202
*Wall Street and the Financial Crisis:
    Anatomy of a Financial Collapse*
    (Senate Permanent Committee on
    Investigations), 84
Wall Street Journal, 29, 155
Walton family, 14
Washington Mutual (WaMu), 37, 84,
    154
Watergate, 67
"What Ails Us about High Frequency
    Trading?" (Saluzzi, Arnuk),
    175–176
Winfrey, Oprah, 6
Wisconsin schools, 79, 81–83, 94,
    103–104, 205, 228, 232
Woodward, Bob, 208
WorldCom, 146
World War II
    Bretton Woods conference (1944)
        and, 57–59, 64–66, 67, 207
    nonsupervisory weekly wages and
        productivity (U.S., 2012 dol-
        lars), *63,* 65 (*See also* income
        distribution)
    taxes and, 194

Zhao, Guannan, 180
Zhou, Dexin, 174–175
Zuckerman, Gregory, 79–80